Nordic Approaches to International Law

Nordic Approaches to International Law

Edited by

Astrid Kjeldgaard-Pedersen

TUTA SUB AEGIDE PALLAS 1683

BRILL
NIJHOFF

LEIDEN | BOSTON

The Library of Congress Cataloging-in-Publication Data is available online at http://catalog.loc.gov
LC record available at http://lccn.loc.gov/2017956462

Typeface for the Latin, Greek, and Cyrillic scripts: "Brill". See and download: brill.com/brill-typeface.

ISBN 978-90-04-34358-0 (hardback)
ISBN 978-90-04-34359-7 (e-book)

This book is printed on acid-free paper and produced in a sustainable manner.

Contents

List of Contributors

Cecilia M. Bailliet
Professor, PluriCourts – Centre for the Study of the Legitimate Roles of the Judiciary in the Global Order, Faculty of Law, University of Oslo, Oslo, Norway

David Thór Björgvinsson
Professor, School of Law, University of Iceland, Reykjavík, Iceland

Ove Bring
Professor (emer.), Stockholm University and the Swedish National Defence College, Stockholm, Sweden

Anders Henriksen
Associate Professor, Centre for International Law, Conflict and Crisis, Faculty of Law, University of Copenhagen, Copenhagen, Denmark

Jakob v. H. Holtermann
Associate Professor, iCourts – Centre of Excellence for International Courts, Faculty of Law, University of Copenhagen, Copenhagen, Denmark

Julie Gjørtz Howden
PhD Candidate, Faculty of Law, University of Bergen, Bergen, Norway

Thórdis Ingadóttir
Associate Professor, School of Law, University of Iceland, Reykjavík, Iceland

Astrid Kjeldgaard-Pedersen
Associate Professor, iCourts – Centre of Excellence for International Courts, Faculty of Law, University of Copenhagen, Copenhagen, Denmark

Martti Koskenniemi
Professor, Erik Castrén Institute of International Law and Human Rights, Faculty of Law, University of Helsinki, Helsinki, Finland

Gregor Noll
Professor, Department of Law, Lund University, Lund, Sweden

Jens Elo Rytter
Professor, Centre for international law, Conflict and Crisis, Faculty of Law, University of Copenhagen, Copenhagen, Denmark

Marlene Wind
Professor, Department of Political Science, Faculty of Social Sciences, University of Copenhagen, Copenhagen, Denmark

Introduction: A Nordic Approach to International Law?

Astrid Kjeldgaard-Pedersen

The Nordic countries have a long-standing tradition of collaboration on a wide range of legal issues. The Nordic Council of Ministers endeavours "to promote basic common principles in Nordic legislation", and extensive inter-Nordic harmonization is now in place in areas as diverse as education, energy, taxation, culture, and gender equality. However, do these 'shared Nordic values' extend to embrace a common perspective on international law and policy beyond the Nordic region? And do international legal scholars in the Nordic countries share a professional outlook enabling us to speak of a distinct 'Nordic approach to international law'? With generous support from The Danish-Norwegian Collaboration Foundation, The Carlsberg Foundation, and The Dreyer Foundation, international legal scholars and expert practitioners from Denmark, Finland, Iceland, Norway, and Sweden gathered at Lysebu outside Oslo for a two-day conference in August 2015 to discuss contemporary issues of international law from a Nordic perspective. In addition to the question of a distinct Nordic tradition within international legal scholarship, the conference call welcomed papers addressing various topics in international law from a Nordic viewpoint. From a wide variety of paper proposals, panels were organized around the following themes: 'The Nordic Approach to International Legal Regulation of Natural Resources', 'Nordic Judges of International Courts', and 'the Nordic Approach to International Human Rights Law'. Moreover, a renowned international legal scholar from each of the Nordic countries was invited to give a key note lecture, and the five directors of legal affairs in each of the Nordic Ministries of Foreign Affairs presented their views on the conference theme in a round-table discussion.

Eight of the papers presented at the conference were published in a special issue of the *Nordic Journal of International Law*, Vol. 86, No. 4 (2016). The present book contains these eight papers as well as five additional contributions from conference participants. All chapters address aspects of the question of a Nordic approach to international law, varying significantly in terms of subject area, methodology and style.

In the opening chapter, *Gregor Noll* claims that the conference was "organized around a phantom pain". Based on three examples concerning central questions in current international law, he first argues that little evidence exists

 | DOI 10.1163/9789004343597_002

of substantive Nordic convergence in today's practice. Noll goes on to show that in the "geopolitical heyday of Nordic international law", the Nordics took a leading role in shaping and articulating an international law of neutrality. This issue, however, is of limited relevance today since the law of neutrality has been replaced by the law of collective security post World War II. The Nordics are therefore left in a state of nostalgia: "a mentality that is acutely mindful of past grandeur and therefore sees and laments present decay". Reading this melancholic longing for a Nordic international law through Andrej Tarkovski's 1983 film, *Nostalghia*, Noll finally asks how it might be transgressed.

Martti Koskenniemi's essay describes the engagement by Finnish jurists with international law in the 20th century. He claims that international law had an exceptionally strong position in Finland in comparison to the other Nordic countries. By way of explanation, he refers to historical events, including the disputes concerning the Åland Islands and Eastern Carelia. Koskenniemi goes on to present the towering figures among 20th century Finnish international lawyers. His account for their principal writings and careers shows a strong tradition among Finnish international lawyers of combining academic endeavours with government service. Koskenniemi finds that, moving with ease between diplomacy and the academy, Finnish international lawyers have predominantly been "doctrinal positivists interested in legal aspects of Finland's international position".

Ove Bring's chapter discusses the life and career of the second Secretary-General of the United Nations, Dag Hammarskjöld. Bring scrutinizes Hammarskjöld's innovative approach to diplomacy in light of his personal background and philosophical outlook. The chapter shows that Hammarskjöld played a key role in shaping and developing the legal framework within which UN continues to operate today. With the examples of Hammarskjöld's efforts relating to peacekeeping operations, humanitarian intervention, and the responsibility to protect, the chapter illustrates how Hammarskjöld – always striving to find the right balance between idealism and realism – exercised significant influence on the development of international law during the Cold War. Finally, Bring's chapter describes the recent reopening of the investigation into the death of Hammarskjöld, thus demonstrating that his memory is indeed still alive.

Also taking a biographical approach, *Astrid Kjeldgaard-Pedersen* studies the voting practice of Nordic judges of the Permanent Court of International Justice and its successor the International Court of Justice. Focusing in particular on dissenting and separate opinions issued by the individual Nordic judges, Kjeldgaard-Pedersen queries whether common traits can be said to exist in their engagement with the World Court that might support the notion of 'a Nordic approach to international law'.

Jens Elo Rytter's chapter studies dissenting opinions of Nordic judges of the European Court of Human Rights (ECtHR). Rytter makes the claim that there exists, to a certain extent, a 'Nordic approach' to the interpretation of the European Convention of Human Rights, which has been remarkably resilient to change since the *Airey* judgment of 1979. Rytter argues that the commonalities between the voting practice of Nordic ECtHR judges correspond to a shared Nordic legal and constitutional tradition characterised by: (1) strict reliance on the ordinary meaning of the text; (2) emphasis on preparatory works as a relevant source for identifying the norm's purpose and scope, and (3) reluctance towards imposing obligations on the national political organs, especially when it comes to question of economic and social policy.

Like Rytter, the authors of the subsequent two chapters address the relationship between international law and domestic law within the field of human rights, but their focus is the reverse of Rytter's: the impact of international judgments on the practice of domestic courts. Despite their common focus, however, Wind's and Björgvinsson's respective approaches – as well as their findings – differ substantially. *Marlene Wind* conducts a quantitative study of the frequency with which Scandinavian supreme courts cite treaties and judgments of international courts. Specifically, she analyses an original, extensive dataset comprising the total number of references made by the supreme courts of Denmark, Norway, and Sweden to decisions of international courts between 1961 and 2014. On this basis, Wind argues that the Scandinavian supreme courts are far less engaging towards international law than what would be expected in light of the common depiction of the Nordic counries as frontrunners, particularly in so far as international human rights law is concerned. Notably, however, her study shows that the Norwegian Supreme Court takes a much more favourable approach to the 'domestication of international law' than its Danish and Swedish counterparts. Wind argues that the reluctance of Scandinavian courts to accommodate international law in domestic judicial practice may be explained by the influence of Scandinavian legal positivism and the strong tradition of majoritarian democracy in the Nordic region.

David Thór Björgvinsson's chapter comprises a qualitative analysis of the effect of judgments of the ECtHR before domestic courts. First and foremost, Björgvinsson examines the status of the principle of *res interpretata* in Iceland with regard to the case law of the ECtHR. For comparison, the paper includes parallel studies of the situation in Denmark and Norway. Björgvinsson concludes that the national courts of all three countries regularly consult the case law of the ECtHR within the framework of *res interpretata* and the rule of presumption.

In the subsequent chapter, *Thórdis Ingadóttir* sets out to examine the implementation of international criminal law into domestic law in the Nordic countries. Ingadóttir begins by arguing that the Nordic countries have all consistently supported the International Criminal Court and the effective enforcement of international criminal law. She goes on to discuss the individual ways in which the Nordic countries have ensured, since the entry into force of the Rome Statute of the International Criminal Court in 2002, that sufficient norms criminalizing international crimes were in place at the domestic level. She describes how, with the exception of Denmark, all Nordic countries have adopted new legislation, either the form of a separate act or a separate chapter of their existing domestic criminal codes. While we have yet to see the effects of these new domestic norms, Ingadóttir expresses hope that they will not only enhance domestic efforts to investigate and prosecute international crimes, but also serve as a deterrent.

Turning towards the law of armed conflict, *Anders Henriksen's* chapter examines – from a Danish viewpoint – how the relationship between international law compliance and the perceived legitimacy of warfare has developed since 11 September 2001. In particular, Henriksen ties the importance of legal arguments to the strategic narratives presented by policy-makers to build popular support for '21st century wars of choice'. He argues that Western states, including Denmark and the other Nordic countries, do not just go to war in places like Kosovo, Iraq, Afghanistan, or Libya to serve national interests, but also to promote or maintain respect for core international norms and values, e.g. democracy, human rights and the rule of law. Henriksen describes the concrete challenges faced by Danish institutions pertaining to international norm compliance, for example as regards the handling of detainees, and discusses how the chosen solutions to these challenges relate to the political decision to contribute to international military operations.

Julie Gjørtz Howden's chapter stands out by examining a concrete example of inter-Nordic cooperation in the field of international water law, namely the newly established Finnish-Norwegian River Basin District. Drawing on the 'community of interest' approach, Howden argues that Norway and Finland could and should have created a more progressive and holistic water management regime. In doing so, Gjørtz Howden claims, the two States would not only have strengthened the peaceful and democratic tradition of Nordic water management. They would also have taken a step towards promoting the Nordic model beyond the region.

Cecilia Bailliet's chapter examines whether there is a Nordic approach to promoting women's rights within international law. Focusing first on 'the external perspective', Bailliet describes the involvement of the Nordic countries in the international promotion of women's rights, including in the drafting of the CEDAW. She then contrasts the Nordic contribution externally with current challenges complicating women's enjoyment of rights from 'the internal perspective'. Bailliet argues that the Nordics have failed to reform their domestic legislation so as to incorporate the equality guarantees they advocated in relation to CEDAW. Finally, she explores 'the myth of a Nordic feminist foreign policy' and the role of Nordic women as creators of international law.

In the final chapter, *Jakob v.H. Holtermann* develops his remarks from the closing round-table discussion at the conference, during which he focused on methodological and theoretical issues in relation to the study of Nordic approaches to international law. Holtermann first queries whether the dismissal by conference participants of a distinctively Nordic approach to international law might suffer from 'the narcissism of small differences'. He then goes on to concentrate on the role of Scandinavian realism in relation to two separate aspects of the question of Nordic approaches, namely the legal political dimension of shaping international law through the adoption of treaties on the one the hand, and the implementation of international law in domestic law on the other. Holtermann argues that Scandinavian realism is 'conspicuously absent' in discussions about the creation of treaties, while it is 'mistakenly present' in discussions about the apparent reluctance among judges of Nordic courts to 'domesticate' the case law of international courts and tribunals.

Nostalghia: A Nordic International Law

Gregor Noll

1 Introduction

Is there a 'Nordic approach to international law'? This question positively rubs me the wrong way. It presupposes another one: 'what is the Nordic?' As any questions of identity would be, this is a dubious question indeed.[1] And if the Nordic is so acutely in question, how could we possibly identify its peculiar way of making, shaping or breaking international law?

I can see two ways of dealing with this problem. I might write a text looking back at the origins of a purported Nordic international legalism, say the 1930s, or the 1950s and 1960s, or any other period which I think reflects authentic Nordicness in international law. There, I would compare the degree of cohesion among Nordic governments, parliaments and institutions in matters of international law existing back then with the currently prevailing one. Today's Nordic approach to international law, I would conclude, is but a shadow of its former self. The temper of this text would be melancholic, and the sentiment impregnating it nostalgic in relation to the origins of Nordic international legalism. Another text I could write would move in the opposite direction; I would seek to show the existence of a new, unprecedented Nordicness and speculate how it might engender a distinct international law for the future.

* I am grateful for comments and criticism from participants of the conference on "A Nordic Approach to International Law?", held 27–29 August 2015 in Oslo, Norway. I remain particularly indebted to its convenor Astrid Kjeldgaard-Pedersen and the *Nordic Journal of International Law's* anonymous reviewer. Thanks are also due to Miran Crnalic and Teresa O'Neill for research assistance. Research for this project was in part conducted when I occupied the Torsten and Ragnar Söderberg Foundations' Chair in Commemoration of Samuel Pufendorf.

1 Why dubious? The literature on the Nordic self-positioning after the Cold War suggests that we still lack any clear-cut reformulation of what being Nordic means today and that (self-) doubt persists. N. Parker's 'Differentiating, Collaborating, Outdoing: Nordic Identity and Marginality in the Contemporary World', 9 *Identities* (2002) pp. 355–381 has aged well and offers a relevant account from a perspective of Nordic marginality even today. The same goes for O. Wæver, 'Nordic Nostalgia: Northern Europe after the Cold War', 68:1 *International Affairs* (1992) pp. 77–102. But asking the question of Nordic identity is dubious for another paramount reason: because the moulding of complex histories into an identitarian cliché always brings with it very real political risks.

 | DOI 10.1163/9789004343597_003

This text would be optimistic in tone, its temper sanguine, and its agenda redemptive. Either of these two texts would be a naive response to the question asked by this special issue.

There is the problem of *method* it engenders. Are we to think of a 'Nordic approach to international law' as a phenomenon akin to a *regional custom*, suggesting that we map the practice and *opinio juris* of Nordic states and other international actors in the region? In doing so, we would appear to apply a 'Nordic positivism', and content ourselves with the formal means of deducing the law well-rehearsed within our discipline. Here, the 'Nordic' would evidence itself strictly through positive law. The chances for such a project are slim.

Or is that a 'Nordic approach to international law' is actually about the *mentality* held by its practitioners and theorists? A kind of *opinio juris* aggregated *across* international law at large, a historically shaped ontology of the law? If the project of explaining the Nordic through its positive law alone were bound to fail, then this would seem to be the only way left. But what method are we to apply when thinking about the mentality of Nordic international lawyers? An ethnology, psychology, sociology or neurobiology of Nordic international law?

Why do I think that the Nordic is something that has become ever more dubious? States do not harmonise their approach to international law just because their territories happen to share roughly the same geographical corner of the world.[2] But states might harmonise their approach to international law to the extent they conceive of their internal and external affairs as being exposed to similar problems and pressures. And, I would think, because it makes sense to form a cartel against what are perceived as antagonistic forces. Thinking about the commonalities of states' approach to international law invariably means to think about their historical, political and personal situation.

The theme of this special issue would be unintelligible to us were it not for the backdrop of 19th century Nordic neutrality politics, including the embrace of *mare liberum* thinking, or the mid-20th century as intense periods of Nordic international legalism. Constellations of antagonistic forces have changed since then, as have other aspects of the personal and political situation of

2 Considering the distance, geographical and otherwise, between Quaanaaq in Greenland and Finnish Imatra, even this suggestion is open to challenge. Greenland is commonly held not to be part of the Nordics (or, more specifically, *Norden*, as the Danish, Norwegian and Swedish term has it, describing a region in the singular rather than a plurality of states). Yet there is no doubt that Danish international legal practice extends to Greenland, notwithstanding the expansion of Greenland's competencies in the area of foreign affairs during the past decade. So any discussion of Nordic international law would seem to extend to Greenland, although it remains outside the Nordic sphere in geographical terms.

the Nordics. So the question of this special issue is of extraordinary complexity. Methodologically it would require a determination of the contemporary politico-historical situation of the Nordics as a preliminary step to identify the Nordic, before embarking on an inventory of the law subsumable under that Nordicness. It is quite a task, and not one that we international lawyers routinely undertake.

For the purposes of this chapter, I will limit myself to a less daunting exercise, combining an argument on decay with an essay on how to overcome this aching for identity. In a first step, I will gather select evidence to indicate that a common Nordic approach to international law hardly exists today. My avowedly limited probing relates to the use of force, to international recognition and to international humanitarian law – all three touching upon the fundaments of international law. There should be reasonably good odds of detecting traces of Nordicness in the conduct of Denmark, Finland, Iceland, Sweden and Norway in the three cases I choose to pursue (section 2).

To give the presence of Nordic international law some contours, I move back in time to sketch up the geopolitical heyday of Nordic international law to make clear that the non-alignment epoch is coming to an end (section 3).

Together, sections 2 and 3 will suggest the absence of a Nordic approach to international law in current state practice other perhaps than an unfulfilled expectation, a nostalgic memory, a phantom pain. But should not the fact that this special issue, and the conference preceding it, is organised around a phantom pain give us pause?

This brings me, second, to ask how the melancholic longing for a 'Nordic international law' might be transgressed (section 4). I read this longing through Andrei Tarkovsky's *Nostalghia* of 1983. It confronts us with the question of what imperatives – legal or other – grow from our melancholia for homelands and persons no longer with us.

2 Substantive Nordic Convergence in Contemporary Practice?

But why start in this sombre mood? Are there not quite a few contemporary indications that Nordic countries continue to coordinate their international legal positions, and quite successfully so?[3] Consider the common statements

3 In the 1990s and the early 2000s, the *Nordic Journal of International Law* published reports on Nordic state practice in coordination, usually authored or co-authored by legal advisers. This laudable form of reporting had to be abandoned by the *Nordic Journal of International Law* as Nordic foreign offices suggested they lacked the necessary resources to continue it.

by the Nordics in the UNGA Sixth Committee, the primary forum for dealing with legal issues in the General Assembly. In a recently concluded four-year period, 16 such statements were presented by Denmark, Finland, Iceland, Norway and Sweden on a rotating basis.[4] As a matter of routine, these common statements move to the top of the speakers' list and are more likely to be quoted by special rapporteurs. Without any doubt, coordination at this and other levels can be successful in making and shaping international law. The separability of impermissible reservations is a material example that has been pointed out to me: drawing on earlier Nordic practice and making use of an article by Jan Klabbers in this journal,[5] the Nordics managed to convince ILC Special Rapporteur Alain Pellet that the ILC Guidelines should contain language supporting the separability approach.[6]

On this level of concretion, I am confident that further evidence could be adduced for the continued pursuit of a Nordic international law. The question is whether the continuation of a formal and bureaucratic coordination practice and its occasional substantive successes are enough.[7] So, let me embark on a brief exploration of whether any commonalities in the approach to international law are traceable in three subject matters that possess some actuality and touch upon central areas to contemporary international law.

One of these is the confrontation between a coalition of states and the Islamic State (hereinafter IS), identified by Denmark as a top priority on the agenda of international security during the 69th session of the UN General Assembly.[8] Sweden, Finland and Iceland joined many other states in stressing

4 I looked at a period stretching from 1 October 2011 to 30 September 2015. Thematically, Nordic common statements in that period dealt with the work of the ILC (which obviously covered a wider array of themes), with international humanitarian law, the responsibility of international organisations and the protection and security of diplomatic missions.

5 J. Klabbers, 'Accepting the Unacceptable? A New Nordic Approach to Reservations to Multilateral Treaties', 69:2 *Nordic Journal of International Law* (2000) pp. 179–193.

6 International Law Commission, *Guide to Practice on Reservations to Treaties*, A/66/10/Add.1. I am grateful to my colleague Marie Jacobsson for making me aware of the causalities in this case.

7 The list of examples on Nordic cooperation on international law issues could evidently be extended. Nordic countries make common statements in the Security Council, *inter alia* on thematic issues, as they do in bodies as UNDP, UNFPA, UNICEF and UN Women. Nordic Heads of Missions to the UN hold a weekly meeting in New York. Every four years, a Nordic country seeks a non-permanent seat in the UNSC.

8 UNGA, Statement by Denmark at the General Debate 24 September 2014, online at <www.un.org/en/ga/69/meetings/gadebate/24sep/denmark.shtml>, accessed on 11 August 2016.

the need for joint action in this area.[9] Three of four Nordic states possessing military capability steer clear from US military action against IS on Syrian territory. Denmark is the only Nordic state that participates in military operations in both Syria and Iraq with a squadron of fighter aircrafts deployed.[10] Denmark, Finland, Sweden and Norway provide military training to Iraqi forces alongside humanitarian assets, while Iceland, lacking armed forces of its own, provides but humanitarian assets.[11] Denmark is clearly an outlier among the Nordics in that it operates militarily on Syrian soil and justifies this with reference to Iraq's right to collective self-defence under Article 51 of the UN Charter.[12] An analogous rift on the legality of the use of force against IS in Syria exists between the US and its Middle Eastern allies on one side, and other Western coalition members on the other. Throughout most of the 20th century, the Nordics have been careful to delimit permissible uses of force under international law. That heritage appears to be insufficient today, as the position taken by Denmark indicates.

Remaining in the Middle East, the status of Palestine is another question whose significance for international peace and security is beyond doubt. Here, Nordic states are far from converging. The Icelandic Parliament passed a resolution in 2011 recognising the statehood of Palestine.[13] The current Swedish

9 UNGA, Statement by Finland at the General Debate 24 September 2014, online at <www.un.org/en/ga/69/meetings/gadebate/24sep/finland.shtml>; UNGA, Statement by Iceland at the General Debate 29 September 2014, online at <www.un.org/en/ga/69/meetings/gadebate/29sep/iceland.shtml>; UNGA, Statement by Sweden at the General Debate 29 September 2014, online at <www.un.org/en/ga/69/meetings/gadebate/29sep/sweden.shtml>, all accessed on 11 August 2016.

10 G. O'Dwyer, 'Denmark to Reinforce Military Fight against ISIS', *Defense News*, 21 April 2016, online at <www.defensenews.com/story/defense/international/2016/04/21/denmark-isis-syria-iraq-military/83338340/>, accessed on 11 August 2016.

11 J. Drennan, 'Who has contributed what in the coalition against the Islamic State', *Foreign Policy*, 12 November 2014, online at <foreignpolicy.com/2014/11/12/who-has-contributed-what-in-the-coalition-against-the-islamic-state/>, accessed on 11 August 2016; D. O'Dwyer, 'Finland to Strengthen Training Mission in Iraq', *Defense News*, 21 April 2016, online at <www.defensenews.com/story/defense/international/2016/04/21/finland-iraq-isis-troops/83332046/>, accessed on 11 August 2016.

12 Danish Ministry of Defence, 'The Effort Against ISIL', online at <www.fmn.dk/eng/allabout/Pages/the-effort-against-isil.aspx>, accessed on 11 August 2016.

13 'Iceland recognises Palestinian state', *The Guardian*, 30 November 2011, online at <www.theguardian.com/world/2011/nov/30/iceland-recognises-palestinian-state>, accessed on 30 August 2016.

government has also recognised Palestine,[14] while the previous one saw the criterion of territorial control as not being fulfilled and precluding recognition. On the other side of the divide, we find Norway, Finland and Denmark. The Norwegian prime minister is on record with making the achievement of a two-state solution a precondition for Norwegian recognition of Palestinian statehood.[15] This practice can be neatly projected on rifts in the international legal doctrine of recognition. These rifts continue to exist, although the pragmatic Nordics have decided in 2013 that Palestine missions to the Nordic countries should have the same status.[16] As self-determination of small states has been a prominent issue for the Nordics since the 19th century, one might have expected a material convergence of sorts here.

Both Israel and Palestine are small and exposed to massive political tectonics. To a degree, the traditional Nordic insistence on the self-determination of small states lends itself to support the Israeli as well as the Palestinian cause. The fact that there is no joint position on the recognition of Palestine – positive or negative – suggests that the material similarity of Nordic history might be exaggerated, or at the very least has lost its traction in our days.

Finally, I choose to add a question from the field of international humanitarian law (IHL), an area in which the Nordics are traditionally seen to have a particular stake. In that field, the advent of new weapons systems that operate with a high degree of autonomy is one of the most significant challenges to IHL. With massive public as well as private investments taking place in robotics in the military sector, the moment for regulation is arguably now. As far as I am aware, there is an industrial interest in the Nordic defence industry, too.[17]

Here, we have the opportunity to follow the nucleus of regulatory deliberations in the records of the 2015 Meeting of Experts on Lethal autonomous weapons systems (or LAWS, as the portentous acronym has it) held under the

---

14 Protocol of the Government's Meeting of 30 October 2014 [*Protokoll vid regeringssammanträde 2014-10-30*] UF2014/68085/UD/MENA, online at <www.regeringen.se/contentassets/6c7d07c17c2241939a2590497424c14f/regeringsbeslut_palestina.pdf>, accessed on 10 August 2016.

15 'Ingen palestinsk stat tross massiv anerkjennelse', *Aftenposten*, 30 October 2014, online at <www.aftenposten.no/verden/Ingen-palestinsk-stat-tross-massiv-anerkjennelse-75635b.html>, accessed on 9 August 2016.

16 *See* Danish Ministry of Foreign Affairs, 'Denmark and Finland to upgrade relations with Palestinians', 4 May 2013, online at <um.dk/en/news/newsdisplaypage/?newSID=0D2BA8C4-D5A1-4503-80A9-7EAA1A72F019>, accessed on 10 August 2016.

17 Saab, the Swedish defence business, has a number of unmanned fixed wing and rotary wing systems on offer or under development.

Convention on Certain Conventional Weapons. The concept of 'Meaningful Human Control' of such systems was discussed at that meeting, with Denmark and Sweden voicing support for it in their respective general statements, while the Finnish concluding statement expressed a measure of scepticism towards its usefulness to clearly define this category of weapons.[18] There seems to have been no intervention by or on behalf of Norway at the meeting. Other statements, as that of Israel, were rather more sophisticated in their categorisation than any of the three intervening Nordics. One needs to acknowledge, though, that the intervention by Israel would seem to counter regulation rather than to promote it. The impression of lacking coordination and shallowness of governmental analysis prevailed at the 2016 meeting, during which Sweden, Finland and Norway intervened.[19] Had the Nordics been interested in articulating the IHL of the future, after an epochal change in fighting wars, this meeting might have been an opportunity to coordinate.

For today, I conclude that it is not warranted to think of Nordic states as pursuing a substantive Nordic approach to international law in any of these areas.

3 The Nordics' International Legalism at the Threshold of an Epochal Shift

Whence these expectations of a Nordic international law? Historically, the Nordics have been extremely productive in shaping and articulating an international law of neutrality in the course of the late 18th, 19th and early 20th centuries. The law of neutrality is in recession today and has to a large extent been replaced by the law of collective security post World War II. So we find ourselves in times where neutrality as the very *topos* that made the Nordics into remarkable international lawmakers approaches its vanishing point.[20] Some of the arenas of Nordic international legalism today – a knack for free

---

18 Delegations' statements, including those of the named states, can be readily consulted at the website of the 2015 Experts' Meeting: <www.unog.ch/80256EE600585943/(httpPages)/6CE049BE22EC75A2C1257C8D00513E26>, accessed on 12 August 2016.

19 Delegations' statements, including those of the named states, can be readily consulted at the website of the 2016 Experts' Meeting: <www.unog.ch/80256EE600585943/(httpPages)/37D5118 9AC4FB6E1C1257F4D004CAFB2?OpenDocument>, accessed on 12 August 2016.

20 H. Lödén's 'Reaching a Vanishing Point? Reflections on the Future of Neutrality in Finland and Sweden', 47 *Cooperation and Conflict* (2012) pp. 271–284 offers an excellent overview of political and academic debates on the current state of neutrality in the two Nordics which stand outside NATO. On the decline of the law of neutrality in international law:

trade, for small states, for humanitarian law – can be properly understood only with that past in mind.

It is, of course, tempting to imagine this former abundance as a product of good statesmanship, political wisdom or social virtue. That benign reading would veil the very real and very material pressures that made weakening Denmark and Sweden to adopt an early form of lawfare as part of its European power politics. The basic tenet of this politics was the growing insight that none of the Nordics could successfully participate in what would become the Concert of Europe: the domination of five major powers in European alliances and conflicts. As lesser powers unable to unite along the nationalist models that would work for Italy and Germany,[21] the Nordics were now looking for a new posture and found it in the international law of neutrality. Articulating the rules of that law and seeking to enforce it to the extent possible would seem to secure both military, political and commercial interests. This would act as a constraint on the use of force in a spirit of legalism.

As both Denmark and Sweden had experienced the growing power of Germany and Russia and their own inability to hold on to exposed territories, it made sense to seek a neutral posture in the dangerous political constellations of the rest of Europe, and to insist on the interest of free trade against hostile interventions by warring parties. In the course of a century ending with the 1907 Hague Conventions and World War I, the Nordics had contained British articulations of neutrality law and in part replaced them with their own versions. The power of warring parties would diminish and the immunity of neutral parties would be confirmed.[22] It was no coincidence that Martin Hübner, one of the great names of the international law of neutrality, was a Dane, and had first-hand experience of negotiating the release of seized Danish and Norwegian vessels with the British government.[23]

With a few strokes of the brush, political scientist Noel Parker draws a picture of the epochal change that the 19th century brought to the Nordics:

> Since the principal axis of European wealth moved north-westward from the 16th century, the Danish, Swedish, Polish, and German political orders

---

M. Gavouneli, 'Neutrality – A Survivor?', 23 *European Journal of International Law* (2012) pp. 267–273.

21 The mid-19th century Scandinavianist movement had unsuccessfully aspired to unite Norway, Sweden and Denmark under one crown.

22 W.G. Grewe, *Epochen der Völkerrechtsgeschichte* (Nomos, Baden Baden, 1984) pp. 433–461.

23 Hübner is given a prominent role in Grewe's account of the formation of neutrality law, *ibid.*, p. 439.

> (the last in the form of Prussia/Germany from late 18th century) have all fought over the wealth and power to be derived from straddling Europe's access to Baltic resources ... Driven back to Scandinavian territory by the 18th century, Denmark and Sweden then reached (uneasy) compromise in their competition over the Baltic.
>
> By the mid-19th century that arrangement was devalued by the intrusion of the two powers with major land-bases outside the area, Russia and Germany. Significantly, it is only then that we find surfacing the romantic vision of a Nordic society, more ancient and quite separate and independent from a "Europe", [sic] which was by then dominated by German and/or French versions of "European Civilization".[24]

This is an important point. The question of Nordicness emerged back then at the threshold to a new and uneasy political constellation, exposing the real weaknesses of the Danish and Swedish realms. The question of Nordicness asked today (not at least by and in this special issue) would then be a sign of an epochal shift, just as the ones that Denmark and Sweden experienced by the middle of the 19th century.

As the last bastion of neutrality, these shifts are perhaps best read through Swedish – and to some extent Finnish – policy reorientation from more pronounced neutrality towards an 'enhancement' of bi- and multilateral defence cooperation. Within the first six months of 2016, Sweden had concluded a Memorandum of Understanding with Denmark on enhanced defence cooperation,[25] signed a Statement of Intent with the US on defence cooperation,[26] and agreed to a Programme on Defence Cooperation with the United Kingdom.[27] Defence ties to Finland have been intensified

24 N. Parker, 'Differentiating, Collaborating, Outdoing: Nordic Identity and Marginality in the Contemporary World', 9 *Identities* (2002) pp. 355–381, at p. 362 (reference and footnote omitted).

25 Government Offices of Sweden, 'Sweden and Denmark sign enhanced defence cooperation agreement', 14 January 2016, online at <www.government.se/articles/2016/01/sweden-and-denmark-sign-enhanced-defence-cooperation-agreement/>, accessed on 11 August 2016.

26 Government Offices of Sweden, 'Statement of Intent between the Secretary of Defense of the United States of America and the Minister of Defense of Sweden', 8 June 2016, online at <www.government.se/globalassets/government/dokument/forsvarsdepartementet/statement-of-intent-swe_us-20160608_signed.pdf>, accessed on 11 August 2016.

27 Government Offices of Sweden, 'Sweden and the United Kingdom enhance defence cooperation', 11 June 2016, online at <www.government.se/articles/2016/06/sweden-and-the-united-kingdom-enhances-defence-cooperation/>, accessed on 11 August 2016.

step-by-step since 2014, culminating in a joint statement of the defence ministers of both countries.[28] And perhaps most significantly, both Finland and Sweden concluded Host Nation Support Agreements with NATO in 2014.[29]

While this is not necessarily the end of military non-alignment for both countries in the formal sense, this process of repositioning gives us pause. Not only does it suggest that non-NATO Nordics are actively preparing for mutual assistance to their neighbours in- and outside NATO on the most concrete technical level, but also that the ties to Western powers and to NATO are now enhanced to such a degree that it is a matter of taste whether to attach a label of 'post-neutrality' or to rescind the use of neutrality terminology at all. Both moves can be seen in a sharper light if we compare them to mid-19th century Nordic politics of military *dégagement* from conflicts in neighbouring Nordics (as vividly exemplified by Swedish non-intervention in the 1863 Danish-German war) and of non-alignment. If the Nordics tried to make a home at the margins of violent European politics by then, their successors appear to seek themselves to their centre right now. In the area of international law, this would mean that the last vestiges of an entrepreneurial legalist role will be evacuated, slowly but surely.

4 *Nostalghia*

This brings us to a point where all the preconditions for a case of nostalgia are in place: a mentality that is acutely mindful of past grandeur and therefore sees and laments present decay. *Algos* is the Greek term for pain, while *nostos* signifies to return home. So nostalgia lives off the difference between our present and our origins. But nostalgia might also provide the springboard for thinking of the potential of our present historical situation: yes, it is different from its origins, but what kind of actions does this difference – and the reflected experience of it – enable?

---

28 Government Offices of Sweden, 'Joint Statement Regarding Deepened Defence Cooperation between Finland and Sweden', 22 May 2015, online at <www.regeringen.se/globalassets/regeringen/dokument/forsvarsdepartementet/2015-05-22-joint-statement---signed.pdf>, accessed on 11 August 2016.

29 NATO SHAPE, 'Finland and Sweden Sign Memorandum of Understanding with NATO', 5 September 2014, online at <www.shape.nato.int/finland-and-sweden-signing-a-memorandum-of-understanding-with-nato-for-operational-and-logistic-support>, accessed on 10 August 2016.

Andrei Tarkovsky was a Soviet film director of international repute, his name associated with works such as *Ivan's Childhood*, *Stalker* and *Solaris*. Tarkovsky's filmmaking is rich in overtones and lives off spiritual and poetic allusions. During the shooting of *Nostalghia* in Italy in the early 1980s, state-owned Mosfilm withdrew support, and Tarkovsky resolved never again to work in the Soviet Union. He died in 1986 in self-imposed Parisian exile, after completing *Nostalghia* and *The Sacrifice*, his final work.

The protagonist of *Nostalghia* is Andrei Gorchakov, a Russian writer researching the biography of Pavel Sosnovsky, a fictional Russian 18th century composer. Sosnovski, who was befallen by nostalgia during a prolonged stay in Italy, decided to return to his oppressive homeland and committed suicide there; and Andrei now visits the places Sosnovsky visited during his Italian stay. In doing so, Andrei's longing for his Russian origins grows to the point of deep melancholy: images of his house, his wife and his family appear in dreamlike sequences; and he recurs to his mother tongue's poetry and ponders its untranslatability.

In a decisive turn, Andrei encounters Domenico, an eccentric mathematician who has withdrawn from the world, lives in a dilapidated house with his German shepherd and is taken to be a madman by the village locals of Bagno Vignoni. Domenico, at first recalcitrant towards Andrei's advances and unsettled by his use of the phrase '*va bene*', explains to Andrei that saving the world is quite easy: it can be done by carrying a burning candle through the pool of the Holy Catherine in the village, an act the local population denies him as a madman. Before letting Andrei go, Domenico hands him a candle stump.

The film eclipses in a double gesture: in the course of his public speech on Rome's Capitol Hill, Domenico exhorts a strangely dispersed audience to listen to the insects before immolating himself. Unaware of Domenico's fate, Andrei simultaneously returns from Rome to Bagno Vignoni in a sudden change of heart and carries the burning candle stump through its pool, failing twice to keep the flame alive in the soft breezes, and succeeds on his third effort. While the camera retains its focus on the burning candle placed atop the pool wall, Andrei suffers a heart attack with locals rushing to his assistance, and only then does the camera move to show the bewildered gaze of a woman witnessing Andrei's fall.

Tarkovsky dedicated *Nostalghia* to his mother, and the sacrifices of caring and love are a central theme. One of its visually most captivating scenes has a young woman kneeling in prayer before a processional figure of the pregnant Mary. Then she buttons open the front of Mary's gown and a swarm of birds is released. The birds turn the air into sheer sound and movement. This image, as others in the film, denies itself to sense making; all its spiritual allusions strike but a tone, dissolve fixity and nudge us towards a possibility.

So, where is the analogy to Nordic international law? Let me imagine an Andrei in our midst, brought up as an international lawyer at a university somewhere in Sweden, having done his grand tour through some of the institutions of our profession, and retaining childhood images of his Nordic upbringing. Perhaps that childhood took place somewhere between the 40s and the 70s of the last century. Perhaps the 90s were an era of great enchantment as much as of a great insecurity for him: an unmooring from a well-rehearsed historical pattern forming his mentality. The internationalism of the 90s now feels stale: the Cold War was followed by the Global War against Terror and yet another Cold War, Bosnian refugees were to be followed by Syrian refugees, and the financial crisis of Sweden, the largest Nordic economy, was followed by a financial crisis of Western economy at large, where austerity overrode economic and social rights. The idea of *folkhemmet,* the people's home – originally invented as a counter socialist move by the Swedish correlate to Carl Schmitt Rudolf Kjellén, but successfully appropriated by Nordic social democracy to a point where it made up much of Nordic identity at home and abroad, was now re-appropriated by scheming nationalists whose nostalgic subliminalities had brought them into four of five Nordic parliaments.

In the domain of the international use of force, Andrei might see the chasm between the 1991 Operation Desert Storm with its express mandate by the Security Council under Chapter VII and the possibly ex post-mandated Operation Enduring Freedom, a failure in which Nordic governments had their military and political share, or, worse still, he might see the chasm between Desert Storm and the illegally waged Iraq war of 2003 to 2011. Andrei might have realised in 2001 that the laws on the use of force cannot be changed by the instant custom of a coalition of the willing. He feels that the engagement of Nordic states in Afghanistan and Iraq is forgetful of formative Nordic experiences – such as the German aggression against and occupation of Denmark and Norway in 1940, or the Swedish prime minister joining a demonstration against the 1972 Christmas Bombings of North Vietnam.

Andrei is very much aware that the Nordics as a region of international law grew out of the experience of being placed where the tectonic plates of two larger geopolitical entities meet. He might think of Nordic self-positioning in the period preceding World War II: Denmark, Finland, Norway and Sweden jointly publishing a Declaration for the Purposes of Establishing Similar Rules of Neutrality in 1938 in the League of Nations Treaty Series, at the brink of war.[30] Or he might think of the 1960s 'Nordic Model' of peacekeeping, drawing on regular meetings by Nordic defence ministers, national stand-by forces and

30 Declaration for the Purposes of Establishing Similar Rules of Neutrality (1938) 188 LNTS 295.

a high willingness to contribute to UN operations.[31] By the end of the Cold War, some 25 per cent of UN peacekeeping personnel were from the Nordics.[32] In UN contexts, Peter Viggo Jacobsen believes the Nordics were regarded a single actor rather than separate states.[33]

It seems, thinks Andrei, the Nordics have now evacuated the friction zone, and climbed onto one of the tectonic plates. This obviously reduces the need for an approach to international law that is distinct and shaped by the need to make the most out of a handful of states with small militaries and a limited population.

Even in other areas Nordic international lawmakers had been vanishing from view. Andrei is still aware of the Nordic Passport Union created by a series of agreements between 1954 and 1957,[34] long before the Schengen Agreement was concluded by five Western European states in 1990.[35] So, was not the free movement of persons and an integrated labour market already a reality in the avant-garde Nordics long before the European Union mainstream started getting serious about it? And was there a *Laval* case in the Nordic labour market at the time?[36] The constituent geometry of polis, market and law seemed to have changed.

Let me move back to Tarkovsky's Andrei now. During his whole stay in Italy, he feels acutely out of place, out of time and out of context. His melancholy grows and he is unable to make contact with the Sosnovski project that brought him there, with the Italian spirituality that Sosnovski once appreciated and with the Italian woman who seeks his love. There is no way back to his origins,

31 P.V. Jacobsen, *Nordic Approaches to Peace Operations* (Routledge, London, 2006) p. 10.

32 *Ibid.*

33 *Ibid.*, p. 1.

34 Agreement between Denmark, Finland, Norway and Sweden concerning a Common Labour Market 199 UNTS 3; Protocol concerning the exemption of nationals of the Nordic countries from the obligation to have a passport or residence permit while resident in a Nordic country other than their own 199 UNTS 29; Convention between Finland, Denmark, Iceland, Norway and Sweden respecting Social Security, 254 UNTS 55; Convention between Denmark, Finland, Norway and Sweden concerning the waiver of passport control at the Intra-Nordic frontiers, 322 UNTS 245 (amended by the agreement of 27 July 1979 and supplemented by the agreements of 2 April 1973 and of 18 September 2000).

35 Agreement between the Governments of the States of the Benelux Economic Union, the Federal Republic of Germany and the French Republic on the Gradual Abolition of Checks at their Common Borders, (1991) 30 ILM 68, also known as Schengen I.

36 Case C-341/05 *Laval un Partneri Ltd* v. *Svenska Byggnadsarbetareförbundet,* [2007] ECR I-11767.

it appears, not even at a point where he is about to be driven to the airport for his return flight. The point of this nostalgia is just that it is suffered, that one is handed over to it. There is no social, political or other imperative to be drawn from it. Then there is Domenico's nostalgia: programmatic and righteous. It is about great ideas, about saving the world and its end point is suicide, just as the end point of Sosnovski's attempt to return to his origins. If Sosnovski and Andrei long for past origins, Domenico longs for future fulfilment and seeks to hasten it violently.

Andrei, our international lawyer, is angry at himself for his melancholic clinging to past Nordicness, because he knows that the 1938 Neutrality Declaration and the peacekeeping of the Nordic Model were gambles growing out of concrete and dangerous geopolitical pressures. This is nothing to cling on to, but he cannot help longing for the intense sensation that the international law and practice of these small states – his small states – actually mattered. Our Andrei knows that there is as little a way forward as there is a way back: to posit the past as the future, to promote an iteration of Nordic international law would seem to be overbearing and ahistorical to him. In a word: idiotic.

In Tarkovsky's *Nostalghia*, the idiot plays a catalytic role. Domenico's gesture does just what our Andrei believes to be impossible: posits the past as the future. His exhortation to listen to the insects is an exhortation to return to the origins of natural creation, and his choice of Marc Aurel's statute as a pulpit for his last speech to the people of Rome points his listeners back to the origins of antiquity and a stoical heroisation of the sage. His speech and *auto-da-fé* is a work of art, a terrifying *Gesamtkunstwerk* whose point is "to gather the polis together by giving form to a projective embodiment of an originary sacred unity".[37]

The same ahistorical overbearing is at work when actors of international law intentionally play out a Nordic legacy to promote a particular norm as the new international *lex ferenda*.[38]

But Domenico, after all, does something important for the storyline of *Nostalghia* before his *auto-da-fé*: he delivers a gesture that Andrei appropriates,

37 S.-O. Wallenstein, 'Tropes of Nostalgia. Winckelmann, Hegel, Heidegger and the Quest for Origins', online at <iloapp.philosophy.se/blog/thinklink?ShowFile&doc=1212586706.pdf>, accessed on 10 August 2016, drawing on Alex Potts' work to characterise Winckelman's agenda in reconstituting the original greatness of Greek art, p. 2.

38 For an example of how Nordic model rhethorics may turn hubristic, *see* M.-L. Skilbrei and C. Holmström, 'The "Nordic Model" of Prostitution Law is a Myth', *The Conversation*, 16 December 2013, online at <theconversation.com/the-nordic-model-of-prostitution-law-is-a-myth-21351>, accessed on 10 August 2016.

and in appropriating it, Andrei converts his own nostalgia into a third form that neither seeks to return to an origin nor to make it into a redemptive future.

Nothing in *Nostalghia* suggests that Andrei is an astute believer, be it in Christianity or in Domenico's hermit spirituality. Nothing suggests that he lets himself be recruited into Domenico's programme for saving the world. What he does is that he executes Domenico's *gesture* – the gesture of carrying a burning candle through the pool of the Holy Catherine. For Domenico, the Mathematician, this gesture might have evoked redemption into that which is divinely determined. Andrei enters the pool without assurances of divine determinism, in fact, without anything but his mood. For him, the gesture is sheer openness, the openness I experience when I join my own longing and suffering into that of another person. This is a way to live in community with the other, an 'other' who has put himself ablaze in a place far away to enforce the fulfilment of the original law.

The question of a Nordic international law is a question of how to live in a true community, and how that community is to live with others. Both questions are normative. The state, as it emerged out of European secularisation processes, is a way to respond to that question. It is no universal form, or so we are reminded by an Islamic state attempting to assert its existence. We have to put it in quotation marks to keep it from contaminating our abstract universal of the state.

So Domenico's gesture turns Andrei's backward longing into openness. What is to be its form? The film ends in this question, culminates in it, as his giving himself over to this question is witnessed by the woman cleaning the pool.

Heraclitus' fragment 119 reads *ethos anthropoi daimon*, or, in a standard English translation, 'for man, character is the demon'. "Once restored to its etymological origin", Giorgio Agamben writes, "Heraclitus's fragment then reads: 'For man, *ethos*, the dwelling in the 'self' that is what is most proper and habitual for him, is what lacerates and divides, the principle and place of a fracture'".[39] Tarkovsky's Andrei encountered fracture in his final effort to carry Domenico's candle. So nowhere is Nordic international law more at home and more itself than at the point where its fracturing is experienced. We are at this point now.

What might an international lawyer learn from *Nostalghia*? Nothing as an international lawyer, nothing as a professional, and everything as one who

39 G. Agamben, '*Se: Hegel's Absolute and Heidegger's *Ereignis*', in G. Agamben and D. Heller-Roazen (trans. and eds.), *Potentialities. Collected Essays in Philosophy* (Stanford University Press, Stanford, CA, 1999) pp. 116–137, at p. 118.

lives in doubt about his profession, the community it implies, and about the personal obligation she or he enters into by assuming it. The question is then, which madman will bequeath us with a gesture that we may execute, thereby opening up our idiotic longing for the Nordic, the Greek, the identic, the authentic and the communal and turn it into openness – an openness that is concrete, historically situated and at work in the world.

Diplomats, Professors, and Then Some: Notes for a History of International Law in 20th Century Finland

Martti Koskenniemi

This little essay has no greater ambition than to describe the engagement by Finnish jurists with international law during the 20th century. The aim is to produce an overview of their principal writings and careers. What will emerge from this is the perhaps surprising ease with which Finnish lawyers have moved between diplomacy and the academy. Politics, government and jurisprudence all play a role in their lives. No attempt is made to produce in-depth analyses of their writings, however. What the effect of their frequent moves between the worlds of practice and academy might have been on their output – or their *habitus* – will have to be discussed elsewhere. This ensuing text will merely point out relevant persons and some of their more interesting academic contributions. Hopefully this might inspire other such overviews and in due course also in-depth analyses to give content to what has recently been emerging as "comparative international law".

Compared to the other Nordic countries, or perhaps to the world at large, international law enjoyed an exceptionally strong position in Finland during the past century. The reasons for this are historical. Having recourse to legal principles and other argumentative devises was adopted as one resistance strategy during the Russification periods (1899–1905 and 1908–1917).[1] Even international audiences were captured by Finland's so-called "autonomy struggle" within Czarist Russia, the effort by the small country to maintain its constitution and other laws dating from the Swedish period and the brief moments of sanity in the Russian leaders' ideological life in the 19th century. International support came most famously in the form of a committee of European international and public law figures, the so-called London Committee in 1910, whose members had decided to make a name for themselves by publishing statements in support of Finland's constitutional autonomy within what the Finns called the Grand Duchy.

* This text is largely a translation of my contribution in the volume U. Kangas (ed.), *Oikeustiede Suomessa 1900–2000-luvulla* (WSOY, Helsinki, 1998) pp. 375–386.

1 *See* O. Korhonen, *International Law Situated: An Analysis of the Lawyer's Stance Towards Culture, History and Community* (Kluwer International, The Hague, 2000).

DOI 10.1163/9789004343597_004

Support was likewise sought from international law in the first years of independence, as the country's political leaders and its small but influential cohort of international lawyers began two operations involving international legal claims to Finland's neighbours. A first problem had to do with sovereignty over the Åland Islands: would the small islands in the middle of the Baltic Sea, consisting of almost exclusively of Swedish-speaking former subjects of the Grand Duke, now belong to Finland or its old imperial master, Sweden? The final opinion of the International Committee of Jurists given to the League of Nations Council in 1921 and the eventual settlement of the question in Finland's favour drew further attention to possibilities offered by international law in framing Finnish independence.[2] Perhaps, indeed, a small, recently independent country could make some use of this late-19th century liberal concoction to its advantage. It is not surprising that ever since those early years, the international status of the Åland Islands has remained a fruitful research topic among Finnish lawyers at the university and in public service (never clearly separated from each other). Another early international law issue implicated relations with Russia. In 1923 Finland brought the interpretation of the Tartu Peace Treaty concerning treatment of the Finnish-related population living in Eastern Karelia to the Permanent Court of International Justice. Did they, too, not deserve autonomy of some sort? Although the Court did not give the desired opinion (but instead decided that using the advisory procedure was inappropriate owing to the absence of the other side, Russia, from the proceedings), the great publicity surrounding these cases, combined with the country's orientation towards the League of Nations, provided the roots for the quite exceptional authority that international law has played in Finland and the way in which respect for it has from the start been understood as in the national interest.[3]

The research profile of the lawyers during the autonomy period and the early years of independence was substantially determined by the effort of advancing the interests associated with autonomy and independence. It may even be said that professors of public and constitutional law at Imperial Alexander University (what had earlier been the Academy of Turku and would later become the University Helsinki) stood at the intellectual forefront of the struggles. These struggles were commenced in 1884 at the University by the professor of cameral and policy law (*kameraali-ja politialainopin professori*), Robert Hermanson, who had just been appointed as a professor of constitutional law.

2 League of Nations, Official Journal, October 1920, Special Supplement No. 3. For the documents, *see also La question d'Isles d'Aland* (Helsinki, 1920).

3 PCIJ, *Eastern Carelia* Advisory Opinion, Ser B 5 (1923).

Hermanson's work *Finlands statsrättsliga ställning* (Finland's Public Law Status, 1892) was designed to demonstrate that within the Russian Empire Finland possessed the status of a non-sovereign, internally independent state. In 1907, two years before Hermanson retired, the title of his professorship was changed into that of "constitutional and international law". But Hermanson had taught international law well before this amendment. A series of lectures by him on international law was published in Swedish under the editorship of Hjalmar Nyqvist in 1901. Those lectures followed the continental mainstream: international law presented there as the sum total of the "absolute" and "relative" rights of states.

But the most prominent Finnish international lawyer in the 20th century was probably Rafael Erich who was appointed, after Hermanson's retirement in 1910, to the chair of constitutional and international law. Two years earlier, Erich had published, in no less than four languages, a work exploring Finland's legal position with the title *Finlands rätt, belyst av utländsk rättslära* (Finland's Law, in the Light of Foreign Jurisprudence). Four years later a wider volume came out on the same subject, with the German title *Das Staatsrecht des Grossfürstentüms Finnland.* Between 1915–1918 Erich was undoubtedly one of the leaders of the independence movement on the side of the academy, with substantive risks to his career and even his personal freedom. That he was largely able to carry out his activism was no doubt to some extent due to his international stature and contacts.

After independence, Erich was elected Member of Parliament. In the years 1920–1921 he even gained the position of prime minister. When his chair in 1921 was divided in two parts, constitutional law and international law, Erich became the holder of a first chair in the country solely dedicated to international law. But he also took assignments as Finnish ambassador in Berne and the League of Nations. That he was permanently transferred to the Foreign Ministry in 1928 did not end his academic activities. Erich was elected member of the Permanent Court of International Justice in 1938, and he was a member of the *Institut de droit international.* He continued to publish widely both at home and abroad. His two series of lectures at the Hague Academy of International Law (1926 and 1929) dealt, appropriately enough, on the emergence of states and the notion of "demilitarized zones".

Hermanson and Erich had both received their intellectual influences from Germany. Hermanson had even been a student of Paul Laband, one of the leading German public lawyers of the late-19th century. In his dissertation *Über Allianzen und Allianzverhältnisse nach heutigem Völkerrecht* (1907), Erich investigated the notions of unions and alliances of states, following not only Laband, but particularly Georg Jellinek's well-known writings. Erich emphasized the freedom international law left to states to conduct their affairs and highlighted the law's relations with "life" in a way that has some resemblance with the writings of the realist school of international politics, including those of its father, Hans Morgenthau. The volume *Kansainvälinen oikeus* (International Law, 1915) used the autolimitation theory (*Selbstverpflichtungslehre*), also received from Jellinek, to explain the way a state was bound by its international obligations. Like most Finnish lawyers at the time, Erich was a follower of the main lines of continental legal positivism. He rejected efforts to maintain any concept of an ethically oriented "just war" as part of international law and always pictured the international "community" in strictly horizontal terms. It was law between, not above, states.

Hermanson and Erich were both active participants in the debates over the Åland Islands and Eastern Karelia questions. Neither they nor their followers ended their interest in international legal research after engaging in political affairs. The same was true of K.G. Idman who published in 1914 an ambitious, historically oriented, interdisciplinary dissertation, *Le traité de garantie en droit international*, at the University of Helsinki. The work did not deal with the question of Finland's legal position, but instead with the concept of a "guarantee agreement" – an institution the usefulness of which might have been at some point entertained among the country's political leaders. In any case, in 1918, Idman took a position at the Ministry for Foreign Affairs where he became a permanent secretary as well as an ambassador in the Tartu Peace negotiations. He was also one of the principal representatives on the Finnish side during the treatment of the Åland Islands question at the League of Nations. In the immediate post-war years Idman became a member of the delegation negotiating the Paris peace agreement as well as the preparation of the 1948 Treaty on Friendship, Cooperation and Mutual Assistance (FCMA) with the Soviet Union. Such official assignments did not prevent him from publishing articles on specific geographical issues such as the legal situation of Danzig and Svalbard. After the war he turned his interests to the codification of international law as well as human rights.

Sigurd von Numers published his doctoral thesis *Kampmedel i sjökrig* (1927) after two years in the service of the Ministry for Foreign Affairs. The dissertation followed the mainstream of Finnish (but also perhaps more widely Nordic and central-European) academic law: its text was inclined in a positivist manner but also designed to end up in suggestions of reform. Subsequent study of humanitarian law in Finland has followed in his footsteps (although rarely with specific acknowledgment). As a member of the Finnish Ministry for Foreign Affairs, von Numers acted as ambassador, and on two occasions occupied a position as the head of the Ministry's legal department (1949–1954 and 1961–1964).

Like Idman, he also continued his publishing activities during those periods. Kaarlo Hiitonen's doctoral thesis *La Compétence de l'Organisation du Travail International I* (1929) likewise adopted a textual approach to its topic and is remarkable for its early human rights orientation. Hiitonen was appointed as the head of the Ministry's League of Nations unit and participated in many delegations to meetings with the League and the International Labour Organisation. He resigned from the Ministry for Foreign Affairs in 1942. After the war he abandoned legal research and joined the Socialist Unity Party, a small faction that separated from the social democrats while also keeping distance to the communists.

S.R. Björksten was appointed professor of international law at the University of Helsinki after Erich in 1931. Bjöksten had never worked as diplomat. His doctoral thesis *Das Wassergebeit Finnlands in völkerrechtlicher Hinsicht* (1925) dealt with the international law of the sea and various other matters related to the administration of Finnish watercourses as well as Finland's maritime boundaries. In 1937, Björksten published a textbook *Kansainvälinen oikeus* (International Law) that with its great detail and personal tone is no doubt one of the most interesting works of Finnish interwar international law. Björksten rejected the voluntarism and the positivism of his colleagues, devoting himself instead to searches for the roots of international law in what he called the legal conviction of humankind. The work was also unique in including a historical outlook on its materials as well as extensive treatments of the status of individuals and minorities in international law. It also took up the great continental theme of "functional cooperation" which, Björksten suggested, was something Finland would be well advised to support. But the war, perhaps logically, persuaded Björksten to end his international law activities and to take up priesthood in Sweden instead.

Finnish international lawyers have not been prone to reflecting on principles of the just war or other types of philosophical speculation. Their outlook has been, generally speaking, that of doctrinal positivists interested in the legal aspects of Finland's international position. Commentaries on international institutions refrain from speculating about a coming international community or other types of federalism. However, in *Om folkrättslig skiljedom* (On International Arbitration, 1912), a commentary on the results of the Second Hague Peace Conference of 1907, Erich did not hide his wish that expanding the use of arbitration might operate as an element of a peaceful international order in the future. But in *Kansainliiton oikeusjärjestys* (The Legal Order of the League of Nations, 1926) he depicted the League as a contractual arrangement between its sovereign members designed to coordinate their activities. It was nothing like an incipient world government. This has continued to be the outlook of most Finnish lawyers ever since. For example, in 1946, Tauno Suontausta published his *Yhdistyneet kansakunnat* (United Nations) where he described the new organization in exhaustively inter-state terms. The thick volume *United Nations*, published in 1990 by Bengt Broms, was predominantly a review of the organization's operational practices. Reviewing the UN system institution by institution, Broms outlined their constitutional basis and expounded their principal operations. None of the Finnish lawyers would follow a continental institutionalism any more than American functionalism. Research has focused on the interpretation of the constitution of the organization and the description of the functioning of the main organs.

By the time Suontausta published his *Valtion alueellisesta puolueettomuudesta* (On the Territorial Neutrality of the State, 1944) he had already worked for the Ministry for Foreign Affairs for a decade. His practical experience was reflected in his doctoral dissertation, which strove to interpret the 1938 Nordic Neutrality Regulations from an international legal point of view. After a period as the head of the legal department of the Foreign Ministry (1944–1947) Suontausta left diplomacy but continued publishing in international law, focusing in his essays on peace-making, mutual defence agreements and the status of the Åland Islands. His theoretical ambitions are visible in the work *La souveraineté des états* (1955) that begins with a reference to the realist Hans Morgenthau. Reviewing doctrines such as the fundamental rights of states, jurisdiction and the recognition of states, Suontausta came to the conclusion that a marked "relativization" of sovereignty had taken place in the 20th century.

Erik Castrén also worked initially at the Ministry for Foreign Affairs (1926–1930) and continued as its legal advisor during and immediately after the war. In 1945 he was appointed professor of international law at the University of Helsinki. Castrén continued his long academic career while being associated with the Ministry for Foreign Affairs as an expert, member of the *Institut de droit international* from 1950, and member of the International Law Commission (ILC) from 1962 to 1972. In addition, he served as a member and president of numerous arbitration tribunals, including the commission on the German external debt and in 1977 as the president of the Court of Arbitration in the continental shelf dispute between Britain and France.

Ilmasota I–II (The Law of Air War, 1938–1939), *The Present Law of War and Neutrality* (1954), *Siviiliväestön suoja maa- ja ilmasodassa* (*The Protection of Civilians in Land and Maritime War*, 1964) as well as the widely read *Civil War* (1966) were works of constructive legal doctrine that sought to systematize and codify the otherwise separate sources and principles available in treaties and customary law in their respective fields. These works manifest Castrén's interest in the development of the laws of war, now increasingly imagined euphemistically as "humanitarian law". Like Erich, Castrén also gave lectures at the Hague Academy of International Law ("Recent Aspects of the Succession of States", 1951). Also Castrén's international law reflected a national experience and a perspective, written into what became the most widely used textbook of international law in the 1960s and 1970s, *Suomen kansainvälinen oikeus* (Finland's International Law, 1959). The work took a consciously Finnish perspective on its subject-matter, providing detailed descriptions of the country's post-war treaty relations with its neighbours. Castrén wrote widely on various technical aspects of international law. He also directed a series of essays to the Finnish audience (in Finnish) designed to defend the reality of international law against sceptical criticism. But he had no ambition to take these arguments to a wider international audience.

Broms was appointed Castrén's successor in 1969. He devoted his research to an approach that could be best described as formal-constructive. Broms' dissertation *The Doctrine of Equality of States as Applied in International Organizations* (1959) was in many ways a "modern" book. It was "empirically" oriented, focusing on the way sovereign states cooperated in the UN system and not on abstract doctrines. The analysis consciously avoided taking a political point of view – including any political theory from "equality". It was a practice-oriented work with an unarticulated commitment to the progress of the institutions that were its object. A large part of Broms' production was directed at international organizations, especially the UN. The focus on the United Nations is clear in his textbook *Yhdistyneet Kansakunnat* (United Nations, 1975), which was published in 1990 in a large English edition, partially revised. Special attention in this work is given to the debates in the UN on the definition of the concept of "aggression", a task in which Broms was personally involved as the chairman of the relevant UN special committee. In 1977 Broms produced a textbook on the basics of international law that was revised in 1995, and his other works included studies on the Suez Canal and the permanent neutrality of Austria. After Broms moved from Turku to Helsinki to take up Castrén's old chair, the professorship in constitutional and international law in Turku went to Toivo Sainio for the period 1971–1997. Sainio's credentials for that job included his doctoral dissertation *Muukalaisen oikeusasemasta erityisesti Suomen oikeutta silmälläpitäen* (On the Legal Situation of Aliens with Special Reference to Finnish Law, vol. I (1959) and vol. II (1968)). The work was situated somewhere between international and domestic Finnish law and perhaps anticipated the future orientation of Finnish constitutional lawyers to human rights research.

The interest shown by von Numers and Castren in international humanitarian law was continued in Allan Rosas' award-winning dissertation *The Legal*

Status of Prisoners of War. A Study of Humanitarian Law Applicable in Armed Conflicts (1976). Rosas was appointed in 1981 professor of constitutional and international law at Åbo Akademi. His doctoral dissertation was largely based on the preparatory work of the 1977 Additional Protocols to the 1949 Geneva Conventions. After the dissertation, Rosas first turned to various political and Cold War topics, but gradually extended his interests in the field of human rights. Under the leadership of Rosas, the Åbo Akademi established a well-known institute of human rights that has continued its activities to this day. Rosas published on the reduction of nuclear weapons as well as on the present role of state sovereignty and has always been interested in the interactions between international law and policy. Rosas has also dealt with the relationship between international and domestic law in Finland, aiming to promote a shift away from basic dualistic attitude. He was also an expert on human rights at the Ministry for Foreign Affairs before joining in 1996 the European Commission's legal department. Today he is a judge at the European Court of Justice.

Lauri Hannikainen's extensive doctoral dissertation *Jus Cogens. Historical Development, Criteria and Present Status* (1988) marked the culmination of the formal-constructivist approach in Finland. Through a systematic study of legal sources in different fields of international law, Hannikainen put together a kind of semi-naturalistic international law constitution. Also Hannikainen began his career in the Foreign Ministry, but soon moved from there to various university positions. Like Rosas, Hannikainen's interest extended way beyond the confines of traditional diplomatic law. His prolific writings cover the fields of humanitarian law, human rights as well as self-determination. Both Rosas and Hannikainen have also written extensively on the Åland Islands. In a volume *Humanitarian Law Applicable in Armed Conflicts* (1992), edited by Hannikainen together with Rosas and Raija Hanski, their ambition was to break out from a purely textual into a more historical approach on the subject-matter.

Towards the end of the century, Finnish international lawyers began to search for influences from the common law world. In 1989, Esa Paasivirta defended his thesis on the *Participation of States in International Contracts* (published in 1990) in Cambridge, and Erkki Kourula in 1987 in Oxford on the *Regional Operations under Chapter VIII of the UN Charter* (not published). Paasivirta's work was a case-analysis, and Kourula's research was targeted at the history and interpretation of Chapter VIII of the United Nations Charter. Both Kourula and Paasivirta were in due course appointed to the Ministry for Foreign Affairs from where they moved to international assignments. Paasivirta joined the European Commission while Kourula was appointed judge at the International Criminal Court (ICC). Mention ought to be made also of Frank Horn's dissertation at the University of Uppsala, *Reservations and Interpretative Declarations in International Law* (1987). This award-winning, practice-oriented and interdisciplinary work used, among other approaches, statistical analyses.

Scholars with non-Finnish backgrounds at Helsinki University included Maurice Andem whose dissertation on *International Economic Cooperation in Developing Countries* (1978) paved the way for a full academic career in Finland, especially the University of Lapland. Ruth Donner's widely read dissertation *The Regulation of Nationality in International Law* (1983) progressed into a second edition, establishing itself as a *Standardwerk* on the laws of citizenship. Donner as well as Andem have worked alongside Hannikainen as associate professors of international law at the University of Helsinki. As an assistant professor at the University of Lapland, Andem was interested in economy and space law. But as domestic priorities changed, lawyers in the new generation began to move from the state-centered "diplomatic" law to human rights. Matti Pellonpää's dissertation *Expulsion in International Law. A Study in International Alien Law and Human Rights with Special Reference to Finland* (1984) joined a textual approach to broader analyses of the case-law and activities of international organizations. Pellonpää became judge at the European Court of Human Rights and the author of the textbook *Euroopan ihmisoikeussopimus* (The European Convention on Human Rights, 2nd edition, 1996). In the 1980s many lawyers began to assess Finnish law from the perspective of international standards. Martin Scheinin's dissertation *Ihmisoikeudet Suomen oikeudessa* (Human Rights in Finnish Law, 1991), as well as many of his prolific later works, used constitutional and comparative law to bring international themes into Finnish debates. Scheinin began his career as a parliamentary secretary in a left-wing party but soon joined the academy and gradually became the country's leading human rights lawyer. He also became a member of the UN Human Rights Committee and special rapporteur on human rights and counter-terrorism.

Finnish international lawyers have also been interested in environmental questions. The above-mentioned Björksten dissertation dealt with the use of water resources. In 1953, Eero Manner, member of the Supreme Administrative Court, defended his doctoral dissertation on this same topic. Manner's wide international contacts prompted the activity of the International Law Association (ILA) in this field and led in 1966 to the adoption of the so-called Helsinki Rules on International Watercourses. Manner also became part-time legal advisor to the Ministry for Foreign Affairs in 1965; he chaired the Finnish delegation to the III United Nations Conference on the Law of the Sea and his work on international watercourses and the law of the sea gained some international attention. Kari Hakapää worked as secretary to the Finnish UNCLOS delegation and in 1981 defended his doctoral dissertation *Marine Pollution in International Law. Material Obligations and Jurisdiction with Special Reference to the Third United Nations Conference on the Law of the Sea* in Helsinki. Hakapää then served as Counsellor at the Ministry for Foreign Affairs before being appointed professor at the University of Lapland. Hakapää's work has been predominantly (though not exclusively) in the field of the law of the sea. Alongside publishing a textbook on the law of the sea, Hakapää also became the author of the most widely used general textbook on international law, *Kansainvälinen oikeus* (International Law, first edition, 1995).

Kari Joutsamo's doctoral thesis, *The Role of Preliminary Rulings in the European Communities* (1979) was the first large academic work in that new field, at the time regarded as exotic if not marginal. This methodologically reflective work included sections on comparative law and opened the doors to study European law and European institutions to a new generation of lawyers. Joutsamo moved from a position in international law in Turku to become professor of European law at the University of Helsinki. In the 1980s many jurists were experimenting with alternative methods and approaches. This was true also of my doctoral thesis *From Apology to Utopia. The Structure of International Legal Argument* (1989) that took its influences from structural linguistics and the US-based critical legal studies movement. At the time I defended the thesis, I had already been an official with the Finnish Foreign Ministry for 12 years. I continued as diplomat until being appointed Broms' successor in Helsinki in 1995. Other works inspired by critical theory include Veijo Heiskanen's doctoral dissertation, *International Legal Topics* (1992), at Harvard University that dealt with the relationship between international and national law, sanctions and the use of force. Heiskanen first worked at international institutions, landing eventually as a partner with the law firm Lalive in Geneva. It may be said that the circle comes to a close with Outi Korhonen's Harvard dissertation *International Law Situated. An Analysis of the Lawyer's Stance towards Culture, History and Community* (2000). A work inspired by hermeneutic philosophy and critical theory, it uses the career and writings of the Finnish independence activist and lawyer Leo Mechelin to examine the "situation" of a lawyer with a political commitment and agenda.

Conclusions

A century of international law in Finland witnessed activism in politics, service in government and engagement with the academy. During the first half of the century, international law teaching was combined with constitutional law, both subjects conceived from the perspective of the German public law tradition, its concerns and methods. The state was not only the central concept of the field but also the focus of commitment and defence. The services of academic jurists were appreciated by the Foreign Ministry and no great gap appeared between the political alignments of jurists working predominantly on the one or the other side. This situation changed somewhat only in the 1980s, some years later than in other European countries, as the field and its priorities expanded and specialized. Rising interest in human rights, the environment and in European law was accompanied by new priorities. In a field previously populated by public-law trained men, an increasing number of women after Donner and Korhonen took positions in international law and international human rights law in the academy as well as the Foreign Ministry. The state could no longer expect unreserved loyalty from the new generation of international jurists growing up in the country's three law faculties. Was the state more the problem than the solution? Overall, the relations between the expanding international law academy and the Foreign Ministry remained good, even if "defending the state" was no longer how either diplomats or academic jurists would have described what they were doing. But if there is one thing Europeans should have learned from their 20th century experience, it is that nationalism, internationalism, cosmopolitanism are entangled in complex configurations and that the best legal institutions are those that can be described alternatively from any such angle. Finland always had an active, even "activist" international law profession. While the points of interest and methods have varied, the sense that international law provides a useful platform for engaging with questions of social and political importance has united generations of Finnish international lawyers.

Dag Hammarskjöld and the "*Ambetsmanna*" Approach to UN Cooperation

Ove Bring

1 Nordics in the United Nations

A number of Nordic civil servants and political personalities have since the start of the United Nations (UN) contributed to the work of the Organization. This article will deal with the second Secretary-General of the UN, Dag Hammarskjöld. As a citizen from a Nordic country he is not alone in having played a role in the history of international cooperation. Hammarskjöld's predecessor as Secretary-General was the former Norwegian foreign minister, Trygve Lie. The former Finnish Foreign Minister Sakari Tuomioja was a UN mediator for Cyprus in the 1960s. Later, Thorvald Stoltenberg (Norway) was the Special Representative of the UN in the former Yugoslavia Conference, while Carl Bildt (Sweden) was the European Union mediator, and Uffe Ellemann-Jensen (Denmark) was the OSCE representative in the same cooperative effort. Former Finnish President Martti Ahtisaari, a winner of the Nobel Peace Award, has been the UN Special Envoy for Kosovo and a mediator in many other conflicts. Jan Egeland (Norway) has been a UN Coordinator for Humanitarian Affairs and Emergency Relief. Kai Eide (Norway) has been Head of the UN Assistance Mission in Afghanistan. Jan Eliasson (Sweden) was a recent Deputy Secretary-General. And so on and on, one is tempted to remark.

Nordic officials have been successful in their role as international civil servants. The question could well be asked if a common intellectual thinking lies beneath. Is there such a thing as a Nordic approach to international cooperation, law and diplomacy – an approach of fairness, impartiality and humanization? Does the "*ambetsmanna*" tradition and rule of law orientation of Nordic societies produce a certain imprint in the civilizing efforts of the international community? Or is the simple putting of this question a manifestation of regional hybris, of a belief that 'we' stick to a higher degree of international morality than 'others'? There will be no attempt in the following to answer these questions. Nevertheless, the questions have been put, and I will let them linger in the air. Again, this article will only deal with Dag Hammarskjöld and his role in global governance.

Hammarskjöld has obviously gone down in history as an inspiring international personality, injecting a dose of moral leadership and personal integrity

 | DOI 10.1163/9789004343597_005

into a world of power politics. He succeeded Trygve Lie as Secretary-General in April 1953, in the midst of the Cold War, and in addition to East–West rivalry he was confronted with Third World problems and the agonizing birth of the new Republic of Congo, a tumultuous crisis, during which he lost his life in the Ndola air crash of September 1961.

2 Background and Personal Philosophy

Dag Hammarskjöld had a flexible approach to international law. On the one hand, he strongly relied on the principles of the UN Charter and general international law, on the other, he used a flexible and balanced *ad hoc* technique, taking into account values and policy factors whenever possible, to resolve concrete problems. Hammarskjöld was inclined to express basic principles in terms of opposing tendencies, to apply a discourse of polarity or dualism, stressing for example that the observance of human rights was balanced by the concept of non-intervention and national sovereignty, and recognizing that principles and precepts could not provide automatic answers in concrete cases. Rather, such norms would serve "as criteria which had to be weighed and balanced in order to achieve a rational solution of the particular problem".[1] Very often it worked.

He was born in 1905 in Jönköping, Sweden, the fourth son of Hjalmar Hammarskjold, President of the Göta Court of Appeal and a member of the Swedish Government. At the time of Dag's birth the father was part of a Swedish delegation that negotiated the dissolution of the union between Sweden and Norway.

Hjalmar Hammarskjöld had studied trade law under Professor Paul Laband in Strasbourg and he later fulfilled his doctorate at Uppsala University with a thesis on contracts of affreightment (1886). He was appointed professor of law at Uppsala in 1891, served as a non-political Minister of Justice in 1901–02, and was appointed member of the Hague Permanent Court of Arbitration in 1904. During most of World War I he served as Prime Minister (1914–17) and pursued

1 O. Schachter, "Dag Hammarskjold and the Relation of Law to Politics", 56 *American Journal of International Law* (*AJIL*) (1962) pp. 2–5. Quotation from p. 5. Hammarskjöld recognized that there was a tension between principles and concrete needs; by taking account of both, he sought to achieve (in his own words) "that combination of steadfastness of purpose and flexibility of approach which alone can guarantee that the possibilities which we are exploring will have been tested to the full". *Ibid.*

a 'strict' policy of neutrality which was widely criticized for being legalistic. In the Prime Minister's own words, he wanted Sweden and the other Nordic countries to stand up for the law of neutrality for the benefit of European civilization. He authored a joint Nordic diplomatic note to the belligerent states to this effect (in November 1914). In 1924 he published the legal treatise *La neutralité en general*.

Dag's elder brother Åke became a member of the League of Nations secretariat and from 1922 until 1936 he was Registrar of the Permanent Court of International Justice in The Hague. In that function he assisted the President of the Court, Judge Max Huber. When Huber was appointed arbiter in the dispute between United Kingdom and Spain in the *Spanish Zone of Morocco Claims* in 1923 he asked Åke Hammarskjöld to function as Secretary of the arbitration commission. They cooperated smoothly in the different decisions that were delivered during 1924 and 1925. Åke Hammarskjöld published a number of articles on international law issues.[2] He was appointed judge of the Permanent Court in 1936, but died prematurely the following year.[3] Dag always held his brother Åke in high esteem.

Dag's eldest brother, Bo Hammarskjöld (1891–1974), was appointed member of the Supreme Administrative Court of Sweden in 1934 and a District Governor in 1935. The father and his sons were groomed in a typical Swedish civil service tradition ("*ämbetsmannatradition*") in which the concepts of 'duty' and 'responsibility' reflected time-honoured values. Oscar Schachter, who was a member of the UN Secretariat between 1953 and 1956, has said of Dag Hammarskjöld that "he had a manifest pride in his family's legal background" and that he "regarded himself as a man of law".[4]

Hammarskjöld had an academic training in both law and economics, and he would later become a professional economist. After initial studies at Uppsala University, he spent the autumn of 1927 at the University of Cambridge and attended the seminars of John Maynard Keynes. He thereafter majored in economics at Uppsala and obtained a Bachelor of Law degree there in 1930. He produced a doctoral thesis in Stockholm on the "business cycle" in 1933 and obtained an assistant professorship in political economy.

2 After his death Åke Hammarskjöld's writings were collected in the book *Juridiction Internationale* (Sijthoff, Leiden, 1938), with a foreword ("In Memoriam") by Max Huber.

3 Åke Hammarskjöld's influential role within the PCIJ is discussed further in Astrid Kjeldgaard-Pedersen's contribution to this volume.

4 Schachter, *supra* note 1, p. 1.

Two years later, Hammarskjöld became an influential civil servant. After some time at the Ministry of Finance, in 1947 he was appointed to a leading function in the Ministry for Foreign Affairs. During this period, his belief was founded that it was of manifest importance to have an impartial civil service, and he later worked hard to realize the goal of an independent international civil service as Secretary-General of the United Nations.[5]

In 1947 and 1948 Hammarskjöld participated in the conferences in Paris on the Marshall Plan and on the structure of European Economic Cooperation. During these negotiations, fellow diplomats discovered his technical and analytical gifts and his talent for finding compromises to complicated problems. In 1951 he joined the Swedish cabinet as (a non-political) Minister without Portfolio. He became, in effect, Deputy Foreign Minister, dealing with economic cooperation. This was his position when he, in the spring of 1953, was approached for the function of Secretary-General of the United Nations.

Hammarskjöld's personal philosophy would play an important role during his time as Secretary-General. He had a very close relationship with his mother Agnes, a pious and religious woman, and from her he inherited a simple wish to 'do good' in concrete cases. Already as a young man he was interested in medieval religious thinking. His early correspondence includes references to mystics such as Meister Eckhart (d. 1327) and Thomas à Kempis (d. 1471). He had received Thomas à Kempis' *De imitatione Christi* from his mother in 1921 and kept the book for the rest of his life. Later he also referred to Thomas Aquinas (d. 1274), the more empiric and realist philosopher who tried to combine Christian doctrine with Aristotelian thinking, and St. John of the Cross (d. 1591), who combined Christian mysticism with religious reformism and poetry. What these thinkers had in common was a focus on meditation and seclusion, a stress on the importance of a man's inner life in relation to God in preparation for individual choices and individual action. Hammarskjöld was through his life attracted to this personal approach to moral decision-making. It also connected to the societal values of 'duty' and 'responsibility' conveyed by his father and the pious-moral influence exerted by his mother.[6] Thus, while the wish to 'do good' seems to be inherited from his mother, it has been said

5 M. Bouman, *Dag Hammarskjöld, Citizen of the World* (Ten Have, Kampen, 2005) p. 26. Bouman also points out that at the same time as Hammarskjöld was Under-Secretary of the Ministry of Finance his brother Bo was Secretary of State for Social Affairs. "It is said that together the two brothers were responsible for working out all the financial and technical details of the Swedish Welfare State". *Ibid.*

6 G. Aulén, *Dag Hammarskjöld's White Book, An Analysis of Markings* (Fortress Press, Philadelphia, 1969) p. 14.

that the ideals of 'duty, righteousness and self-less service' were inherited from the Swedish paternal tradition.[7]

After Hammarskjöld's death, the manuscript of a diary was found in his New York apartment. Together with it was a letter addressed to a Swedish friend and diplomat, where Hammarskjöld described the text "as a sort of *white book* concerning my negotiations with myself – and with God".[8] The diary was published in Sweden in 1963 as *Vägmärken* (Roadmarks). An English translation was published in 1964 under the title *Markings*.[9] The entries do not tell us anything about Hammarskjöld 'on the job' as Secretary-General (other than obliquely), but they tell us something about his thinking on values and personal guidelines. His religious and moral reliance on Meister Eckhart and Thomas Aquinas (in that order) was confirmed. In addition, it became clear (or was confirmed) that he had an intense relationship to world literature. He used the works of Joseph Conrad, Herman Hesse, Henrik Ibsen, Fyodor Dostoyevsky and others for personal reflection in situations where decisions needed to be taken. It was manifest from his correspondence and diary that these and other authors played a significant role in his world of ideas since his student years.[10]

Dostoyevsky's *The Brothers Karamazov* includes references to each individual's universal responsibility for other individuals, to the ideas of 'service to mankind' and 'brotherhood and inclusiveness of men', and to individual action 'for the sake of the future'. Dostoyevsky's novel foreshadowed the ethics of Albert Schweitzer, and Hammarskjöld always kept a copy of it in his apartment. Hammarskjöld was much attracted to the idea of moral individual action. He also felt that Joseph Conrad's novels *Lord Jim* and *Heart of Darkness* conveyed strong moral messages, and that Herman Melville's *Moby Dick* and Henrik Ibsen's *Brand* caught the dilemmas of strong-willed individuals who frantically pursue their chosen path of life in constant uphill battles.

Hammarskjöld was not afraid of uphill battles. He saw the appointment as Secretary-General as a challenge and a chance to be of real service to the international community. At last he was in a position to put into action the ethics of Albert Schweitzer embraced by himself, the ideal of service to man. His diary entries following 7 April 1953 (the day of his election by the General Assembly upon the recommendation of the Security Council) express a

7 *Ibid.*

8 The letter is rendered on the introductory page in Dag Hammarskjöld, *Markings* (translated from the Swedish by Leif Sjöberg and W.H. Auden) (Alfred A. Knopf, New York, 1964).

9 *Ibid.*

10 See K.E. Birnbaum (ed.), *Dag Hammarskjöld: Ungdomsårens vittnesbörd: Brev och uppteckningar 1925–1931* (Swedish Science Press, Stockholm, 2001).

certain self-confidence: "To say Yes to life is at one and the same time to say Yes to oneself".[11] He was ready to take on a role of leadership vis-à-vis the international community.

3 In the United Nations

Not long after Hammarskjöld's appointment as Secretary-General in 1953 it was already becoming clear that he had an innovative approach to the possibilities of the UN. He was not a formalist, he wanted to go forward and act in line with the purposes of the UN Charter. The purposes of the Charter were fixed and binding, but the working methods of the Organization had to be flexible and innovative. He did not feel fettered by concrete provisions of the Charter that did not explicitly provide for things he wanted to do, options he wanted to test in his capacity as Secretary-General. If he felt that the purposes of the UN made it possible, he would envision a mandate flowing from the Charter to act in accordance with his conscience as an international civil servant.

Hammarskjöld set out his views on the role of the UN Organization and his approach to the UN Charter in the Annual reports to the General Assembly. In this context, he developed a doctrine on the independence of the international civil servant, including an active role for the Secretary-General under an expansive interpretation of Articles 97–100 of the Charter. He introduced new mechanisms for a UN presence in conflict areas, for example, the appointment of Special Representatives of the Secretary General (SRSGs).

He did not make a very sharp distinction between law and politics. Nor did he look upon international law as mainly 'written law', but emphasized, in the vein of Myres McDougal, "the whole international pattern of rules and behavior".[12] Even before Wolfgang Friedman had published his famous book *The Changing Structure of International Law* (1964), Hammarskjöld used the distinction between the traditional 'law of coexistence' and the more dynamic

11 See Hammarskjöld, *Markings, supra* note 8, p. 92. On Hammarskjöld's use of the phrase "to say Yes", see Henry P. van Dusen, *Dag Hammarskjöld: The Statesman and His Faith* (Harper & Row, New York, 1967) pp. 99–102.

12 Wilder Foote (ed.), *The Servant of Peace, A Selection of Speeches and Statements of Dag Hammarskjold* (The Bodley Head, London, 1962), p. 242. The quoted words may indicate an intellectual link to the New Haven school, but at the same time as Hammarskjöld was guided by universal "policies and goals" (including the concept of human dignity), he nevertheless gave priority to the legal elements over the political ones in the decision-making process. Schachter, *supra* note 1, p. 2.

'law of cooperation'. The world, in his view, was slowly moving into the latter more advanced area, which included supranational decision-making.

During his time as Secretary-General Hammarskjöld set forth a number of general themes regarding the role of the UN, but he did not articulate specific doctrines on human rights, intervention, or security. Nevertheless, as we shall see, he developed new methods for the functioning of the system of collective security, and he was a frontrunner in the field of what today is called human security.

One of Hammarskjöld's first tasks as Secretary-General was to negotiate, in the aftermath of the Korean War, the release of American pilots taken prisoners by China. In this context, he felt the support of the wisdom of the Jewish philosopher Martin Buber as expressed in the book *Ich und Du* (1923). Buber stressed the importance of human dialogue and Hammarskjöld's visit to Beijing in January 1955 was marked by fruitful intellectual dialogue with Chinese Premier Chou En-lai. The chemistry between the two men made the conversation sparkle. Later the same year the US airmen were released. The release coincided with Chou En-lai's personal congratulations to the Secretary-General on his 50th birthday. Hammarskjöld is famous for having coined the concepts of preventive and quiet diplomacy, but in this case, it was more a matter of personal diplomacy.

4 The Introduction of Peacekeeping

Hammarskjöld is best known for his innovative approach to the UN Charter. The first example here is the matter of peacekeeping, which was not, and still is not, mentioned in the Charter.

Hammarskjöld elaborated the new concept during the Suez crisis of 1956. As the Security Council was blocked by a joint British and French veto, the Secretary-General had to rely on the General Assembly. As a procedural mechanism he used the Uniting for Peace resolution of 1950 to summon an extra Emergency Session of the Assembly. Together with the Canadian External Affairs Minister, Lester Pearson, he thereafter introduced the option of a UN mandated military peace operation in the conflict area, with the consent of the parties to the conflict. On 7 November 1956, the General Assembly adopted a resolution which launched the first peacekeeping operation in UN history, the UN Emergency Force in the Middle East (UNEF).

Although UN observer missions had been fielded in 1948 and 1949, the deployment of *armed troops* to assist in the implementation of agreements reached between the UN and parties to a conflict added a new dimension to international relations. To govern these operations Hammarskjöld laid down three principles: (1) consent from the territorial state and other parties involved; (2) impartiality on the UN side to secure credibility in the operation; and (3) non-use of force by the UN side, unless in individual self-defense or collective mission defense.

Over the years, it became clear that the Security Council should be the UN body to decide on all forms of UN peace operations, not only with regard to peace *enforcement* under Chapter VII of the Charter, but also with regard to cooperative peacekeeping.

When UNEF was established, Hammarskjöld considered it a new departure. "It is", he said, "certainly not contrary to the Charter, but is in a certain sense outside the explicit terms of the Charter".

Thus, peacekeeping operations, PKOs, were not foreseen under either Chapter VI or VII of the Charter, but fell somewhere in between, and not surprisingly the unwritten Chapter VI ½ has been suggested as their legal basis. It is submitted that this "VI ½ perception" is appropriate and useful; appropriate because PKOs *are* a more ambitious involvement than anything provided for in Chapter VI; and politically useful because it shows that innovations, even without textual support, can be legitimized under the system of the Charter if they fulfil the purposes of the UN Organization.

5 Hammarskjöld on Idealism and Realism

Dag Hammarskjöld was appointed Secretary-General five years after Hans Morgenthau had published his influential realist opus *Politics among Nations*. In a speech in 1956 Hammarskjöld had reason to comment on the divide between idealism and realism. Assertions that the UN had failed were often misleading, he said:

> Do we refer to the purposes of the Charter? They are expressions of universally shared ideals which cannot fail us, though we, alas, often fail them. Or do we think of the institutions of the United Nations? They are our tools. We fashioned them. We use them. It is our responsibility to remedy any flaws there may be in them.

And he continued:

> This is a difficult lesson for both idealists and realists, though for different reasons. I suppose that, just as the first temptation of the realist is the

> illusion of cynicism, so the first temptation of the idealist is the illusion of Utopia.[13]

Hammarskjöld was an idealist in the sense that he believed in the purposes and principles of the UN Charter and in the possibilities of the UN Organization. At the same time, he was a realist in the sense that he did not want to stretch the potential capacities of the Organization too much if member states were not ready for it. For example, he opposed the idea of a standing UN military force, because he felt it was politically premature in view of the strong feelings related to national sovereignty, and also because he felt it was impractical to have a ready-made military unit standing by when it was much better to tailor a unit to the specific demands of an impending situation.[14]

It goes without saying that he wanted the UN to respond to the demands of the international community, and in reflecting how that should be done he again fell back on a distinction between existing legal norms and innovative procedures. On the one hand, he could refer to the UN normative framework in a natural law-oriented manner that included an implicit static element. Thus, in 1956 he stated that:

> the principles of the Charter are, by far, greater than the Organization in which they are embodied, and the aims which they are to safeguard are holier than the policies of any single nation or people.[15]

On the other hand, he often used a dynamic and evolutionary approach to the system of the UN Charter, repeatedly arguing that although the objectives and rules of the Charter were binding, the working methods of the system could be supplemented by new procedures. As he put it in 1959:

> As is well known, such an evolution has in fact taken place, and it has (...) been recognized that (...) new procedures may be developed when they prove productive in practice for (...) the objectives of the Charter. In this respect, the United Nations, as a living organism, has the necessary scope

13 "An International Administrative Service", from an address to the International Law Association at McGill University, Montreal, 30 May, 1956. See Wilder Foote (ed.), *supra* note 12, p. 116.

14 B. Urquhart, *Hammarskjold* (The Bodley Head, London, 1973), p. 230.

15 Statement during the Suez Crisis, 31 October 1956. *Official Records of the Security Council*, 751st meeting. Quoted in *ibid.*, p. 174.

> for a continuous adaptation of its (...) [system] to the needs [of the international community].[16]

This organic approach was in line with his views on the Uniting for Peace resolution and the establishment of UNEF. But Hammarskjöld developed it further into a dynamic conception of the UN Organization. His successor, U Thant, once remarked that Hammarskjöld was prone to use his great gift for innovation and improvisation. He "discovered new ways to help keep the peace" – an emergency force in one situation, an observer group in another, and a UN presence in a third context.[17]

The dynamic approach of Hammarskjöld was also stressed by his collaborator in the UN Secretariat, Ralph Bunche. Bunche indicated in a speech in 1964 that Hammarskjöld consciously strove to make the UN a progressive force for human advancement. Wherever there was a conflict situation, actual or threatening, he believed the UN should actively seek to contain or avert it:

> [B]y quiet diplomacy when the circumstances permitted, in the form of good offices if the parties themselves demonstrated an inability to deal with the situation; and, if necessary by overt United Nations action.

Bunch added that Hammarskjöld saw clearly that the UN "must do more than hold meetings and talk and adopt resolutions".[18] Hammarskjöld himself said at a press conference in early 1959 that the UN simply must respond to those demands which might be placed upon it. If those demands would go beyond the "present capacity", that must not in itself be a reason to exclude action. The capacity of the UN could prove to be greater than expected. He referred to the Organization as a machine, thrusting its way through the terrain of international politics. He said: "I do not know the exact capacity of this machine. It did take the very steep hill of Suez; it may take other and even steeper hills".[19]

Hammarskjöld was not confronted with the issues of human security and UN intervention until the summer of 1960, but he had reason before that to comment upon some of the elements of that discourse. With regard to the protection of national sovereignty he referred in a speech in 1953 to the classical

---

16 From the Introduction to the Annual Report of the Secretary-General on the Activities of the Organization 1958–59, 22 August 1959. Wilder Foot, *supra* note 12, p. 223.

17 U Thant, 'Looking ahead', Address given at Columbia University, January 7, 1964. See A.N. Cordier and Wilder Foote (eds.), *The Quest for Peace, The Dag Hammarskjöld Memorial Lectures* (Columbia University Press, New York, 1965), p. 40.

18 R.J. Bunche, 'The United Nations Operation in the Congo', in *ibid.*, p. 121 *et seq.*

19 Quotation by Lester B. Pearson in *ibid.*, p. 100.

Chinese philosopher and poet Tao-Tse Tung, who is reported as stating that whoever wants to grip the world and shape it will fail, because the world is a spiritual thing that cannot be shaped. Hammarskjöld later in his speech made clear that the UN

> ...has no power to encroach upon the national sovereignty of any state against the will of its government and people. It would indeed not only be against the letter and the spirit of the Charter (...) to attempt to impose its will in domestic matters. It would also be against the elementary wisdom expressed (...) [by] Tao-Tse Tung.[20]

With regard to the protection of human rights, Hammarskjöld said at one point that behind the Universal Declaration of Human Rights, "we find literally thousands of people who directly or indirectly participated actively in its drafting".[21] He thereby implied that the Declaration was *not* mainly a contribution of the West. He further stated that the Declaration could be called a "universal expression" on the subject in a world where the memory was still fresh of some of the worst infringements of human rights ever experienced in history.

With regard to the principle of collective security, Hammarskjöld sometimes referred to the Chapter VII procedure as a necessary requirement for armed action. At the same time, he was prone to relate the matter of collective peacemaking to the other objectives of the Charter. Not surprisingly, he then used a contextual approach. In his view, peace was not solid without human rights, and human rights could not be fully realized unless peace was at hand.[22]

In similar vein, he also saw the creation of the UN as something going beyond the exclusive interests of states and governments. In 1958 he made the point that a global cooperative project – a universal body – was not a new idea. The UN Organization was a body for collective efforts established after centuries of human struggle. He said:

> It is the logical and natural development from lines of thought and aspiration going far back into all corners of the earth since a few men first began to think about the decency and dignity of other men.[23]

20 Wilder Foote, *supra* note 12, p. 43.

21 "The International Significance of the Bill of Rights", Address at Celebration of the 180th Anniversary of the Virginia Declaration of Rights 1776–1956, Williamsburg, Virginia, 14 May 1956. *Ibid.*, p. 106.

22 Address in New York, 10 April 1957. *Ibid.*, p. 127.

23 "The Uses of Private Diplomacy", Address in the Houses of Parliament, London, 2 April 1958. *Ibid.*, p. 174.

The choice of emphasis on 'men' instead of 'states', and on 'dignity' instead of 'security', is perhaps telling about how Hammarskjöld regarded the objectives of the UN Charter. Collective security included human dignity. Or, as we would express it today, collective security is not only state security but also human security. The interests of the international society of states could and should not differ from the interests of mankind.

6 The Issue of UN Humanitarian Intervention in Peace Operations, a 'Responsibility to Protect'

When the political situation in the Republic of Congo deteriorated in the summer of 1960 a UN peace operation, ONUC, was launched. In August there were tribal massacres in the province of Kasai. Hundreds of Balubas were killed by Government soldiers. Villages had been pillaged and burned and their inhabitants, including children, killed simply for the reason of their ethnicity.

Hammarskjöld felt – and made clear to his associates – that the UN could not stand aside and remain passive in what he called "a case of incipient genocide". He indicated that the Central Government had to accept this responsibility of the UN.

True, the Kasai situation was a delicate one for the UN to interfere in, against the background of an unclear mandate and the non-intervention principle of Article 2(7) of the Charter. But, on the other hand, Hammarskjöld concluded in a cable to his emissary in Leopoldville: "Prohibition against intervention in internal conflicts cannot be considered to apply to senseless slaughter of civilians or fighting arising from tribal hostilities".[24]

After a meeting with his advisers in New York, he authorized the interposing of UN troops, using force if necessary, to stop the massacres.[25] As it happened, in the beginning of September 1960, the situation calmed down and there was no need to act upon these instructions. In reporting to the Security Council on 9 September Hammarskjöld referred to the atrocities as international crimes. He stated:

> They involve a most flagrant violation of elementary human rights and have the characteristics of the crime of genocide since they appear to be directed towards the extermination of a specific ethnic group, the Balubas.[26]

24 Unpublished statement quoted by Urquhart, *supra* note 14, p. 438.

25 *Ibid.*

26 *Security Council Official Records,* 896th Meeting, 9 September 1960, para 101.

Hammarskjöld did not at this point ask for an extended ONUC mandate to deal with the humanitarian threats. His moral gut reaction was – as is shown by the cable to Leopoldville – that it was not necessary. But diplomatic prudence would of course have it that any humanitarian crossing of the borderline between peacekeeping and peace enforcement should be mandated by the Security Council, and if there is no time for that, that Council approval should at least be registered *ex post facto*.

Hammarskjöld's position in principle was clear. We can assume that it was not exclusively a legal position. His moral 'do good' inclination was probably influenced by his Christian values and he was not prepared to compromise with his personal conviction. In his report to the General Assembly he made clear: "You try to save a drowning man without prior authorization".[27]

There was probably also a policy element of human rights involved. Hammarskjöld was normally not a driving force in the field of human rights. The issue was tainted with Cold War controversy and he regularly approached it with caution. In this case, however, he was prepared to use the Secretary-General's power of interpretation to protect human rights and play the card of 'incipient genocide' to increase his power of persuasion. To him, obviously, it was a matter of values and a mix of law and morality. He was not alien to the incorporation of extra-legal elements in the process of international law. Although he laid heavy emphasis on the non-intervention principle of Article 2(7) of the Charter, he nevertheless thought that the Kasai massacres were outside the scope of that provision. His personal ethics coincided with the natural law proposition that *lex scripta* had to be reconciled with a law of higher order.

Hammarskjöld's policy related instincts, focused on a kind of "UN responsibility to protect" perception, did not leave a significant imprint in the peacekeeping discourse during the Cold War. It is noteworthy, though, that the principle of protecting civilians during peace operations has been brought into the present millennium by the Brahimi report (2000)[28] and through the broader concept of Responsibility to Protect (2005).[29] Hammarskjöld's instinctive approach to the matter has come to stay and is now codified in the peacekeeping doctrine of the United Nations.[30]

---

27 Statement on UN Operations in Congo before the General Assembly, 17 October 1960.

28 Report of the Panel on United Nations Peace Operations, chaired by Ambassador Lakhdar Brahimi (Algeria), transmitted to the Secretary-General on 17 August 2000. UN Doc. A/55/305-S/2000/809.

29 General Assembly Resolution 60/1, World Summit Outcome Document (2005), paras. 138–139.

30 Report of the Secretary-General, Implementation of the Recommendations of the Special Committee on Peacekeeping Operations, UN Doc. A/60/640 (2005). See also O. Bring, 'Dag Hammarskjöld and the Issue of Humanitarian Intervention', in J. Petman and

7 Leadership and Legal Development

The future of the UN Organization lies, as always in the case of intergovernmental organizations, in the hands of Member States. Political will is essential, as is international leadership. Unfortunately, the world today suffers from a lack of both. As to political will, Hammarskjöld did not expect it to surface in multilaterally negotiated documents, he saw it develop through precedents created by a responsible international leadership. Thus, the Hammarskjöld approach to the UN and international law was not to rely on drawn out political compromise, but on *ad hoc* arrangements responding to urgent and concrete needs in line with the purposes of the UN. As Hammarskjöld's biographer Brian Urquhart has pointed out, the then Secretary-General believed that a just and reliable world order had to rely on precedents (state practice) made possible through political acquiescence.

Hammarskjöld's contribution to international law, beyond his value based decision-making and his innovative and flexible use of the UN Charter, lies in this development feature. He realized that a progressive development of international law could not be achieved exclusively through multilateral treaty-making, but that, in addition, an element of 'development through practice' would be needed. However, development through precedents presumes that those international actors which are prepared to take the lead, statesmen of governments and organisations, can inspire confidence in their initiatives vis-à-vis the rest of the international community. Hammarskjöld had this gift of inspiring confidence.

8 The New Investigation into the Death of Hammarskjöld

The name of Dag Hammarskjöld is topical today, not due to the substance of his leadership, but due to the unclear circumstances of his death. On 17 September 1961, Hammarskjöld was flying from Leopoldville, Congo, to Ndola, Northern Rhodesia, to meet with the Katanga leader Moise Tshombe. The intention was to mediate in the Katanga crisis. At ten minutes after midnight, Hammarskjöld's plane, the Transair DC6 *Albertina*, informed the Ndola control tower that the airfield lights were in sight. The aircraft passed the airfield to turn around and start its landing approach from the west. The tower never

J. Klabbers (eds.), *Nordic Cosmopolitanism, Essays in International Law for Martti Koskenniemi* (Martinus Nijhoff, Leiden, 2003), pp. 485–518.

saw or heard from the plane again. About three minutes later, the *Albertina,* after having turned and started its descent, brushed the treetops and cut a swath through the forest. As the left wing touched the ground, the aircraft cartwheeled and was transformed into a mass of flame.

In the control tower nothing was known about this. Everyone was waiting in vain for the plane to land. At last Lord Alport, the British High Commissioner in Rhodesia, who was present in the tower, uttered the famous words that the Secretary-General must have decided "to go elsewhere". Alport's conclusion was that everyone could leave, whereupon the airport manager closed down the airport. It took four hours after daybreak to start a search and it took fifteen hours to find the missing aircraft.

On 26 October the General Assembly set up a Commission of Investigation into the circumstances of the crash. Evidence was analysed and the wreckage of the plane examined. The possible causes were sabotage, attack from air or ground, material failure, and human failure. The UN Commission submitted its report on 24 April 1962, and reached no firm conclusion as to the cause of the crash. There was no evidence of foul play, but this possibility could not be excluded.

Decades later, in 2011, Susan Williams of London University published her book *Who killed Hammarskjöld?* Through its new evidence, Williams' book inspired the setting up of an independent commission of jurists. The report of this commission, the Hammarskjöld Commission, was published in September 2013. The Commission concluded that the United Nations would be justified in reopening its 1961–62 inquiry into the cause of the Ndola crash. Possible evidence included recorded cockpit conversations, monitored, recorded, and archived by the US National Security Agency (NSA).

The Secretary-General of the United Nations received the Report of the Hammarskjöld Commission in September 2013 and later made the report available to the General Assembly. In his covering note to the UN Document in question, dated 21 March 2014, the Secretary-General referred to new evidence. In paragraph 4 of his Note he obviously had in mind the possible Cyprus recordings:

> [I]t also appears that additional new evidence may exist which, for national security reasons, was and remains classified … more than 50 years after the fact. I trust that the General Assembly may wish to encourage Member States, in the light of the passage of time, to seek to declassify any relevant records in their possession in accordance with their respective national legislation.

Mr Ban Ki-moon further advised the General Assembly on its future handling of the situation. Among the possible options were (a) to establish an independent panel of experts to examine the new evidence, (b) to reopen the 1961–62 inquiry, or (c) to establish a new inquiry. As the Secretary-General summarized the situation:

> The unparalleled service and sacrifice of Dag Hammarskjöld and his legacy within the United Nations and beyond compels us to seek the whole truth of the circumstances leading to his tragic death and that of the members of the party accompanying him.

On 29 December 2014, the General Assembly adopted Resolution 246 authorizing the Secretary-General to appoint an independent Panel of Experts to examine all the evidence and report back to him. The Resolution was adopted by consensus of all 193 Member States of the UN. The memory of a Nordic contributor to international peace and security is still alive.

Nordic Judges of the Permanent Court of International Justice and the International Court of Justice

Astrid Kjeldgaard-Pedersen

1 Introduction

This chapter was presented at the conference "A Nordic Approach to International Law?" held in Oslo in August 2015 as a part of a panel on "Nordic Judges of International Courts". It sets out to examine whether it is possible to ascertain distinctive common features in the voting practice of Nordic judges of the Permanent Court of International Justice (PCIJ), and its successor the International Court of Justice (ICJ), that might support the idea of 'a Nordic approach to international law'.

Several studies have looked into potential biases of the World Court.[1] A regional bias is indeed presumed in the appointment of judges. There is an informal understanding that "[t]he Court as a whole must represent the main forms of civilization and the principal legal systems of the world".[2] In practice, this principle manifests itself in the distribution of judges among the main regions of the world. The Nordic countries fall into the category of "Western Europe and other States" to which five out of 15 seats are allocated. Of the five seats, however, three are traditionally ascribed to the states in the category that are also permanent members of the Security Council, *i.e.* the United States, the United Kingdom and France. This effectively leaves two positions open to Nordic judges – two positions for which the five Nordic countries compete with 21 other states.[3]

Statistics show that ICJ judges vote in favour of their home state 90 per cent of the time.[4] While there is little evidence that this bias extends to neighbouring countries, studies have presented some evidence that judges favour states that are similar to their own in terms of wealth level, political system, language

1 *See*, for example, E.A. Posner and M.F.P. de Figueiredo, 'Is the International Court of Justice Biased?, 34 *Journal of Legal Studies* (2005) p. 599, at p. 615.

2 See <www.icj-cij.org/court/index.php?p1=1&p2=2>, visited on 7 August 2016.

3 For a complete list of the States included in the category of "Western Europe and other States", *see* <www.un.org/esa/govwest.htm>, visited on 7 August 2016.

4 *See further* Posner and de Figueiredo, *supra* note 1.

 | DOI 10.1163/9789004343597_006

and religion.[5] If this holds true, Nordic judges are presumably biased towards the other Nordic states. There have only been few cases, however, where a Nordic judge has heard a dispute between a Nordic neighbour state and a third state. The Norwegian Helge Klaestad was president of the ICJ when the Court issued *Application of the Convention of 1902 Governing the Guardianship of Infants* (*Netherlands* v. *Sweden*) in 1958 and voted in favour of Sweden together with the majority, which included Swedish *ad hoc* judge Fredrik Julius Christian Sterzel. In contrast, Swedish judge Sture Petrén did not vote with Danish *ad hoc* judge Max Sørensen in *North Sea Continental Shelf* (*Federal Republic of Germany* v. *Denmark*) of 1969.[6] Thus – even if we were to ignore the fact that presumptions based on a limited number of judgments would be of little value – there is no evidence of an inter-Nordic bias.[7]

Instead of attempting to document the existence of an inter-Nordic bias, we might ask whether, statistically, Nordic judges of the World Court have a tendency to 'vote together'; that is to conduct parallel legal analyses and propose similar solutions when presented with the same dispute. This, however, is also impossible to assess since there have only very rarely been two Nordic judges on the bench at the same time[8] – except of course in disputes between two Nordic states where, unsurprisingly, the Nordic judges, *ad hoc* as well as permanent, have demonstrated a strong inclination to vote in favour of their respective home states.[9]

All in all, statistics are a less interesting object of research for present purposes. This chapter will therefore concentrate on whether it is possible to identify common traits in the way in which the Nordic judges have engaged with the World Court, focusing in particular on their respective approaches to treaty

---

5 *Ibid.*, p. 615 *et seq.*

6 *North Sea Continental Shelf* (*Federal Republic of Germany* v. *Denmark*), 20 February 1969, ICJ, Judgment, ICJ Reports 1969, p. 3.

7 Notably, the Danish judge, Didrik Nyholm, dissented when the PCIJ denied a request for an Advisory Opinion on the *Status of Eastern Carelia* in 1923. Russia was not a member of the League of Nations at the time, and, according to the majority, had therefore not consented to the jurisdiction of the Court. While Nyholm's dissent thus favoured Finland, he did not append any opinion which makes it difficult to assess his rationale. *See Status of Eastern Carelia*, 23 July 1923, PCIJ, Advisory Opinion, PCIJ Ser. B, No. 5.

8 *See* further section 2.3 *infra*.

9 *See Case Concerning the Legal Status of the South-Eastern Territory of Greenland*, PCIJ, Orders, 2 and 3 August 1932, PCIJ Series AB, No. 49, *Case Concerning Passage through the Great Belt* (*Finland* v. *Denmark*), Order, Provisional Measures, 29 July 1991, ICJ, Order, *ICJ Reports* (1999), p. 12, and *Maritime Delimitation in the Area between Greenland and Jan Mayen* (*Denmark* v. *Norway*), Judgment, 14 June 1993, *ICJ Reports* (1993), p. 38.

interpretation. The judges are discussed in chronological order. The chapter takes account of academic and biographical publications by and about each of the Nordic judges, but the primary sources of the study are of course the decisions of the PCIJ and the ICJ. Since there are no records of deliberations, however, the Nordic judges' individual dissenting and concurring opinions merit particular attention.

2 The Permanent Court of International Justice

By way of introduction, it is worth noting that the Nordic countries played an active role in the establishment of the PCIJ in the aftermath of World War I. In fact, a committee set up by the Danish, Swedish, and Norwegian governments prepared a joint proposal published in January 1919 in the so-called *Avant projet de Convention* (*sur une Organisation Juridique Internationale*) which was essentially a first draft of the PCIJ Statute.[10]

It also deserves mention that Francis Hagerup – who in addition to being a diplomat and professor of law had served as prime minister of Norway at the turn of the 20th century – was member of the Advisory Committee of Jurists appointed by the Council of the League of Nations in 1920 to be responsible for the development of a PCIJ. In that capacity, Hagerup, *inter alia*, voiced strong opinions about the necessary qualifications of the future judges of the Court. Some members of the Advisory Committee believed that not only lawyers should be eligible to sit on the bench. One member advocated against the exclusion of "practical men", and another stated concurringly that "statesmen of great ability in international law, who had never published scientific works on the subject" should not be barred from the Court.[11] Hagerup, however, "insisted upon the necessity of a definite statement in the text to the effect that judges must have a thorough knowledge of the law".[12] In the adopted version, Article 2 of the Statute of the PCIJ reads:

10 J. Evensen, 'The International Court of Justice: Main Characteristics and Its Contribution to the Development of the Modern Law of Nations', 57 *Nordic Journal of International Law* (1988) p. 3, at p. 4.

11 Advisory Committee of Jurists, *Procès-verbaux*, 1920, p. 447. Available at <archive.org/details/procsverbauxofooleaguoft>, visited on 1 September 2016.

12 *Ibid.*, p. 449. *See* further O. Spiermann, "Who Attempts Too Much Does Nothing Well': The 1920 Advisory Committee of Jurists and the Statute of the Permanent Court of International Justice', 73 *British Year Book of International Law* (2002) p. 187, at pp. 224–226.

> The Permanent Court of International Justice shall be composed of a body of independent judges, elected regardless of their nationality from amongst persons of high moral character, who possess the qualifications required in their respective countries for appointment to the highest judicial offices, or are jurisconsults of recognized competence in international law.

As will become apparent in the following, the Nordics judges of the PCIJ and the ICJ count both former domestic judges, politicians and career diplomats.

2.1 *Sverige: Åke Hammarskjöld (Registrar 1922–1936, Judge 1936–1937)*

The most influential Nordic person during the foundational period of the PCIJ was apparently not a judge, but the Swedish Registrar Åke Hammarskjöld. Hammarskjöld was involved in activities connected to the PCIJ for a total of 17 years. As member of the Secretariat of the League of Nations, he worked with the Advisory Committee of Jurists on the drafting of the Statute of the PCIJ in 1920. He later became the first registrar of the PCIJ, serving from 1922 to 1936, when he was elected judge.

As registrar, Hammarskjöld had exercised considerable influence on the work of the PCIJ. In 1935, when Hammarskjöld was up for election as judge, then President Hurst said as follows about him:

> (a)s Registrar he has become too powerful, and it would be good for the Court and for him that after thirteen and a half years of service as Registrar he should be elected to a judgeship. I cannot say that he is a popular person: he is formal and rigid, and possesses no sense of humour; but of his qualifications for the post I entertain no doubt.[13]

It seems that Hammarskjöld formed a sort of 'triumvirate' with judges Huber and Anzilotti.[14] This allowed Hammarskjöld to play a key role in the drafting of a number of the PCIJ's landmark decisions. Siding with Huber, Anzilotti, and also Norwegian deputy-judge Beichmann,[15] Hammarskjöld took part in

13 Hurst to Malkin, 31 March 1935. Here cited from O. Spiermann, *International Legal Argument in the Permanent Court of International Justice* (Cambridge University Press, Cambridge, 2005) pp. 369–370.

14 O. Spiermann, 'Judge Max Huber at the Permanent Court of International Justice', 18 *European Journal of International Law* (2007) p. 115, at p. 116.

15 *See* further section 2.3 *infra*.

the production of landmark decisions such as the *Case of the SS Lotus* of 1927,[16] *Jurisdiction of the Courts of Danzig* of 1928,[17] and *Serbian Loans* of 1929.[18] His role in these rulings indicates that Hammarskjöld favoured objective and effective – as opposed to restrictive – interpretation of treaty provisions.[19] *Jurisdiction of the Courts of Danzig* provides and illustrative example. The PCIJ stated that "according to a well-established principle of international law ... an international agreement, cannot, as such, create direct rights and obligations for private individuals".[20] However, while the Permanent Court in this way paid lip-service to the orthodox notion that international legal personality is reserved for states only, it subsequently applied the international agreement in question, the *Beamtenabkommen*, directly to Danzig railway officials without interpreting it restrictively. Had the PCIJ wished to do so, it could have conveniently construed the relevant Article 9 "in a manner which would make the applicability of the provisions of the *Beamtenabkommen* depend on their incorporation into a Polish Regulation".[21] The Court did exactly the opposite. The PCIJ thus effectively refuted the notion that there is a presumption against the international legal personality of individuals. According to Hersch Lauterpacht, the Advisory Opinion "dealt a resounding blow to the dogma of the impenetrable barrier separating individuals from international law ...".[22]

It is notable that Hammarskjöld not only influenced the Court's work from within the Peace Palace walls. During the first years of the PCIJ's existence, he would also publish comments on the Court's work under various pseudonyms such as 'Paul de Vineuil' and 'Michel de la Grotte'[23] – at times adding

16 *The Case of the SS Lotus*, 7 September 1927, Judgment, PCIJ Series A, No. 10.

17 *Jurisdiction of the Courts of Danzig*, 3 March 1928, Advisory Opinion, PCIJ Series B, No. 15.

18 *Case concerning the Payment of Various Serbian Loans issued in France*, 12 July 1929, Judgment, PCIJ Series A, No. 20. *See* also *Case concerning the Payment in Gold of Brazilian Federal Loans contracted in France*, 12 July 1929, Judgment, PCIJ Series A, No. 21.

19 *See further* Spiermann, *supra* note 13, pp. 401–402.

20 *Jurisdiction of the Courts of Danzig*, *supra* note 17, p. 17.

21 *Ibid.*, p. 20.

22 H. Lauterpacht, 'The Subjects of the Law of Nations', in E. Lauterpacht (ed.), *International Law – Being the Collected Papers of Hersch Lauterpacht* (Cambridge University Press, Cambridge, 1975), Vol. II, p. 487, at pp. 511–512. In response to proponents of interpreting the Opinion as compatible with the traditional view of individuals in international law, Lauterpacht stated that "the departure from the established view was effected with such ingenious restraint that some have been led to believe that the decision of the Court amounts to a solemn affirmation of the established doctrine". H. Lauterpacht, *The Development of International Law by the Permanent Court of International Justice* (Stevens & Sons Limited, London, 1934) p. 52.

23 *See further* Spiermann, *supra* note 13, p. 214.

a rationale to the Court's *motifs* which had been rejected by the majority of judges.[24]

When Hammarskjöld was eventually elected judge in 1936, a number of the first judges, including Huber, had left the PCIJ and been replaced by judges who were more prone to restrictive treaty interpretation.[25] Supposedly, this shift did not please Hammarskjöld, and he might have become a great dissenter had it not been for his untimely death at the age of 44 – after only nine months on the bench.[26]

2.2 *Denmark: Didrik Nyholm (Judge 1922–1930)*

Didrik Nyholm from Denmark was one of the first judges of the PCIJ and sat on the bench from 1922 to 1930. Nyholm had begun his career in the Danish Ministry of Justice and had served in the Danish domestic court system for a number of years, before he was appointed to the mixed courts at Cairo in 1896. Based on his main publication from 1918, in which he aired a rather idealistic plan for the Permanent Court,[27] he had high hopes for the future of international law. Nevertheless, some of his activities at the Court, for example his Dissenting Opinion to the *Readaptation of the Mavrommatis Jerusalem Concessions* judgment of 1927[28] and his observations to the 1928 *Factory at Chorzów* judgment,[29] reveal that Nyholm was inclined to interpret international law in a way that made it resemble domestic law. In the latter judgment, the Court had ruled on Germany's claim to indemnity so as to settle the dispute concerning the factory at Chorzów, but the majority of the judges found that Poland's claims to a set-off against Germany's claims fell outside the PCIJ's jurisdiction. They noted "that jurisdiction as to reparation due for the violation of an international convention involves jurisdiction as to the forms and methods of payment".[30] Yet, the Court's jurisdiction to award monetary compensation did not, according to the majority, extend to "any question whatever of international law even

24 *See* further Spiermann, *supra* note 14, p. 126.

25 *See* further Spiermann, *supra* note 13, Chapter 7.

26 M.O. Hudson, 'In Memoriam: Åke Hammarskjöld', 31 *American Journal of International Law* (1937) p. 703.

27 D.G. Nyholm, 'La Cour permanente de Justice internationale', in P. Munch (ed.), *Les Origines et l'œuvre de la Société des Nations* (Copenhagen, 1924), Vol. 2, p. 241. *See further* Spiermann, *supra* note 13, p. 138.

28 *Case of the Readaptation of the Mavrommatis Jerusalem Concessions (Jurisdiction)*, 10 October 1927, PCIJ, Judgment, Series A, No 11, Dissenting Opinion of Nyholm.

29 *Case concerning the Factory at Chorzów (Claim for Indemnity)(Merits)*, 13 September 1928, PCIJ, Judgment, Series A No. 17.

30 *Ibid.*, p. 61.

quite foreign to the convention under consideration, for the sole reason that the manner in which such question is decided may have an influence on the effectiveness of the reparation asked for".[31] Nyholm disagreed with the majority on this point. Drawing an explicit analogy to domestic law, he stated as follows:

> It appears, however that the Court, which has jurisdiction as regards the sums in dispute, will also have the right to hear and determine the objections. To those which relate to the extinction of the credit claimed may be added the declaration of a set-off which cancels out the credit. In international law no principle can be raised which would establish on this subject a difference between national and international law.[32]

Nyholm's rather domestic-oriented and conservative approach, which is also reflected in his Dissenting Opinion to the *Lotus* judgment,[33] might explain why there was not much inter-Nordic sympathy between him and Åke Hammarskjöld. In 1925, for example, Nyholm expressed his dissatisfaction to judge Moore that "(t)he whole court is in the hands of the Registrar".[34]

2.3 *Deputy-judge: Norway: Frederik Beichmann (1922–1930)*

The first term of the PCIJ was the only time in the history of the World Court with more than one Nordic judge on the bench. Frederik Beichmann, who served together with Nyholm from 1922 to 1930, came from a position of president of the Court of Appeals of Trondheim in Norway, and he was one of the first four deputy-judges to be elected. Based on various 'behind the scenes' material, Beichmann supported the Huber-Anzilotti-Hammarskjöld faction of the first PCIJ.[35] For example, Judge Huber wrote the following about the drafting of the 1923 *Nationality Decrees* Advisory Opinion:[36]

> The opinion was drafted by me and the final product was almost entirely due to my drafting, despite widespread deletions, which I, Anzilotti

---

31 *Ibid.*, pp. 61–62.

32 *Case concerning the Factory at Chorzów (Claim for Indemnity)(Merits)*, 13 September 1928, PCIJ, Judgment, Series A No. 17, Observations by Nyholm, p. 98. *See further* Spiermann, *supra* note 13, p. 225.

33 *The Case of the SS Lotus, supra* note 16, Dissenting Opinion by M. Nyholm.

34 Nyholm to Moore, 23 November 1925, Moore papers 177. Here cited from Spiermann, *supra* note 13, p. 214, note 20.

35 *See* further section 2.1 *supra*.

36 *Nationality Decrees Issued in Tunis and Morocco*, 7 February 1923, Advisory Opinion, PCIJ Series B, No. 4.

> and Beichmann regretted. ... Only by threatening to append a separate opinion did Anzilotti, Beichmann and I arrange for the thoughts that we regarded as being most important to be included, though in a form so compressed that it became almost unintelligible. Subsequently Hammarskjöld has explained our thoughts in an article by Vineuil in the *Revue de Droit International*.[37]

2.4 *Finland: Rafael W. Erich (Judge 1938–1942, Deputy-judge 1931–1936)*

When Beichmann's and Nyholm's term ended 1930, the Finnish lawyer, politician and diplomat Rafael Erich was elected deputy-judge.[38] He served in this capacity until 1936 and later took over Åke Hammarskjöld's seat on the bench. Erich only participated in five PCIJ decisions. In the 1939 *Panevezys-Saldutiskis Railway* case, he submitted a Dissenting Opinion indicating that he preferred objective and effective interpretation of treaty provisions over judicial restraint. Erich conducted a material assessment of the effectiveness and actual exhaustion of local remedies;[39] whereas the majority granted the national courts a wide margin of appreciation in the determination of this matter. The same kind of caution was exercised by the majority in *The Electricity Company of Sofia and Bulgaria* judgment of 1939 to which Judge Erich also appended a Separate Opinion.[40]

3 The International Court of Justice

At no point in time has there been more than one permanent Nordic judge on the ICJ, and there have also been long periods of time with no Nordics at all. At present, it has been more than 20 years since Jens Evensen left the ICJ as the last representative of the Nordic region.

---

37 M. Huber, *Denkwürdigkeiten* (Orell Füssli, Zürich, 1974) p. 276. Here cited in translation from Spiermann, *supra* note 13, pp. 157–158. *See* further *ibid.*, pp. 149–160, 239–240; and Spiermann, *supra* note 14.

38 *See further* Martti Koskenniemi's chapter 'Diplomats, Professors, and Then Some: Notes for a History of International Law in 20th Century Finland' in this volume.

39 *The Panevezys-Saldutiskis Railway Case*, 28 February 1939, Judgment, PCIJ Series AB, No. 76, Dissenting Opinion by Erich, pp. 51–55.

40 *The Electricity Company of Sofia and Bulgaria* (*Preliminary Objection*), 4 April 1939, Judgment, PCIJ Series AB, no 77, Separate Opinion of Judge Erich.

3.1 *Norway: Helge Klaestad (1946–1961, President 1958–1961)*

The first Nordic judge of the ICJ was another Norwegian, Helge Klaestad. When he was elected to the new bench in 1946, Klaestad was a judge of the Supreme Court of Norway. He had previously been president of the Anglo-German Mixed Arbitral Tribunal and member of the Permanent Court of Arbitration. He served as judge of the ICJ from 1946 to 1961, the last three years as president.

In the early days, the ICJ issued a number wide-ranging and innovative decisions. Klaestad was a part of the majority in landmark Advisory Opinions such as the *Reparations for Injuries* of 1949,[41] *International Status of South-West Africa* of 1950[42] and the *Reservations to the Genocide Convention* of 1951,[43] which indicates that he supported further detachment of international law as a legal discipline from domestic law. This finds support in the first of two cases involving Norway that the ICJ heard during Klaestad's years on the bench. In the 1951 *Anglo-Norwegian Fisheries* judgment, Klaestad was a part of the majority advancing the 'straight baseline doctrine' now codified in Article 7 of UNCLOS, which lead to the conclusion that Norway's delimitation of fisheries zones did not violate international law.[44] However, the other case involving Norway during Klaestad's time, *Certain Norwegian Loans* (*France* v. *Norway*), which was decided in 1957, points in a more conservative direction. Klaestad again voted with the majority finding – in favour of Norway – that the ICJ lacked jurisdiction. By virtue of the condition of reciprocity, Norway was entitled to invoke a reservation made by France to the ICJ's compulsory jurisdiction under Article 36(2) of the ICJ' Statute. With this reservation France had excluded from the ICJ's jurisdiction "matters which are essentially within the national jurisdiction as understood by the Government of the French Republic". The majority gave effect to the reservation as it stood, and found that it excluded the jurisdiction of the ICJ in the concrete case.[45] Judge Lauterpacht, however, submitted a Separate Opinion arguing that the French reservation was invalid because it was contrary to Article 36(6) of the ICJ Statute according to which

41 *Reparation for Injuries Suffered in the Service of the United Nations*, 11 April 1949, ICJ, Advisory Opinion, *ICJ Reports* (1949), p. 174.

42 *International Status of South West Africa*, 11 July 1950, ICJ, Advisory Opinion, *ICJ Reports* (1950), p. 128.

43 *Reservations to the Convention on Genocide*, 28 May 1951, ICJ, Advisory Opinion, *ICJ Reports* (1951), p. 15.

44 *Fisheries* (*United Kingdom* v. *Norway*), 18 December 1951, ICJ, Judgment, *ICJ Reports* (1951), p. 116.

45 *Certain Norwegian Loans* (*France* v. *Norway*), 6 July 1957, ICJ, Judgment, *ICJ Reports* (1957), p. 9.

the Court itself is entitled to settle matters concerning its own jurisdiction.[46] Shortly after the *Norwegian Loans* case, the ICJ was faced with another question concerning a reservation to Article 36(2) with regard to domestic jurisdiction. The *Interhandel* case concerned the validity of a reservation made by the United States, which was very similar to the French reservation in *Norwegian Loans*. Interestingly, Klaestad this time submitted a Dissenting Opinion[47] in which he invoked Lauterpacht's argument and found that the reservation was indeed in conflict with ICJ's power to decide disputes concerning its own jurisdiction. One might speculate that Klaestad's leaning towards objective and effective treaty interpretation was overruled in the *Norwegian Loans* case by his inclination to vote in favour of his home state.[48]

Klaestad's perhaps most remarkable Dissenting Opinion is attached to the 1953 *Nottebohm* judgment.[49] The question was whether international law regulated the manner in which, and under what conditions, a state may confer nationality on aliens. Klaestad disagreed with the majority that international law required a genuine link between the state and alien in question. Instead, he maintained a strict separation between international law and national law, and argued that the ICJ should refrain from pronouncing upon matters that are solely within the competence of national authorities.

Whereas Klaestad was seemingly a popular judge and eventually elected president by his colleagues at the ICJ, the next Nordic judge, the Swede Sture Petrén, had a quite different experience.

3.2 *Sweden: Sture Petrén (1967–1976)*

When Sture Petrén was elected to the ICJ in 1967, he had had a long career in the Swedish court system, ultimately as president of Svea Hovrätt, the Court of Appeal in Stockholm. Although he also had considerable experience with diplomacy, he was first and foremost a judge. This is clearly reflected in his voting habits at the ICJ. Petrén frequently voiced his disapproval in dissenting and separate opinions when the ICJ overstepped the boundaries of what he believed to be the proper function of a court. In the 1971 *Namibia* Advisory

46 *Ibid.*, Separate Opinion of Sir Hersch Lauterpacht, p. 43.

47 *Interhandel* (*Switzerland* v. *United States of America*), 21 March 1959, ICJ, Judgment, *ICJ Reports* (1959), p. 6, Dissenting Opinion of Klaestad.

48 In should be noted, however, that Klaestad expressly distinguished the *Norwegian Loans* and the *Interhandel* cases given that the validity of the reservation was only disputed in the latter.

49 *Nottebohm* (*Liechtenstein* v. *Guatemala*), 6 April 1955, ICJ, Judgment, *ICJ Reports* (1955), p. 4, Dissenting Opinion by Judge Klaestad.

Opinion, for example, Petrén criticised the Court for rejecting South Africa's request for an *ad hoc* judge.[50] He also expressed his regret that the majority had decided to retain a member on the bench who had – when he was a delegate of his country to the UN – participated actively in drafting a Security Council resolution, which was a part of the case now before the ICJ.

Petrén's concerns regarding procedural issues before the ICJ not only had to do with administration of justice. He was clearly uncomfortable with the way in which the Cold War impacted the General Assembly's use of the Court's advisory competence,[51] and he was generally very sceptical towards admitting cases that he found to involve political rather than legal questions. This was readily apparent in his Separate Opinions to the 1974 *Nuclear Tests* judgments[52] as well as his Separate Opinion to the 1975 *Western Sahara* Advisory Opinion. In the latter, he stated as follows:

> In my view, a request for an advisory opinion cannot be regarded as admissible unless the question which it submits to the Court relates either to the existence or the content of rights or obligations of international law, or to the conditions which, if fulfilled, would result in the coming into existence, the modification or the termination of such a right or obligation.[53]

In general, Petrén strongly advocated that the ICJ should not admit cases unless its jurisdiction was firmly established. In the 1974 *Fisheries Jurisdiction* cases, for example, Petrén believed that the majority had gone too far in its interpretation of an agreement between the parties.[54] He favoured a narrow

50 *Legal Consequences for States of the Continued Presence of South Africa in Namibia (South West Africa) notwithstanding Security Council Resolution 276 (1970)*, 21 June 1971, ICJ, Judgment, ICJ Reports (1971), p. 16, Separate Opinion of Judge Petrén.

51 *See*, for example, Shabtai Rosenne, 'The Cold War and the ICJ', 35 *Virginia Journal of International Law* (1994–1995) 669, pp. 671–674.

52 *Nuclear Tests (Australia* v. *France)*, 20 December 1974, ICJ, Judgment, Separate Opinion of Petrén, *ICJ Reports* (1974), p. 253, and *Nuclear Tests (New Zealand* v. *France)*, 20 December 1974, ICJ, Judgment, Separate Opinion of Petrén, *ICJ Reports* (1974), p. 457.

53 *Western Sahara*, 16 October 1975, ICJ, Advisory Opinion, Separate Opinion of Judge Petrén, *ICJ Reports* (1975), p. 108.

54 *Fisheries Jurisdiction (United Kingdom* v. *Iceland)*, 25 July 1974, ICJ, Judgment, Dissenting Opinion by Petrén, *ICJ Reports* (1974), p. 3, and *Fisheries Jurisdiction (Federal Republic of Germany* v. *Iceland)*, 25 July 1974, ICJ, Judgment, Dissenting Opinion by Petrén, *ICJ Reports* (1974), p. 175.

interpretation of said agreement, which would have excluded the cases from the Court's jurisdiction.

Petrén's somewhat conservative approach brought him into conflict with a number of his colleagues in The Hague. By the end of his term at the ICJ, he had become quite unpopular and – to his disappointment – he was not re-elected for a second term in 1975.[55]

3.3 *Norway: Jens Evensen (1985–1994)*

As mentioned above, the last Nordic ICJ judge to date was another Norwegian, Jens Evensen, who sat on the bench from 1985 to 1994. His election to the ICJ followed an impressive career as a lawyer, civil servant, diplomat, and politician. Evensen led the Norwegian Foreign Ministry's legal department from 1961 to 1973, and he is famous for his work on securing Norway's rights to offshore resources. Rumour has it that Evensen was the one who convinced the Danish foreign minister, Per Hækkerup, to have 'just one more glass of whisky' at the crucial meeting in 1963, where Norway got exclusive rights to *inter alia* Ekofisk oil field. From 1979 to his election to the ICJ in 1984, Evensen was member of the International Law Commission.

Evensen was part of the majority in the ground-breaking *Nicaragua* judgments of 1986, in which the ICJ not only invoked a controversial interpretation of the United States' acceptance of the Court's jurisdiction, but also significantly developed the rules on the prohibition against the use of force.[56] He was also a part of the majority in the important *ELSI* judgment of 1989, where the ICJ elaborated on the 'exhaustion of local remedies'-criterion in the doctrine of diplomatic protection.[57] However, Evensen submitted very few individual dissenting and separate opinions that might have provided insights into his legal reasoning.[58] One example, seemingly corroborating the idea that Evensen favoured objective and effective interpretation, is his Separate Opinion to the

55 M. Sørensen, 'Sture Petrén: In Memoriam', 46 *Nordisk Tidsskrift for International Ret* (1977) p. 3, at p. 5.

56 *Military and Paramilitary Activities in and against Nicaragua* (*Nicaragua* v. *United States of America*) (*Jurisdiction*), 26 November 1984, ICJ, Judgment, *ICJ Reports* (1984), p. 392, and *Military and Paramilitary Activities in and against Nicaragua* (*Nicaragua* v. *United States of America*) (*Merits*), 27 June 1986, ICJ, Judgment, *ICJ Reports* (1986), p. 14.

57 *Elettronica Sicula S.p.A.* (*ELSI*) (*United States of America* v. *Italy*), 20 July 1989, ICJ, Judgment, *ICJ Reports* (1989), p. 15.

58 Before he became a permanent judge, Evensen had served as judge *ad hoc* in *Case concerning the Continental Shelf* (*Tunisia/Libyan Arab Jamahiriya*), 24 February 1982, ICJ, Judgment, *ICJ Reports* (1982), p. 18. In his Dissention Opinion, he stated *inter alia* that the majority had failed to take sufficiently account of "the 200-mile exclusive economic zone

1989 Advisory Opinion on the *Privileges and Immunities of the United Nations,* in which he advocated a wide interpretation of Article VI, Section 22, of the 1946 Convention on the Privileges and Immunities of the United Nations so as to encompass a right to respect for a person's family and family life:

> The respect for a person's family and family life must be considered as integral parts of the 'privileges and immunities' that are necessary for "the independent exercise of their functions" under Article VI, Section 22, of the 1946 Convention on the Privileges and Immunities of the United Nations.[59]

4 Conclusion

The PCIJ and ICJ have not exactly been overrun by judges from the Nordic region. However, with seven out of a total of 141 of permanent judges and deputy-judges[60] – equivalent to 5 per cent – the Nordic region has arguably held its fair share of seats. Whereas Sweden, Denmark, and Finland dominated the PCIJ, Norway has certainly exercised greater influence on the ICJ compared to its Nordic counterparts. In addition to Judges Klaestad and Evensen, the registrar of the ICJ from 1946 to 1953 was also a Norwegian named Edvard Hambro. Some of the Nordic judges have been more powerful than others. Hammarskjöld and Klaestad appear to have been particularly influential in the early days of respectively the PCIJ and the ICJ. Petrén, on the other hand, was seemingly a rather unpopular figure during his term at the ICJ.

So, what does the voting practice of the Nordic judges of the PCIJ and the ICJ tell us about a possible Nordic approach to international law? Well, perhaps not that much. Indeed, one could reasonably object that the chapter has taken on an impossible endeavour because relevant material available to scrutiny is so scarce. It is hardly safe to draw any conclusions on the basis of the limited number of judges and cases; except perhaps that Nordic judges are uniformly biased towards their respective home states. But that is true of judges of all nationalities. Moreover, the lack of records of deliberations significantly

concept as a new accepted trend in the Law of the Sea Conference". *See ibid.*, Dissenting Opinion of Judge Evensen, p. 288.

59 *Applicability of Article VI, Section 22, of The Convention on the Privileges and Immunities of the United Nations*, 15 December 1989, ICJ, Advisory Opinion, *ICJ Reports* (1989), p. 177, Separate Opinion of Judge Evensen, p. 211.

60 35 at the PCIJ and 106 at the ICJ.

complicates any attempt at a qualitative analysis of whether the nationality of the individual judges has had any influence on the substance of their decisions. With these significant caveats, however, the image that does appear from the material is that Nordic judges of the World Court have predominantly favoured objective and effective treaty interpretation as opposed to restrictive interpretation and judicial restraint. But it would be a huge overstatement to conclude that the voting practice of Nordic judges at the PCIJ and the ICJ reflects the existence of a distinctive Nordic approach to international law.

A Nordic Approach to the Interpretation of the European Convention on Human Rights?

Jens Elo Rytter

1 Introduction

It might seem heretical even to ask the question whether there might exist a specific Nordic approach to the interpretation of the European Convention on Human Rights (ECHR). As a matter of principle, such a phenomenon would seem incompatible with the fact that the ECHR is an international treaty and thus subject to the customary international methods and principles of treaty interpretation as codified in the 1969 Vienna Convention.[1] These are also the methods and principles, which guide the Strasbourg Court in its institutional role as the authoritative interpreter of the Convention. In practice, however, it may not be so simple.

The Vienna principles on treaty interpretation do not provide a strict formula that can be applied in just one fashion. Within the boundaries of interpretation "in accordance with the ordinary meaning to be given to the terms of the treaty in their context and in the light of it subject and purpose" there is a room for manoeuvre. What is more, there may not even be general agreement as to where the outer boundaries of interpretation lie. The Strasbourg Court consists of judges from all 47 Contracting States. International judges, too, are products of their national background – shaped by national legal culture and constitutional tradition. It might thus seem somewhat naïve to imagine that an international judge, once appointed, should suddenly leave his or her national 'heritage' behind and enter the realm of treaty interpretation with an entirely open mind. This includes judges coming from one of the Nordic countries – Sweden, Finland, Norway, Iceland, and Denmark.

This article makes the claim that a specific Nordic interpretative approach to the ECHR does indeed exist to a certain extent. I do not mean to say that such a Nordic approach is always visible – far from it. Rather, the specific Nordic approach occasionally reveals itself in certain cases of principle and controversy.

---

* The author wishes to thank law student Anders Svane for excellent assistance in researching for this chapter.

1 Vienna Convention on the Law of Treaties, Art. 31–33.

 | DOI 10.1163/9789004343597_007

In this article I will not be able to scientifically prove that my claim is correct. My ambition is merely to substantiate my claim with such circumstantial evidence that it might be regarded a reasonable assumption that a Nordic approach to the interpretation of the Convention exists. The suspicion of a Nordic approach to the interpretation of the ECHR came to me when reading a couple of dissenting opinions delivered, or joined, by the Danish Strasbourg judge in controversial cases touching upon issues of principle relating to interpretation. It seemed that in such cases the Danish judge would often be dissenting together with other Nordic judges to the extent that Nordic judges took part in the decision at all.

I started looking more broadly for what could be termed 'Nordic' dissenting opinions, *i.e.*, dissenting opinions joined by all the Nordic judges (sometimes just one) taking part in the Court's decision in the case.

As a *caveat* it should be emphasized that my search has not been systematic and I have identified only a relatively small number: Ten 'Nordic' dissenting opinions. It should also be clear from the outset that the vast majority of Strasbourg judgments do not support the idea of a special 'Nordic' interpretative approach. Obviously, this holds true for cases decided unanimously with Nordic judges taking part; it also holds true for judgments decided by a majority in which Nordic judges stand divided.

When I still dare to claim that the few cases I have identified are indicative of a special Nordic approach to the interpretation of the ECHR, it is because of the substance and common features of these 'Nordic' dissenting opinions. Together, they seem to reveal a common approach to interpretation, which is not only shared predominantly (though not always exclusively) among Nordic judges, but which also corresponds very well to what may be labelled Nordic legal culture or tradition.

In what follows, I will first provide a very sketchy description of Nordic legal and constitutional tradition. Then, I turn to analysing the 'Nordic' dissenting opinions that I have found in search of a possible 'Nordic' interpretative approach. Finally, I offer my overall assessment of the findings as well as some concluding perspectives.

2 Nordic Legal and Constitutional Tradition

Despite obvious differences between the Nordic countries, it is possible to identify a (core) common Nordic legal tradition as well as a common overall constitutional tradition. What is more, the *legal* and the *constitutional* traditions in the Nordic countries seem to be mutually reinforcing.

Nordic legal systems are typically considered to be part of the Germanic law family. However, there are several aspects which suggest that Nordic law has special features distinguishing it from the Roman-German legal tradition. Notably, Nordic legal tradition is said to be more pragmatic, lending perhaps in this respect from Anglo-Saxon common law tradition. Thus, Nordic law may be described as a mix between "powerful Germanic and weaker common law elements".[2] Accordingly, Nordic law is generally considered to constitute a legal family of its own.[3]

Three characteristics of Nordic legal and constitutional tradition stand out:

Legal positivism. Like Germanic law, Nordic law systems are characterised by a culture of legal positivism, only less formalistic and more pragmatic in nature.[4] The essence of this is that the text provides a binding limit on the interpreter. The Scandinavian legal realism adds to this approach, by rejecting moral absolutism, considering moral values to be emotions which should not form part of legal thinking.[5]

Importance of preparatory work. Generally speaking, preparatory work is considered an extremely important source of law in Nordic legal systems. Thus, the teleological interpretation is focused on studying the preparatory work of legislation in order to clarify its intended purpose. This is in accordance with positivism and the way in which Scandinavian tradition emphasises the role of the legislature and her will.[6] By thus constantly searching for the legislator's intentions in case of doubt, the Nordic tradition leaves less room for the judge to develop his or her own vision of a norm's object and purpose.[7]

Relatively weak constitutional role of courts. In the Nordic constitutional tradition, courts exercise restraint vis-à-vis the legislature and other political

2 J. Husa, K. Nuotio and H. Pihlajamäki, 'Nordic Law – Between Tradition and Dynamism', in J. Husa, K. Nuotio and H. Pihlajamäki (eds.), *Nordic Law – Between Tradition and Dynamism* (Intersentia, Antwerp 2007) pp. 1–39 (7–8).

3 *Cf.* J. Husa, 'Nordic Constitutionalism and European Human Rights – Mixing Oil and Water?', 55 *Scandinavian Studies in Law* (2010) pp. 101–124 (p. 105, with further references in footnote 14 to, among others, Konrad Zweigert and Hein Kötz).

4 *Cf.* Husa et al., *supra* note 2, pp. 9–10.

5 *Cf.* D. Tamm, 'The Danes and their legal heritage', in B. Dahl, T. Melchior, L.A. Rehof and D. Tamm (eds.), *Danish Law in a European Perspective* (GadJura, Copenhagen, 1996) pp. 33–52 (49); T. Malminen, 'So You Thought Transplating Law is Easy? Fear of Scandinavian Realism in Finland, 1918–1965', in Husa et al. (eds.), *supra* note 2, pp. 75–87 (78); Husa et al., *supra* note 2, pp. 32–34.

6 *Cf.* D. Tamm, *supra* note 5, pp. 49–50; Husa et al., *supra* note 2, p. 34; J. Niemi-Kiesiläinen, 'The Structure of Legal Argument', in Husa et al. (eds.), *ibid.*, pp. 89–108 (94).

7 *Cf.* Husa et al., *ibid.*

organs. Generally speaking, Nordic courts (although to a varying extent) have kept a 'low-profile' and tried to avoid conflict with the political organs. Nordic courts not only seek to avoid acting in a political way but may even often "seem to feel a great deal of *loyalty* toward the Parliament".[8] This cautious tradition may likely have been supported and preserved by the absence of constitutional courts in the Nordic countries. Presumably, ordinary courts lacking the political mandate and expertise of specialised constitutional courts are less likely to take an activist approach.

Clearly, the Nordic approach to legal interpretation and constitutional balance of power is likely to sit somewhat uncomfortably with any advanced development of human rights law by a judicial organ such as the Strasbourg Court. From a Nordic perspective human rights norms have an air of being 'political'; not only do they limit the freedom of the political organs, they are also often couched in broad and imprecise terms and thus need filling-out to a larger extent than many other legal norms.

3 'Nordic Approaches' in Strasbourg Case Law

The time has come to present the 'Nordic' dissenting opinions which in my view are indicative of a special Nordic approach to the interpretation of the ECHR; an approach very much corresponding to the characteristics of Nordic legal and constitutional tradition.

As mentioned above, I have found 10 'Nordic' dissenting opinions[9] – *i.e.*, dissenting opinions joined by all the Nordic judges (sometimes just one) who actually take part in the Court's decision (sometimes together with other judges as well; five of the ten dissenting opinions found are purely 'Nordic').

The examples span from 1979–2016 (but with a big 'gap' from 1981–2005, and the majority from the last ten years). They concern altogether 8 different Convention rights (right to a fair trial, prohibition of retroactive punishment, right to respect for private and family life, freedom of religion, freedom of expression, freedom of association, protection of property, right to free elections). They involve nine different Nordic judges (three Danish, two Norwegian, two

8 Husa, *supra* note 3, p. 108. See also as regards Danish judges having a "fear of trespassing into the field of the legislator…", O. Due, 'Danish Law in a European Context', in Dahl et al. (eds.), *supra* note 5, pp. 13–31 (21).

9 The 10 opinions stem from just 9 cases since, as will be seen below, there are two 'Nordic' dissenting opinions in the case *Bélâné Nagy* v. *Hungary*, one from the Chamber judgment the other from the subsequent Grand Chamber judgment.

Icelandic, one Swedish, and one Finnish), providing a total of 16 Nordic votes (seven from Danish judges, five from Icelandic judges, two from Norwegian judges, one from a Swedish judge, and one from a Finnish judge) out of 33 dissenting votes in all.

In its landmark judgment in *Airey* (1979)[10] the Court held that even Convention freedoms may exceptionally oblige states to provide financial assistance, finding that Ireland had violated Article 6 (right to fair trial) and Article 8 (right to respect for private and family life) by not providing the applicant with legal aid without which she was not able to obtain a judicial separation from her husband. Judge Vilhjálmson (Iceland) dissented, referring to the textual limits of the Convention as well as the danger of stepping into a complex political area outside the Court's competence:

> The ideas underlying the Convention, as well as its wording, make it clear that it is concerned with problems other than the one facing us in this case. The war on poverty cannot be won through broad interpretation of the Convention.... Where the Convention sees financial ability to avail oneself of a right guaranteed therein as so important that it must be considered an integral part of the right, this is so stated.... When this is not the case, the Convention has nothing to say on how, when and if the financial means should be made available. Any other interpretation of the Convention, at least at this particular stage of the development of human rights, would open up problems whose range and complexity cannot be foreseen but which would doubtless prove to be beyond the power of the Convention and the institutions set up by it.[11]

In another landmark case, *Young, James and Webster* (1981)[12] on mandatory trade union membership, the Court held that Article 11 (freedom of association) also to some extent protects the freedom not to be compelled to become a member of a specific association (negative freedom of association). This was despite the fact that it emerged from the preparatory works that – due to the existence of 'closed shop' agreements in certain states – the question of negative freedom of association was deliberately left out when the provision was negotiated. In a harsh dissenting opinion Max Sørensen (Denmark), Thór Vilhjálmson (Iceland), and Lagergren (Sweden) rejected the majority's findings

10 *Airey* v. *Ireland*, 9 October 1979, ECtHR, judgement.

11 *Ibid.* Dissenting opinion of Judge Thór Vilhjálmson.

12 *Young, James and Webster* v. *the United Kingdom*, 13 August 1981, ECtHR, plenary judgement.

concerning a negative freedom of association as transgressing the limits of interpretation:

> [T]he States Parties to the Convention must be considered to have agreed not to include the negative aspect, and no canon of interpretation can be adduced in support of extending the scope of the Article (art. 11) to a matter which deliberately has been left out and reserved for regulation according to national law and traditions of each State Party to the Convention.[13]

In the much debated *Hirst* (2005),[14] the Court held that it was incompatible with Article 3 of Additional Protocol 1 (duty to hold free and democratic elections) that prisoners in the United Kingdom were banned from voting while serving their criminal sentence. Judge Lorenzen (Denmark) dissented with four colleagues, referring to the textual limits of the provision as well as the political sensitivity of the issue:

> We do not dispute that … a "dynamic and evolutive" approach may in certain situations be justified. However, it is essential to bear in mind that the Court is not a legislator and should be careful not to assume legislative functions. …Taking into account the sensitive political character of this issue, the diversity of the legal systems within the Contracting States and the lack of a sufficiently clear basis for such a right in Article 3 of Protocol No. 1, we are not able to accept that it is for the Court to impose on national legal systems an obligation either to abolish disenfranchisement for prisoners or to allow it only to a very limited extent.[15]

In *Sørensen and Rasmussen* (2006),[16] the Court further extended the protection of the negative freedom of association – so to speak finishing the process it began in 1981 with *Young, James and Webster* – holding that even an obligation of trade union membership existing at the time of employment violated Article 11 (freedom of association). Judge Lorenzen (Denmark) dissented, referring – as had his three Nordic colleagues in 1981 – to the incompatibility with the

13 *Ibid.* Dissenting opinion of Judge Sørensen, joined by Judges Thór Vilhjálmson and Lagergren, para. 5.

14 *Hirst* v. *the United Kingdom (no. 2)*, 6 October 2005, ECtHR, Grand Chamber judgement.

15 *Ibid.* Joint dissenting opinion of Judges Wildhaber, Costa, Lorenzen, Kovler and Jebens, para. 6 and 9.

16 *Sørensen and Rasmussen* v. *Denmark*, 11 January 2006, ECtHR, Grand Chamber judgement.

travaux préparatoires to the Convention, while also expressing concern that the Court was involving itself in sensitive social and political issues:

> It transpires from the travaux préparatoires ... that the member States were not prepared to accept the inclusion in the Convention of a provision ... which would have expressly granted the right not to belong to an association.... [T]he margin of appreciation in the field of closed-shop agreements is now considered to be "reduced". As justification for this change, the majority referred to the need in a democracy to achieve "a balance ... which ensures the fair and proper treatment of minorities and avoids any abuse of a dominant position". I fail to see how such a principle ... constitutes a convincing argument for increasing the Court's involvement in the assessment of delicate social and political matters such as those in issue in the instant case.[17]

Scoppola (2009)[18] concerned Article 7 (prohibition of retroactive punishment) which in the second sentence of its first paragraph states that: "Nor shall a heavier penalty be imposed than the one that was applicable at the time the criminal offence was committed". The Court in this case held that Article 7 (now) also includes a right to be sentenced to a new and more lenient penalty than the one applicable at the time the criminal offence was committed in situations where the relevant legislation has subsequently been changed in favour of the accused – *lex mitior*. Judge Lorenzen (Denmark) dissented with five colleagues, arguing that the interpretation of the majority in fact invented a novel right, overstepping not only the textual limits of Article 7 but also extending its prohibition beyond what had been intended:

> In our opinion Article 7 § 1 does not admit of such interpretation. ...The *lex mitior* principle does not form part of nor can it be considered an extension or a corollary of this rule of law requirement. It is a different kind of norm. ...It remains, in the absence of some specific provision, a matter of policy or choice in the discretionary area enjoyed by the State in criminal matters. It is clear that when Article 7 § 1 was adopted the *lex mitior* principle was not included in it; and it has not been suggested that anyone had then thought that it was covered by the *nullum crimen nulla poena sine lege* principle. ...The Travaux Preparatoires of Article 7 § 1 reveal ... that the possibility had been canvassed of adding to it the

17 *Ibid.* Dissenting opinion of Judge Lorenzen, paras. 2 and 4.

18 *Scoppola* v. *Italy* (*no.* 2), 17 September 2009, ECtHR, Grand Chamber judgement.

> *lex mitior* principle but that it was abandoned. ...The majority has ... had [Art. 7] re-written in order to accord with what they consider it ought to have been. This, with respect, oversteps the limits.[19]

Vilnes and Others (2013)[20] concerned a somewhat more practical issue: Private divers who had incurred health problems that might well be related to deep-sea diving. The human rights question was whether Norway – by not adequately ensuring that divers received timely and understandable information regarding decompression tables – had violated the divers' rights under Article 8 (right to respect for private life) by failing to fulfil the state's positive obligation to protect the applicants' health. The Court answered this question in the affirmative. However, Judges Nordén (Norway) and Lorenzen (Denmark) dissented, finding that this was taking the doctrine of positive obligations too far, placing a too heavy burden on states in a technical field, where it was easy to blame the state in retrospect: "I emphasise that an unrealistic burden should not be imposed on the authorities, and that their conduct should not be evaluated with the wisdom of hindsight".[21]

In *Magyar Keresztény Mennonita Egyház and Others* (2014)[22] the Court held that a Hungarian reform act regarding religious communities violated the applicants' freedom of religious association – Article 11 (freedom of association) read in the light of Article 9 (freedom of religion). The applicants had all previously been registered as churches with special benefits and privileges but as the reform had introduced new criteria, they no longer qualified for registration. The new act did not limit the freedom of every religious community to practice their religion but merely affected the future access of religious communities like the applicants' to financial support from the State.[23] Judge Spano (Iceland) dissented with his Italian colleague, holding that there was no interference with freedom of religious association as this freedom does not entail any right to benefits from the state – and warning the majority of the inherent risk of too expansive interpretations:

---

19 *Ibid.* Partly dissenting opinion of Judge Nicolaou, joined by Judges Bratza, Lorenzen, Jociené, Villiger and Sajo.

20 *Vilnes and Others* v. *Norway*, 5 December 2013, ECtHR, judgement.

21 *Ibid.* Partly dissenting opinion of Judge Nordén, joined by Judge Lorenzen.

22 *Magyar Keresztény Mewnonita Egyház and Others* v. *Hungary*, 8 April 2014, ECtHR, judgement.

23 In this respect, the act would seem to discriminate in favour of old, long-established churches in Hungary. However, since the majority found a violation of Article 11, *cf.* Article 9, they never took a stand on Article 14 (discrimination).

> Today's judgment enlarges the scope of Article 9, taken alone and in conjunction with Article 11, as regards associative religious activity, to an extent that conforms neither to the text or purpose of these provisions nor to their development in the case-law of this Court. ...the Court has never held before today that the decision of the State to withhold previously afforded material benefits from religious entities which are duly registered and afforded legal personality status constitutes, as such, interference with the freedom to manifest a religion or a belief under Article 9, interpreted in the light of Article 11. ...this Court must be ever mindful that the scope of the rights and freedoms guaranteed by the Convention is not without limits. As rules of law, their scope must be defined within the text of the relevant provision, as interpreted reasonably in the light of their object and purpose. The unrestrained expansion of the substantive reach of the Convention runs the risk of undermining the legitimacy of this system of European supervision of human rights.[24]

In *Magyar Helsinki Bizottság* (2016)[25] the Court held for the first time that Article 10 (freedom of expression), which includes, *inter alia*, the right to "receive information and ideas without interference by public authority", implies – on certain conditions – a right of access to information held by public authorities and thus obliges the State to provide such information. The majority relied on a dynamic interpretation taking into account subsequent developments in international and national law. Judge Spano (Iceland) and Judge Kjølbro (Denmark) provided a lengthy dissenting opinion, arguing that the majority's interpretation was incompatible with the text as well as the purpose of Article 10 as clarified in the preparatory works:

> [T]he role of this Court is not to imbue every positive development in the field of European human rights with the binding force of law by incorporating such developments into the Convention, irrespective of the limits laid down by the Convention's text and structure. The Court's role is rather to determine whether, as a matter of law, the Convention can be interpreted to include a particular right.... Words matter when interpreting a legal text. ...The text of Article 10 § 1 of the Convention is limited to the freedom to receive information and ideas without governmental

24 *Supra* note 22, Dissenting opinion of Judge Spano joined by Judge Raimondi, para. 5 and 14–15.

25 *Magyar Helsinki Bizottság* v. *Hungary*, 8 November 2016, ECtHR, Grand Chamber judgement.

> interference. In other words, the text does not include the freedom to seek information. The verb to receive, in its ordinary everyday meaning and when applying simple common sense, cannot be understood to include a right of access to information that the holder does not want to impart. ...it transpires from the preparatory work that the modality of seeking information ... was deliberately omitted in the final text. ...the methods of exercising the freedom in question are couched explicitly in negative terms, thus they shall not be "interfered [with] by public authorities". ...In sum, when one examines in good faith the ordinary meaning of the words used in Article 10 § 1 of the Convention, in their context and in the light of the preparatory work as a supplementary means of interpretation, one must conclude, at least as a starting point, that Article 10 § 1 does not, and was not meant to, encompass a right to access information held by public authorities that they are not willing to impart or obliged to disclose under domestic law.[26]

Finally, in *Béláné Nagy* v. *Hungary* (2015–2016)[27] the Court held that Hungary had violated Article 1 of Additional Protocol 1 (right to property), which includes, *inter alia*, the right of every person to "the peaceful enjoyment of his possessions", by enacting in 2012 a new law on disability benefits as a consequence of which the applicant lost her previous right to a disability pension as she could not fulfil the new conditions. According to the court, by entirely depriving the applicant of her previous access to disability pension the act had constituted a disproportionate interference with her legitimate expectation of being able to receive disability pension in the future. The case was adjudicated first by a Court Chamber and subsequently by the Grand Chamber; in both instances the case was decided in favour of the applicant by a slim majority, and in both judgments all the Nordic judges taking part in the case dissented. In the Chamber Judge Spano (Iceland) and Judge Kjølbro (Denmark) together with their Swiss colleague delivered a harsh dissenting opinion, arguing that there was no possession to be interfered with and therefore there could be no violation of the right to property and further alleging that the majority had overstepped the Court's competence with unforeseen political consequences in the Contracting States:

> Article 1 of Protocol No. 1 to the Convention has never, before today, been interpreted by this Court as obliging member States to provide persons

26 *Ibid.* Dissenting opinion of Judge Spano joined by Judge Kjølbro, paras. 2, 4, 6, 9 and 11–12.

27 *Béláné Nagy* v. *Hungary*, 13 December 2016, ECtHR, Grand Chamber judgement, preceded by chamber judgment in the same case of 10 February 2015.

> with the right to social security benefits, in the form of disability pensions, independently of their having an assertable right to such a pension under domestic law. The majority have thus expanded the scope of the right to property under the Convention in a manner that is flatly inconsistent with this Court's case-law and the object and purpose of Article 1 of Protocol No. 1. As the right to property under the European Convention on Human Rights is not an autonomous repository for economic and social rights not granted by the member States, we respectfully dissent. ...It is undisputed in the present case ... that the applicant had no assertable right under domestic law to the disability pension she requested in February and August 2012.... This irrefutable legal fact should, in our view, have been the end of the matter, as the existence of an arguable claim under Article 1 of Protocol No. 1, in the field of welfare benefits, is firmly conditioned on the existence of a right to such benefits under domestic law. ...The majority cannot ... [invent] a substantive right to a disability pension under the Convention, where none exists, with unforeseen consequences for the social security and welfare systems of the 47 member States of the Council of Europe.[28]

When the case came to the Grand Chamber, Judge Hirvelä (Finland) and Judge Møse (Norway), together with six colleagues dissented, essentially on the same grounds:

> [T]he applicant's claim had no basis in domestic law as it stood.... There was thus no claim under domestic law that could be considered an asset protected by Article 1 of Protocol No. 1. In our opinion, therefore, the applicant did not have a "possession" within the meaning of Article 1 of Protocol No. 1, and the guarantees of that provision do not apply in the present case.[29]

4 Assessment and Conclusion

Contours of a 'Nordic' approach to the interpretation of the Convention seem to emerge from the abovementioned cases. What is more, the picture emerging is one very much in line with Nordic legal and constitutional tradition. This approach is notably characterised by:

---

28 *Ibid.* Joint dissenting opinion of Judges Keller, Spano and Kjølbro, paras. 1, 7–8, 14.

29 *Ibid.* Joint dissenting opinion of Judges Nussberger, Hirvelä, Bianku, Yudkivska, Møse, Lemmens and O'Leary, para. 39.

- Reluctance to move beyond the textual limits of the relevant provision, *i.e.*, an insistence that some basis in the ordinary meaning of the text is required (*Airey, Hirst, Scoppola, Magyar Keresztény Mennonita, Magyar Helsinki Bottzag, Béláné Nagy*).
- Reliance on preparatory works – rather than on more autonomous and free considerations – as a relevant source for identifying the purpose and extent of a provision when these are unclear (*Young, James and Webster, Sørensen and Rasmussen, Scoppola, Magyar Helsinki Bottzag*).
- Resistance towards imposing (without a solid legal basis) obligations on the national political organs, notably in the field of economic and social policy (*Airey, Hirst, Sørensen and Rasmussen, Vilnes, Béláné Nagy*).

Many of the dissenting opinions also testify to the mutually reinforcing influence of, respectively, the positivist Nordic legal tradition and the Nordic constitutional tradition of courts exercising caution in its role vis á vis the legislature and other political organs:

The positivist and realist emphasis on a clear textual basis and/or support in the preparatory works supports the constitutional tradition of staying away from interfering with the domain of politicians. According to Jaakko Husa, when the Strasbourg Court steps outside the text of the Convention it acts in a "political way" which Nordic courts would not do.[30] In the same vein Robert Spano, the current Icelandic judge in Strasbourg, has stated that while he does not disagree with the "living instrument doctrine" of the Strasbourg Court, he finds it valid to sometimes criticise "the Court's interpretational results".[31]

The constitutional tradition, in turn, supports the positivistic legal approach by warning against expansive interpretations that place burdens on politicians, especially in the field of economic and social policy. As emphatically noted by former Danish Strasbourg judge, Peer Lorenzen: "The Strasbourg Court is not a legislative organ and should refrain from taking on a legislative role".[32]

A final observation is the apparent resilience of the Nordic tradition over time. The cases mentioned above span more than 35 years and they do not

30 Husa, *supra* note 3, p. 122.

31 R. Spano, 'The European Court of Human Rights and National Courts: A Constructive Conversation or a Dialogue of Disrespect?', 33:1 *Nordic Journal of Human Rights* (2015) pp. 1–10 (9).

32 P. Lorenzen, 'Dissenser og dissentierende dommere i Menneskerettighedsdomstolen', in Børge Dahl, Michael Hansen Jensen and Søren Højgaard Mørup (eds.), *Festskrift til Jens Peter Christensen* (Jurist- og Økonomforbundets forlag, Copenhagen, 2016) pp. 879–897 (897 – my translation from Danish).

seem to indicate any tendency of Nordic judges abandoning their heritage and converging towards a 'common Strasbourg' approach to interpretation. On the contrary, the material seems indicative of a diehard Nordic tradition continuing to influence the Nordic judges in Strasbourg even after all those years. A recent statement by the former president of the Danish Supreme Court, Børge Dahl, fits this picture and even lends it support. Børge Dahl writes that the Danish approach to the delimitation between law and politics is based on democracy and that the international development should not become too dynamic and creative, adding with some sense of common Nordic resistance:

> As matters stand in Denmark and the other Nordic countries, we may safely rely on our own approach to the questions raised by the internationalisation. Nordic legal pragmatism is a common value, which it is worth guarding, and we should not give in to others' out of hand.[33]

---

33 B. Dahl, 'Hvad skal vi med Højesteret?', in Dahl et al. (eds.), *ibid.*, pp. 619–634 (634 – my translation from Danish).

Who Cares about International Law? A Study of How Scandinavian Judges Cite International Law and Courts

Marlene Wind

1 Introduction

In his book *Political Order and Political Decay* from 2014, Francis Fukuyama spends quite some time on what he calls "the getting to Denmark problem".[1] Denmark is, according to Fukuyama, an 'idealized place' that all countries should strive to come to look like and he underscores how Denmark successfully made the transition from patrimonial to modern state without having rulers falling into the trap of mixing personal and public interests.[2] The description of Denmark could just as well have been of the other Nordic countries. In particular, since the Second World War, the Nordic states have often been portrayed as "champions of international law and human rights",[3] as "moral superpowers",[4]

* From 2012–2015 the author was Professor II in Public Law at the PluriCourts Centre, at the University of Oslo. This research is funded by the Danish National Research Foundation Grant no. DNRF105 and conducted under the auspices of the Danish National Research Foundation's Centre of Excellence for International Courts (iCourts). I would like to thank colleagues at iCourts and Pluricourts for valuable comments to this chapter and to my evolving research on citations and legitimacy of ICs in general over the past years. I would also like to thank commentators at a conference on Nordic exceptionalism at the EUI in May 2016 and for comments at other international conferences over the past four years and of course to the anonymous review conducted by the *NJIL*. Most gratitude goes, however, to my research assistant Kristoffer Kohn Schaldemose for helping me with the collection of data and the designing and presentation of results and to Majka Holm for helping with the fine tuning of the manuscript. Any remaining faults or mistakes rest of course with me alone. Apart from a few changes, this chapter is identical to: Marlene Wind, 'Do Scandinavians Care about International Law? A Study of Scandinavian Judges' Citation Practice to International Law and Courts', *Nordic Journal of International Law*, Vol. 85, No. 4 (2016) pp. 281–302.

1 F. Fukuyama, *Political Order and Political Decay: From the Industrial Revolution to the Globalization of Democracy* (Profile Books Ltd., London, 2014) pp. 40, 751.

2 *Ibid.*, p. 41.

3 J. Christoffersen and M.R Madsen, 'The End of Virtue? Denmark and the Boomerang of the Internationalisation of Human Rights', 80:3 *Nordic Journal of International Law* (2011) p. 259.

4 A.S. Dahl, 'Sweden: Once a Moral Superpower, Always a Moral Superpower?', 26:4 *International Journal* (2006) pp. 859–908.

 | DOI 10.1163/9789004343597_008

and as "global good Samaritans".[5] The three Scandinavian countries, Sweden, Denmark and Norway, together of course with their Nordic brothers, Finland and Iceland, are in other words examples to be followed. They have been presented (and presented themselves) as frontrunners when it comes to human rights, the handing over of peace prizes but also when it comes to signing up to international courts, international law treaties and conventions. At least this has been the official picture. What is much less known is that the Scandinavians have displayed an enormous hesitance when it comes to the frequency by which they have domesticated the values they themselves stand for. For instance, the case law of those international courts they helped set up after the Second World War. The research and data presented in this chapter try to document this 'lacking domestication' quantitatively for the first time. It also deciphers the differences among the three Scandinavian countries (which are significant) and gets behind the more trivial explanations of their hesitance and the variance among them. The research presented here is unique as it draws on a newly established database, which has traced citations to international law in Danish, Swedish, and Norwegian Supreme Courts as far back as the 1950s. The empirical data presented shows that Norway sticks out as much closer to the conventional image of the Nordic states when it comes to citing the treaties it has signed up to and the case law of treaty-monitoring bodies. Sweden and Denmark do far worse falling surprisingly behind the Norwegian court's domestication of international law.

The chapter starts off by presenting the global context in terms of an explosion in international courts and international adjudication since the Second World War. In this period states have also accepted a general juridicalisation at the *national level* with the establishment of strong constitutional courts. Interestingly this evolution has not been reflected in the Nordic countries. After setting the stage in section 2, the chapter discusses and defends the theoretical (and methodological) claim promoted in this research, namely that the legitimacy of international courts and conventions can be attributed to how much they are cited by national judges. As the role of precedence is central to citation studies in general, the following section discusses the role of precedence in international law, and in relation to the Scandinavian countries[6] having a strong dualist tradition. The chapter then presents the data and the methodology behind the quantitative data set and presents some descriptive

5 A. Brysk, *Global Good Samaritans. Human Rights as Foreign Policy* (Oxford University Press, New York, 2009).

6 I use Nordic and Scandinavian more or less interchangeably in this chapter, knowing of course, that the two are often distinguished.

statistics comparing the three Scandinavian countries. Finally, the chapter ends by discussing the differences among the three Supreme Courts by drawing on my own previous research on the importance of national judicial review for international engagement,[7] as well as the role of Scandinavian legal positivism as it has been understood by the academy as a possible explanatory factor for understanding the strong emphasis of the lawmaker and preparatory work for judges and national courts in Scandinavia.

2 The Rise of International Courts and the Lacking Domestication of International Law in Scandinavia

Since the first permanent international court (IC) was set up in 1922, states have established almost 25 international judicial bodies. Altogether four global courts and 20 regional courts have emerged, and many more are in the making.[8] At the same time within the past 15 years more than 150 countries around the world have introduced constitutional democracy defined as "democracy where constitutional judicial review of legislation by strong constitutional courts" is regarded as a corner stone.[9]

This is quite a dramatic global development, which is replicated (and in some cases even originating) in Europe where most countries, including the new democracies in Central and Eastern Europe, have embraced German-style constitutional democracy in the post war period.[10] Both the setting up of an increasing number of ICs and the establishment of strong national constitutional structures with significant review powers to courts can be attributed to the general rise and spread of international human rights after the Second World War. It is perhaps a bit of a paradox as Christoffersen and Madsen put it, that it

7 *See* M. Wind, 'When Parliament comes first: The Danish Concept of Democracy meets the European Union', *Nordic Journal of Human Rights* 2 (2009) pp. 272–289; M. Wind, D.S. Martinsen and G.P. Rotger, 'The Uneven Legal Push for Europe', 10:1 *European Union Politics* (March 2009) pp. 63–88; M. Wind, 'The Nordics, the EU and the reluctance towards supranational judicial review', 48:4 *Journal of Common Market Studies* (2010) pp. 1039–1063; J.E. Rytter and M. Wind, 'In Need of Juristocracy? The Silence of Denmark in the development of European Law', 9:2 *International Journal of Constitutional Law* (2011) pp. 470–504.

8 C. Romano, K. Alter and T. Shany (eds.), *The Oxford University Press Handbook of International Adjudication* (Oxford University Press, Oxford, 2013); K. Alter, *The New Terrain of International Law* (Princeton University Press, Princeton, 2014).

9 R. Hirschl, *Towards Juristocracy* (Harvard University Press, Cambridge, 2004).

10 A. Stone Sweet, *Governing with Judges: Constitutional Politics in Europe* (Oxford University Press, Oxford, 2000).

was in Europe that the human rights convention was invented and designed[11] as we are dealing with a continent which had committed an excessive number of human rights atrocities during the war. It was also a continent, which after the war with its imperial ambitions "manipulated the very same notion [of human rights] limiting its applicability to a selected group of individuals and instrumentalized human rights as part of their self-described 'mission civilisatrice' abroad".[12]

The Scandinavian countries joined the European Convention of Human Rights (ECHR) at a fairly early stage in the beginning of the 1950s. However, it soon became clear that the Convention was mainly for external consumption and not directed at these countries themselves.[13] Scandinavians such as Dag Hammarskjöld,[14] who was a prominent figure in the United Nations (UN) as the second secretary general from 1953–1961, came to "embody the notion that small states should seek to exploit international forums such as the UN and therefore generally support the drafting of binding international law as a means for international peace and cooperation".[15]

In other fields of the social sciences like international relations, which emerged as an independent discipline after the Second World War, the narrative that Scandinavians had a special humanitarian approach to international law, human rights and peaceful coexistence also became prominent. Wæver and Kristensen[16] argue that the Scandinavian IR discipline started out with a strong focus on peace studies and a deep-felt criticism of power politics – a fact that underscored also the academic community's commitment to a special Nordic focus on peace operations, human rights and international cooperation in general.[17] However, also here the dominant hidden assumption seemed to be that human rights were primarily for export and not something that the Scandinavians themselves needed to address. Even after the human rights

---

11 *See* E. Bates, 'The Birth of the European Convention of Human Rights – and the European Court of Human Rights', in J. Christoffersen and M. Rask Madsen (eds.), *The European Court of Human Rights between Law and Politics* (Oxford University Press, Oxford, 2011); M. Rask Madsen, 'The protracted institutionalization of the Strasbourg Court: From Legal Diplomacy to Integrationist Jurisprudence', in Christoffersen and Rask Madsen, *ibid.*

12 Christoffersen and Rask Madsen, *ibid.*, p. 1.

13 Christoffersen and Rask Madsen, *supra* note 4, p. 258.

14 And before him, the Norwegian Trygve Halfdan Lie who was the first secretary general.

15 Christoffersen and Madsen, *supra* note 4, p. 259.

16 O. Wæver and P.M Kristensen, 'Scandinavian IR – Less Identity, More Influence?', forthcoming.

17 Wæver and Kristensen argue among other things that Norway is the country in the world with the largest number of IR scholars signing up to liberalism.

convention was incorporated into national law in the beginning of the 1990s, more than 40 years (!) after it was signed, the Scandinavian countries avoided to fully embrace it. But what would a true domestication of human rights have entailed? Following Christoffersen and Madsen it would be:

> taking international law down from its elevated position in terms of a universal commitment to peace and international cooperation, which had marked most of the 20th century Scandinavian legal internationalism, and instead bringing it into the everyday practice of law and politics.[18]

One way of "taking international law down from its elevated position" was for domestic courts to start citing it and thus rely on the convention and the Strasbourg Court's case law in their own decisions. Something that the Scandinavian courts have turned out to be very hesitant to do – even today. Fig. 1, which is generated from an iCourts database collecting citations from all European courts, illustrates that the Nordic countries' courts are among those least likely to cite the oldest and most well-known human rights court in the world: the European Court of Human Rights (ECtHR).

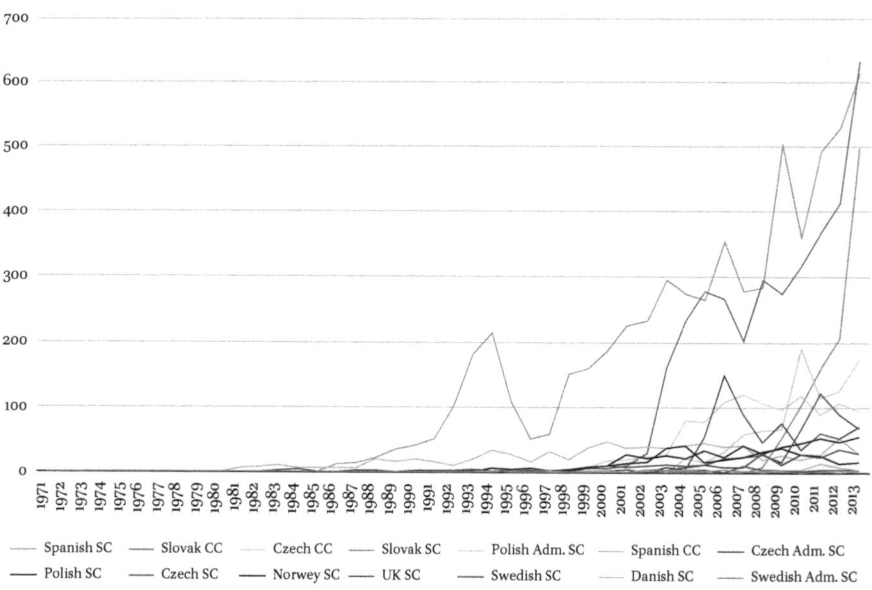

FIGURE 1 *Selected Supreme Court citations to the ECtHR*

18 Christoffersen and Madsen, *supra* note 4, p. 258.

Neglecting those international court-decisions that your own government has signed up to by not citing them is a rather clear statement as we are to see below.

However, it was not only the domestication of human rights and international law that never really penetrated the Scandinavian countries. It was also the general idea of constitutionalism. Apart from Norway, which actually adopted a constitutional court with rather strong review functions already in 1866,[19] Denmark and Sweden preserved strong parliaments and no constitutional courts. The Supreme Courts of the latter two democracies have over the years conducted no or only very weak constitutional review.

In Denmark it has only happened once in 170 years that the Supreme Court has set aside a piece of legislation adopted by parliament. It was in the case of the Tvind law in 1999, which was considered unconstitutional.[20] In Sweden judicial review was explicitly forbidden in the Constitution until 1979 and is even today significantly limited.[21]

The same goes for Finland where constitutional review was forbidden until 2000.[22] The mantra has thus been 'no one over or above the parliament' in the Nordic countries[23] – a mantra that is still highly dominant in the public discourse. Following the distinction between constitutional and majoritarian democracies presented by legal philosopher Ronald Dworkin this means that the Scandinavian countries – perhaps with the important exception of

19 *See* A. Kierulf, Taking *Judicial Review Seriously: The Case of Norway* (Oslo University Press, Oslo, 2014) p. 6.

20 J.P. Christensen, *Domstolene – den tredje statsmagt* (Aarhus Universitets forlag, Aarhus, 2003).

21 J. Nergelius, 'Judicial review in Swedish law', 27:2 *Nordic Journal of Human Rights* (2009) pp. 142–160.

22 T. Ojanen, 'From Constitutional Periphery toward the Center – transformation of Judicial Review in Finland', 27:2 *Nordic Journal of Human Rights* (2009) p. 195.

23 Until 1979 judicial review was forbidden in Sweden (and very restricted until 2001), and in Denmark there is no mentioning of this role to the courts in the Constitution. Only once in 170 years has the Danish Supreme court set aside a piece of legislation adopted by the Danish Parliament. This was in the *Tvind* case handed down by the Danish Supreme Court on 19 February 1999 (U 1999.841 H). *See* J. Nergelius, 'North and South: Can the Nordic States and the European continent find each other in the constitutional area – or are they too different?' in M. Scheinin (ed.), *The Welfare State and Constitutionalism in the Nordic Countries*, (Nordic Council of Ministers, Nord, Copenhagen, 2001); *see also* Wind, 'When Parliament Comes First: The Danish Concept of Democracy Meets the European Union', 2 *Nordic Journal of Human Rights* (2009) pp. 272–289; Rytter and Wind, *supra* note 8, pp. 470–504.

Norway – can be categorised as majoritarian democracies.[24] More specifically, what characterises a majoritarian (as opposed to constitutional) democracy is exactly that there is no tradition[25] for conducting judicial (constitutional) review by courts and that the vision of the majority in parliament (elevated above the other branches of government) holds strong.[26] The point that I am making here, and have made elsewhere, is thus that the absence of a solid review institution in these countries has significant repercussions, not just for the conception of democracy in these countries but also for their relationship to supranational regulation in terms of international and European law.[27] This is not meant to imply that we are dealing with a static situation but, as Ran Hirschl has pointed out, the Scandinavian countries constitute in this respect an unexplored laboratory of countries, which have deliberately rejected constitutionalism.[28]

While in previous research attention has been paid to the limited number of preliminary questions forwarded to the European Court of Justice from the Nordic states, explained in part by the lack of a solid judicial review tradition,[29] no attention has been given to the much broader debate of international law. We in fact have very little systematic knowledge about how, whether and to what degree the three Scandinavian countries have domesticated and 'downloaded' the international law treaties and ICs' case law that their governments have signed up to in their own national legal orders. The question could also be asked as McCrudden does in his article on national courts' citation to the Convention on the Elimination of Discrimination Against Women (CEDAW).

---

24 A similar distinction as the one presented by Dworkin is found in a more recent book by Richard Bellamy from 2007 who distinguishes between legal and political constitutionalism where he strongly defends political constitutionalism (i.e. majoritarian democracy). *See* R. Bellamy, *Political Constitutionalism* (Cambridge University Press, Cambridge, 2007).

25 It is important to emphasise here that I am not claiming that constitutional or judicial review never takes place or is still forbidden. My point is merely – but never the less importantly – that constitutional review is rarely practiced and considered problematic by politicians as well as the judges themselves.

26 R. Dworkin, *Freedoms Law: The Moral Reading of the American Constitution* (Harvard University Press, Cambridge, MA, 1996).

27 Wind, *supra* note 8, pp. 1039–1063.

28 R. Hirschl, 'The Nordic counter narrative: Democracy, human development, and judicial review', 9:2 *International Journal of Constitutional Law* (2011) pp. 449–469.

29 *See* the author's previous research which is also the subject of Ran Hirschl's comment: Wind, 'When Parliament Comes First', *supra* note 8, pp. 1039–1063; Rytter and Wind, *supra* note 8, pp. 470–504.

Do national judges primarily act as domestic actors "who use international law in order to advance domestic goals"?[30]

In the following I will take a closer look at the role citations and precedence play in national and in particular in international law. This part draws on recent American political science research investigating the role of citations and precedence in international law. What this research demonstrates is that: how and whether judges cite international courts and conventions can be seen as a proxy for the acceptance and perceived legitimacy of the normative international judicial development since the Second World War. The link between citations to international courts and conventions and their perceived legitimacy will also be a central assumption in the present chapter where the Nordic countries are in focus.

3 Citing International Cases and the Question of Legitimacy

It is sometimes argued that it is less problematic whether national judges cite the case law of those international courts that their government has signed up to as IC decisions are 'one shot' events that concern only the parties involved. As the International Court of Justice points out in Article 59 of its founding statute "[t]he decision of the Court has no binding force except between the parties and in respect of that particular case".[31] The dogma that international courts do not create precedent is however strongly contested as ICs' case law is increasingly cited, not only by the ICs themselves but also by legal practitioners, national courts and scholars.[32] If we look at the European courts alone, both the ECtHR and the European Court of Justice (ECJ) have already a long tradition for creating precedent through their case law. This also goes for more specialized courts. Krzyztof Pelc has put it more bluntly, referring to ICs and international law in the following way "[b]inding precedent [in international law] may be a legal fiction, but it is one that courts and countries tacitly accept

30 C. McCrudden, 'Why do National Court Judges Refer to Human Rights Treaties? A Comparative International Law analysis of CEDAW', *Public and Legal Theory Research Papers*, paper no. 482, 26 October 2015, online at <SSRN.COM/ABstract=2680458>, visited on 5 July 2016.

31 Statute of the International Court of Justice, online at <www.icj-cij.org/documents/?p1=4&p2=2>, visited on 5 July 2016.

32 *See also* A.M. Slaughter, *A New World Order* (Princeton University Press, Princeton, 2004); K. Alter, *The New Terrain of International Law* (Princeton University Press, Princeton, 2014).

to be bound by".[33] Things are thus very different today, and it makes sense to say that judges in civil as well as common law systems[34] cite previous cases from both the national and the international level to build a persuasive and legitimate argument. Doing so is, however, not only about persuasion and consistency. It is also about lending legitimacy to the cited court. Any specific reference may thus mirror the reputation of the specific court cited and its judges.[35] Helfer and Slaughter also argue that courts "enhance each other's prestige" by citing each other's decisions.[36]

Lupu and Voten have shown that "judges cite precedent at least in part to provide strategic legitimation for their decisions".[37] In their very interesting study of the citation practice of the European Court of Human Rights, they moreover demonstrate that the court cites about ten of its own previous cases in each new case.[38] The fact that international courts cite their own cases tells us that precedence is important to ICs themselves when trying to foster influence and establish a coherent, predictable and legitimate body of law. Since treaties and IC case law is also collected in large prestigious volumes and studied in law schools all over the world, one must assume not only that precedence plays an increasing role in modern international law, but also that national courts deciding international law related cases will take the case law into account and even cite it when appropriate. In particular, if the national judges come from countries with a solid international law tradition.

The Nordic countries and their national courts would most certainly be expected to belong to such a category and to be in the forefront when it comes

33 K. Pelc, 'The Politics of Precedent in International Law: A Social Network Application'. 108:3 *American Political Science Review* (2014) pp. 547–564; *see also* Slaughter, *ibid.*; Alter, *ibid.*

34 There used to be a great divergence in the use of precedence between the two different types of legal systems. This is however no longer considered the case.

35 *See* W. Sandholtz, 'How domestic courts use international law', 38:2 *Fordham International Law Journal* (2015) pp. 596–536; C. McCrudden, 'Why Do National Court Judges Refer to Human Rights Treaties? A Comparative International Law Analysis of CEDAW', *Public and Legal Theory Research Papers*, paper no. 482, 26 October 2015, online at <SSRN.COM/ABstract=2680458>, visited on 5 July 2016.

36 L.R. Helfer and A.-M. Slaughter, 'Toward a Theory of Effective Transnational Adjudication', 107 *Yale Law Journal* (1997) pp. 325–326; M. Wind, 'Do Scandinavian judges care about international law?', in M. Wind (ed.), *International Courts and Domestic Politics* (Cambridge University Press, Cambridge, forthcoming).

37 Y. Lupu and E. Voten, 'Precedent in International Courts: A Network Analysis of Case Citations by the European Court of Human Rights', 42 *British Journal of Political Science* (2011) p. 438.

38 *Ibid.*

to lending legitimacy to ICs, treaties and conventions by citing them. However, as we are to see below, the number of treaties signed as well as the growing caseload from ICs since the 1970s has gone more or less unnoticed by the Scandinavian judges.[39] A liked and often used explanation (or even excuse) for this among Nordic lawyers has been the dualist approach to international law which has dominated all legal thinking in this part of the world for centuries.[40] Here decisions by ICs (or international treaties) are not considered part of national law unless national legislative acts have turned them into legal sources in national law through legislation.[41] Alf Ross (1899–1979), an internationally recognized Danish legal philosopher who was generally critical of international law due to its natural law origins, saw national law and international law as representing two irreconcilable legal realms.[42] As a consequence, international law could never establish precedence in Danish law in its own right.[43] You still find this point of view represented among Scandinavian judges and civil servants. However, in particular since the incorporation of the European Convention of Human rights into national law, the classical dualist conception has often been described as increasingly challenged. Not because politicians and judges suddenly changed their view on the requirement that the Convention could only have effect in national law when adopted through a legislative act in parliament (though only with ordinary and not constitutional law status), but probably more because the Strasbourg Court has been effective in clarifying the Convention in its own case law and thus confronted the excuse used by many Nordic judges and politicians that the Convention was too unclear and unspecific to be applied by national courts. In Norway one thus gradually

39 Christoffersen and Rask Madsen, *supra* note 4, pp. 257–258.

40 O. Bing, 'Monism och dualism i går och i dag', in R. Stern and I. Österdahl (eds.), *Folkrätten i svensk rätt* (Liber, Malmö, 2012).

41 H. Palmer Olsen, 'Præjudikatværdien af internationale domstoles afgørelser', in J.H. Danielsen (ed.), *Max Sørensen 100 år* (Djøf, Copenhagen, 2013) p. 102.

42 *See* the analysis of Ross and international law in M. Wind, *Sovereignty and European Integration: Towards a Post-Hobbesian Order* (Palgrave, London, 2001), p. 9.

43 H. Zahle, *Dansk Forfatningsret 2: Regering, forvaltning og dom* (Christian Eijler's Forlag, Copenhagen, 2001) p. 211 refers to Alf Ross for this understanding. H. Palmer Olsen cites former Supreme Court judge Torben Jensen for the same point of view as Ross in an article from 1990. "Under the current legal state of affairs the European Convention of Human Rights and its decisions … is just as any other international regulation (apart from EU law) by the Human Rights Court non-binding in Denmark. In order to be so incorporation is necessary. The international law obligations deducible from the convention or the court will be irrelevant until this happens". Author's own translation from Danish.

started talking about a new 'semi-monism' or 'sector-monism'[44] indicating – at least among international law friendly legal scholars – that international law and international decisions had or perhaps rather would gradually take over as *the* national source of law.[45] In the late 1990s when all three Scandinavian countries were on board in the sense that they had all become firm partners of the European human rights regime, national judges could thus legitimately have used the Convention as well as the ECtHR's case law as a source in their own cases. Things did not turn out to be that easy however. Counter to what one might have expected Scandinavian Supreme Courts have been very conservative and hesitant when it comes to taking this new instrument into use. In Denmark politicians even spelled out in their preparatory works to the incorporation of the Convention that national courts should be careful not to independently develop the law on the basis of the Convention or the Strasbourg Court's case law.[46] One classical argument has as mentioned above been that conventions have been considered too broad and imprecise and thus unfit to be a serious source of law. However, if Supreme Courts (in agreement with politicians) initially abstained from relying on or even mentioning the European Human Rights Convention because it was too imprecise, this argument became obsolete as the ECtHR started clarifying the Convention's provisions in its own case law in the 1980s and onwards, making the Convention judiciable.[47] As Palmer Olsen puts it with regard to the Danish courts: "International courts' decisions – also those that do not concern Denmark specifically – ... should thus gain precedence in Danish law to the degree these decisions are used as precedents by these international courts themselves".[48]

This has however not happened. In fact, quite the contrary as we are to see below. The conception of international law as a foreign element *and* the classical scepticism towards strong courts and constitutionalism in general contribute to a rather peculiar situation, where in particular Danish and Swedish

44 In Danish legal theory, Professor Henrik Zahle called it 'practical monism'. *See* Zahle, *ibid.*, p. 21.

45 *See* D.T. Björgvinsson, *The Intersection of International Law and Domestic Law: A Theoretical and Practical Analysis* (Edward Elgar, Cheltenham, 2015); *see also* S.O. Johansen, *Den internasjonale rettens påvirkning på norsk rett* (The Effect of International Law on Norwegian Law) (6 February 2014), PACTA nr. 23, available online on SSRN: <ssrn.com/abstract=2391683>; J. Helgesen, *Teorier om "Folkerettens stilling i norsk rett"* (Oslo, 1982); and J. Helgesen's chapter 12 on the role of international law in the domestic legal system in T. Eckhoff and J. Helgesen, *Rettskildelære*, 5. utgave (Universitetsforl., Oslo, 2001).

46 *See also* Rytter and Wind, *supra* note 8, pp. 470–504.

47 *See* Palmer Olsen, *supra* note 42, pp. 114–115.

48 *Ibid.*, p. 106.

judges – still – largely ignore international law. In the following the results of the data analysis will be presented together with some words about how the citations were collected. In the concluding section the findings will be debated and some tentative explanations as to why Scandinavian judges have never fully embraced the international courts and treaties that their governments have signed up to will be put forward.

4 Results and a Few Words on Methodology

Mattias Kumm once asked "[s]hould national courts in liberal constitutional democracies enforce international law even when there is no specific authorization from the legislative or executive branches to do so?"[49] The question is provocative because it questions the so-called internationalist approach to international law that "[n]ational courts should enforce international law, irrespective of national law".[50] But, according to Kumm, whether national courts actually play this role is an *empirical* and not a normative question. The main concern of this project is however *not* whether Scandinavian courts enforce international law, but rather whether they have deliberately domesticated and thereby legitimized it by citing it in their own case law. The project presented here however raises similar questions to those presented by Kumm about the interaction between the two legal spheres. It moves from normative assumptions about how things ought to be (and perhaps are assumed to be) to trying to understand to what degree Scandinavian judges in the Supreme Courts actually have embraced the treaties and conventions that Sweden, Denmark and Norway have signed up to since the 1950s.

Below the preliminary findings from a huge data set is presented. The data has been collected by a team of researchers at the Centre of Excellence for International Courts (iCourts) at the University of Copenhagen. In order to count the citations made by the Scandinavian Supreme Courts to ICs' case law, a comprehensive and original quantitative data set has been assembled from scratch. The goal has – as mentioned briefly already – been to count how many times the Supreme Courts in the three Scandinavian countries have cited an IC's case law, a treaty or a convention in their own case law since the 1950s. The aim has been to be able to distinguish between the different courts, treaties and conventions, and thus determine exactly which specific court, treaty or

49 M. Kumm, 'The International Rule of Law and the Limits of the Internationalist Model', 44:1 *Virginia Journal of International Law* (2003) p. 21 *et seq.*

50 *Ibid.*

convention was cited.[51] Finally, to show developments over time, the date of the citation was coded for as well.

As the Scandinavian Supreme Courts have delivered thousands of judgments since 1950, coding all the judgments manually would be extremely time-consuming. To overcome this challenge, parts of the coding process had to be automatized based on innovative computer software. The automatic coding process has thus been an essential and innovative part of this project.[52]

The citations by the national Supreme Courts to the ICs were detected by using a method based on legal keywords. The relevant keywords were essential and not identical to the different variables in the codebook. In order to detect all the citations made to, for example, the ECtHR in the Danish Supreme Court cases, all possible ways in which a particular national court refers to the ECtHR had to be included. Obviously it had to be taken into account that Supreme Courts do not cite the different courts in a uniform or standardised way. For instance, the Danish Supreme Court uses expressions such as 'EMK', '*Den Europæiske Menneskerettighedsdomstol*', '*Domstolen i Strasbourg*' (the Court in Strasbourg). Consequently, detecting all the relevant keywords was a difficult task and had to be individualised from country to country. Through legal consultancy and advice from experts the keywords were identified manually by coding a large sample of Supreme Court decisions. All the different expressions used when citing the different ICs, treaties or conventions were written down and this work continued until a reasonable amount of keywords for all the relevant ICs had been identified. There is of course always the risk of capturing so-called 'false negatives', meaning that your analysis may capture citations that cannot be regarded as a 'true' precedent in support of a previous case. It can be argued, however, that even citations that (explicitly) criticise the

51 The aim was as well to be able to determine whether it was the court, the parties or both the court and the parties to the case that made the citation in any given Supreme Court's decision.

52 The first step in the automatized coding process was to create a codebook. A codebook is a detailed statement of instructions to coders on how to facilitate the coding. The codebook is a tool to increase the possibility of replicating the study in a reliable way at a later point in time. That is, different coders should be able to replicate the study and get the same results. This clearly adds to the quantitative methodology's validity. There are many different ways in which to formulate a codebook. In this case the codebook presents and describes all variables, and all the possible values these variables might take. It further presents the numbers (*i.e.* codes) that should be typed in the coding scheme given the different possible values of the variables. The complete codebook, "Codebook – Scandinavian Supreme Courts' citations to international courts" was developed by Kristoffer Schaldemose at iCourts in 2014.

cases cited – what Fischman refers to a 'negative references'– demonstrates the specific IC's impact if not its perceived legitimacy. If a national court really perceives a given IC as illegitimate, why bother to cite case law from the IC at all? In other words, while 'negative references' might not be 'true' precedents, the project build on the notion that they certainly imply that the national court accepts the IC as a legitimate source of law.[53]

Based on the manually detected keywords, it was thus possible using a specific computer software to search for and find these keywords, and hence automatically code the court decision or judgment. Variables such as date, ID-number and so on were also coded.[54]

Fig. 2 presents the total number of citations to international courts made by Scandinavian Supreme Courts in their judgements and court decisions covering the time period 1961–2014. Although the present study only includes *three* countries (Denmark, Norway and Sweden) results of four Scandinavian Supreme Courts are included due to the fact that Sweden has two Supreme Courts: the 'regular' Supreme Court and the Administrative Supreme Court.

Fig. 2 clearly shows that the Norwegian Supreme Court refers much more frequently than both its Danish and Swedish counterparts, with 450 citations against 71 (DK) and 126 (the two Swedish courts put together). These findings support the hypothesis put forward in previous research that Norway with a strong national judicial review tradition will be more inclined to cite to international courts than majoritarian democracies with no such tradition like Denmark and Sweden.[55]

Where Fig. 2 presented the number of citations to international *courts*, Fig. 3 focuses on the many international *conventions* and *treaties* that the

53 *See* J. Fishman, 'Reuniting "Is" and "Ought" in Empirical Legal Scholarship', 162:1 *University of Pennsylvania Law Review* (2013) pp. 117–168; R. Anderson, 'Distinguishing Judges: An Empirical Ranking of Judicial Quality in the United States Courts of Appeal', 76:315 *Missouri Law Review* (2011) pp. 318–373.

54 Although a significant part of the coding process has been automatized, a considerable amount of manual test-coding has been necessary in order to increase the reliability in the study. In other words, the coding was constantly improved by adding new and improved keywords, which optimised the computer script. The process is truly iterative: The keywords were detected manually and created a computer script, which then was used to code a random sample of court decisions. Thereafter, a random set of these court decisions were coded manually and the findings compared with the automatized coding. This was done over and over again. Following this technique, errors can be found and corrected thereby improving the reliability of the study significantly.

55 See A. Kierulf, *Taking Judicial Review Seriously: The Case of Norway* (Oslo University Press, Oslo, 2014).

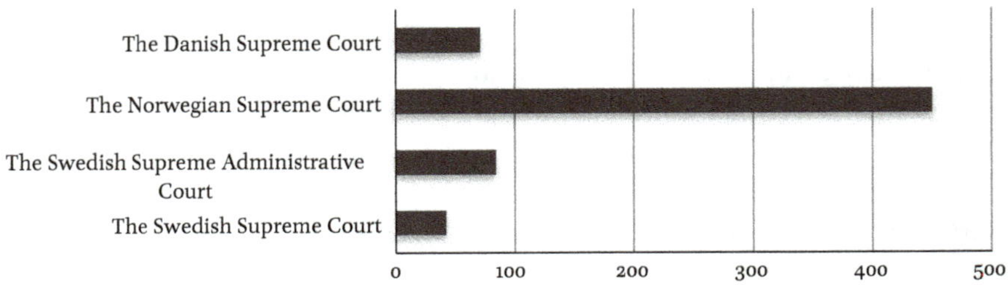

	The Swedish Supreme Court	The Swedish Supreme Administrative Court	The Norwegian Supreme Court	The Danish Supreme Court
■ Total number of citations to international courts, 1961–2014	42	84	450	71

FIGURE 2 *Total number of citations to international courts, 1961–2014*

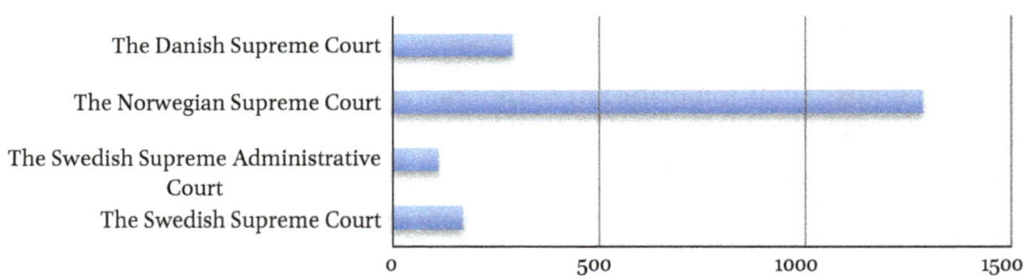

	The Swedish Supreme Court	The Swedish Supreme Administrative Court	The Norwegian Supreme Court	The Danish Supreme Court
■ Total number of citations to international conventions and treaties, 1961–2014	169	111	1285	291

FIGURE 3 *Total number of citations to international conventions and treaties, 1961–2014*

Scandinavian countries have signed up to. It is rather interesting (but perhaps not surprising) that the Scandinavian courts refer much more often to the conventions and treaties than to international courts. While the Scandinavian Supreme Courts all together made 647 citations to international courts, they referred to conventions and treaties no less than 1756 times in the same period of time. This suggests that international law and treaties – which are based on 'legislation' and thus explicit 'government/parliamentary consent' – are perceived to be more legitimate than those international courts, which actually enforce international law.

As in the case of international courts, Norway is however also far ahead when it comes to making explicit citations to international conventions and treaties compared to its neighbouring countries. Norway thus run ahead with 1285 citations in the period from 1961–2014 compared to 291 in Danish case law and 280 in Swedish case law.

The extensive data set takes all relevant international courts into consideration. However, it is clear from Fig. 4 that only very few are considered relevant for the Nordic countries. In Norway, the ECtHR is clearly the most cited court. While the Danish and Swedish courts also cite ECtHR, they both cite the European Court of Justice more often.

While Norway generally cites international courts' case law more frequently than Denmark and Sweden, both Denmark and Sweden cite the ECJ more often than Norway, which is not a member of the EU. It is interesting, however, that the Norwegian Supreme Court actually does cite the ECJ. This underscores of course that Norway is fundamentally penetrated by EU law although the European Free Trade Association (EFTA) court is the European Economic Area's (EEA) own court (which normally sticks closely to the ECJ's legal practice). It could be argued, that the ECJ should not be part of this study at all as EU law no longer reasonably can be considered to be characterised as international law.[56] It is moreover interesting that Scandinavian courts practically only cite two courts altogether: the ECtHR and the ECJ – though Norway has also cited the ICJ and the EFTA court. No other courts are deemed relevant by the judges in the Scandinavian Supreme Courts.

Fig. 5 shows the number of citations by the four Scandinavian Supreme Courts to three selected courts and treaties, namely the ECHR, the ECtHR and the ECJ. The graph is rather interesting as it clearly shows that the Norwegian Supreme Court use international human rights case law in its own cases much more often than its Scandinavian neighbours. The causes for this clearly need to be studied more qualitatively as well, but it does raise some interesting

56 J.H.H. Weiler, 'The Transformation of Europe', 100:8 *Yale Law Review* (1991) pp. 2403–2483.

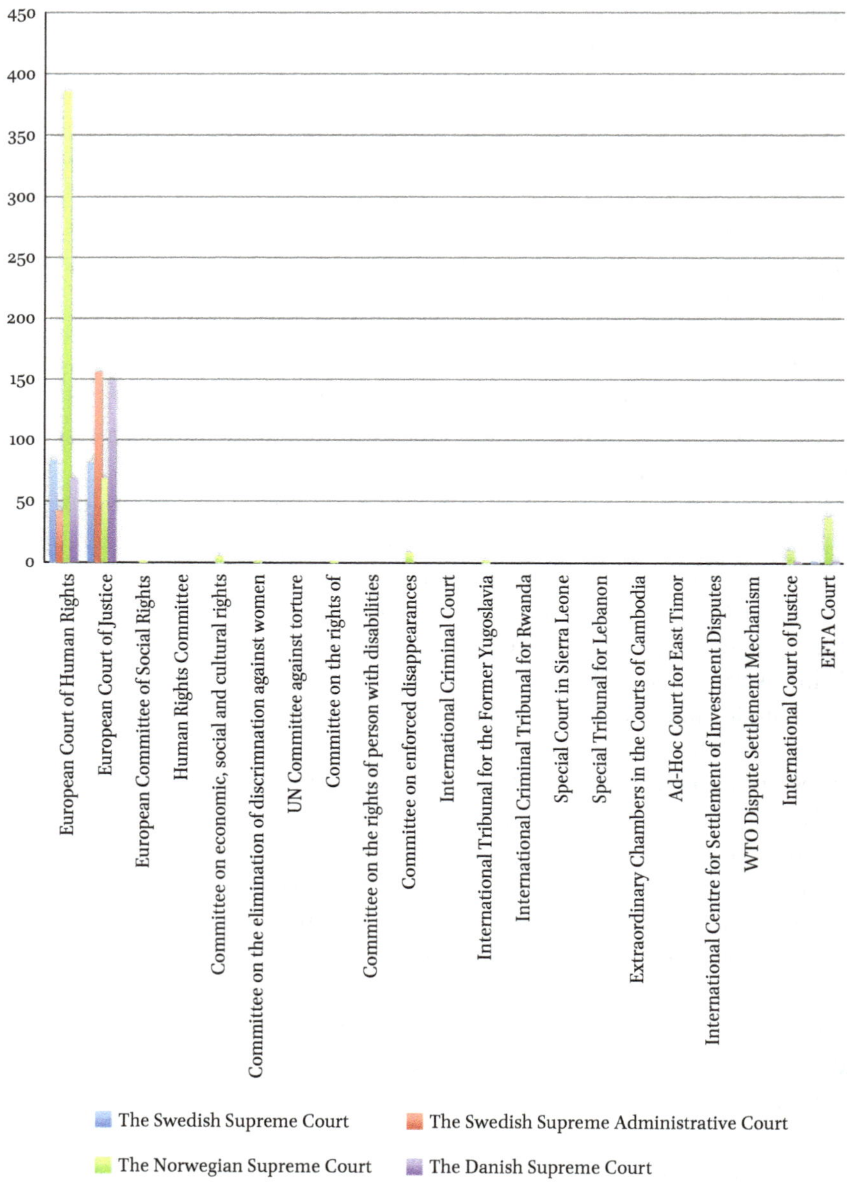

FIGURE 4 *Number of citations to different international courts, 1961–2014*

questions about potential differences in the levels of human rights protection in the Scandinavian countries. It also urges us to look more into: legal and political traditions, the dominance of Scandinavian legal positivism where international law in general plays a somewhat inferior role, legal teaching in the

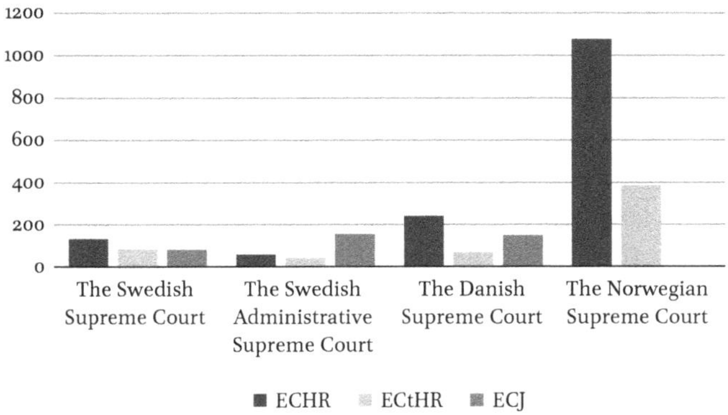

FIGURE 5 *Number of citations (selected conventions and courts), 1961–2014*

universities, and transparency in the judiciaries. I will not be able to go into any of these explanations in detail here, but only suggest two elements, which are important and closely linked: the missing judicial review tradition at the national level, and the dominant positivist approach to law in general in Scandinavia, where statutes and preparatory works seem to be the most important sources of law for national judges.

5 Conclusions: Does the Influence of Legal Positivism and Majoritarian Democracy Explain Citation Frequency?

To what degree can legal traditions, ideas and visions about the role and status of international law in legal science explain the Scandinavian Supreme Courts' citation practice? Before we get too far down this ally it is probably important to emphasise that how we think and traditionally have thought about the status of international law only partially explains the apparent ambivalence towards international law by the judges. However, when courts are hesitant to cite or rely on international legal sources, in particular courts' case law and less so treaties adopted through legislative acts by the contracting parties, this may – I will argue – have to do with the strong emphasis in this part of the world on legal statutes and the parliament as the prime lawmaker. The elevated position and role of the parliament *vis-à-vis* other branches of government is clearly also important when trying to understand the special Nordic rejection (apart perhaps from Norway) of a solid judicial review tradition at the national level, which otherwise has been a global phenomenon the past 25–40 years. Majoritarian democracy is and continues to be an almost indisputable value in the Scandinavian countries, also among judges themselves and the majority of professors who write the legal textbooks – though often only implicitly as they are only rarely explicit about their own conception of democracy.[57]

In line with my previous research on the 'Reluctance towards supranational judicial review' among the Nordics in the EU,[58] the data collected here broadens the perspective to encompass international law supporting the thesis put forward previously that the presence or absence of a solid judicial review tradition at the national level potentially has strong implications for the willingness of national judges to cite, domesticate and lend legitimacy to international law (in particular ICs' case law) in their own legal practice.

Closely linked to majoritarian democracy is the special version of Scandinavian legal positivism[59] where positive law – seen as parliamentary statutes and legislative acts – are absolutely central. Courts play a very reticent role in political life in this part of the world at least when it comes to being active in striking down and scrutinising law-making.[60] A survey from 2006 concluded that judges in Sweden and Denmark see themselves as closer to a '*Bouches de la loi*'-conception than as lawmakers, or active constitutional guardians, and that they felt quite comfortable with this.[61]

The legal text, as represented by statutes and other legislative documents, is thus the most important framework of interpretation for judges. Reliance on

---

57 We have conducted a systematic but not yet published analysis of the description of international law (compared to national law) in legal textbooks in the Scandinavian countries. We explicitly excluded text-books by international lawyers as they would obviously be biased and much more positive about international law than the average and thus only included those describing the legal field in general. See Wind, *supra* note 36.

58 Wind, *supra* note 8, pp. 1039–1063.

59 See J. Bjarup, 'The Philosophy of Scandinavian Legal Realism', 18:1 *Ratio Juris* (March 2005) pp. 1–15. It is here argued that (in order to destroy the distorting influence of values) one should destroy the metaphysics and normative aspects of legal and create a scientific theory of law. Central figures were Axel Hägerström and the Danish philosopher and legal scholar Alf Ross. They both focused on positive law as a system of rules in terms of behavioural regularities among human beings. It builds on the idea of positive law as based on statutes and leaves very little room for the normativity of the law.

60 One way of putting it would be to say that in a positivist system of law, litigants or other legal actors would always know what the law is and thus not be surprised by an unwritten obligation or rule. Legal positivism in the Scandinavian version would also be very skeptical of judicial discretion. Legal positivism would expect judges to decide cases in accordance with the law (*bouches de la loi*), and not their personal preferences or moral considerations. See more in *West's Encyclopedia of American Law* (2nd edition, The Gale Group, Inc., Farmington Hills, MI, 2008).

61 Wind, *supra* note 8, pp. 1039–1063.

considerations other than the political intention of the legal provision is often (but not always) regarded as judicial policymaking, which judges ought to abstain from as far as possible. This also explains why the *travaux préparatoires* become very central for the judges because they inform about the intentions and the will of the legislature, and thus the political majority in parliament. Following former Professor J.P. Christensen – now a judge at the Danish Supreme Court – the understanding of the unconstrained legislature as the essence of democracy can to a large degree be attributed to the Danish legal philosopher and legal positivist Alf Ross, an understanding which has dominated law students in Copenhagen for generations.[62] As Christensen puts it, "[f]or almost 40 years did this idea dominate the law faculty at the University of Copenhagen".[63] As he further puts it in a footnote: "Not until the 2nd edition of Henrik Zahle's *Dansk Forfatningsret* from 1996 did anyone claim that the §3 in the constitution limits the power of the legislator ...".[64]

Alf Ross has played and continues to play a central role for many Scandinavians' conception of international law. In particular Ross' unease with international law's natural law origins has played a role. Though Ross has also been misinterpreted,[65] he was very clear in his views about the differences between international as opposed to national law and about the hierarchy of legal sources. What later jurists paid attention to was thus the fragments of Ross' work where he emphasised that the most valid sources of international law were positive sources like treaty and customary law.[66] Common to these sources is that they are explicitly adopted by the states through legislation and practice, which is what defines them as 'positive'. Ross clearly did not exclude more justice-based sources but what later generations of lawyers focused on was the 'positive' elements of legal norms, that is, those elements that were actually referred to and used by states, legal practitioners and judges. The status and role of law is based on whether the law is in fact respected and not due to their natural law origins. The specific point made by Ross is often referred to as

62 See J.P. Christensen,' Ross og statsforfatningsretten', in Jakob von Holderstein Holtermann and Jesper Ryberg (eds.), *Alf Ross. Kritiske gensyn* (Djøf, Copenhagen, 2006). As he writes: "With Ross the division of power theory became a theory of the legislative branch's all-encompassing power. For almost 40 years this doctrine dominated the legal studies programme at the University of Copenhagen", p. 81, the author's translation from Danish.

63 *Ibid.*, p. 81, my translation from Danish.

64 *Ibid.*, p. 103, my translation from Danish.

65 UdgivetJ. Holtermann, 'Naturalizing Alf Ross's Legal Realism: A Philosophical Reconstruction', 24 *Revus: Journal for Constitutional Theory and Philosophy of Law* (2014) pp. 165 –186.

66 A. Ross, *International Law: An Introduction* (Nyt Nordisk Forlag, Copenhagen, 1984); Wind, *Sovereignty and European Integration, supra* note 43.

saying that "[a] realist theory of legal sources builds on experience".[67] Among later academic lawyers this emphasis legitimized a specific (convenient) conception of law putting most emphasis on treaties adopted by states rather than court cases. Court cases could also be important in this understanding but only to the degree that they created precedence and were perceived of as authoritative. The great scepticism against the natural law origins of international law is clear but also implies that human rights – and their natural law origins – were problematic for at least the version of Scandinavian realism that lived on among most scholars and later students of the Scandinavian school. Human rights were certainly not unimportant, in particular if they were positivized in the sense of being put into treaties, customary law and adopted/practiced by states. It is in other words clear that in this conception of Scandinavian positivism the state as a source of law plays an enormous role. Also in Sweden the legal positivism of Axel Hägerström (who strongly inspired the young Alf Ross) has been incredibly influential and often called the father of Scandinavian legal realism together with other Scandinavian scholars such as Herbert Tingsten and Karl Olivecrona.[68] The fact that Hägerström, like his later followers, were critical of natural law, arguing that all law should be based on experience, may have influenced, although to a varying degree, legal education in the Nordic states. Perhaps this also made judges sceptical towards more normative international law sources. It is thus telling that at the Faculty of Law at the University of Copenhagen there is neither a professor of human rights nor of international law.

I fully recognise that it is difficult to verify how Scandinavian legal positivism may have directly influenced Supreme Court judges' citation practice. Much more research needs to be done in particular into how international law is taught in Scandinavian universities – both within law and political science. There is little doubt, however, that at least in Denmark and Sweden the division between positive/natural law rhetoric (law as morals vs law as facts) has had an impact on the way students, civil servants, politicians and judges have looked at international law and courts. It may thus also help us explain the weak domestication of international law among Supreme Court judges in Scandinavia.

67 Ross, *ibid.*, p. 110.

68 J. Nergelius, 'North and South: Can the Nordic States and the European Continent Find each other in the Constitutional arena – or are they too different?', in M. Scheinin (ed.), *The Welfare State and Constitutionalism in the Nordic Countries* (Nord, Copenhagen, 2016) p. 81.

The Effect of the Judgments of the ECtHR before the National Courts – A Nordic Approach?

David Thor Björgvinsson

1 Introduction

Under Article 46 of the European Convention on Human Rights (ECHR), the contracting parties undertake to abide by the final judgment of the European Court of Human Rights (ECtHR) in any case to which they are parties. This means that the judgments are binding *inter partes*. The wording, however, does not support *erga omnes* effect. Nevertheless, in a recent report of the Steering Committee on Human Rights (CDDH) on the long term future of the system of the Convention, in order to prevent future violations, the contracting parties are encouraged to consider the conclusions to be drawn from a judgment finding a violation of the Convention by another state, where the same problem of principle exists within their own legal system, and to integrate the case law of the ECtHR into national law. It is said that in this respect a reference is often made to the principle of *res interpretata*,[1] whereby it is argued, based on Articles 1, 19, 32 and 46 of the Convention, that national authorities *should* take account of the Convention as interpreted by the Court.[2] Scholars have also argued for the importance of the *res interpretata* principle as an important tool in reinforcing the principle of subsidiarity underlying the entire Convention

---

* The chapter draws inspiration from the author's presentation at the conference: *A Nordic Approach to International Law?*, held in Oslo on 27 to 29 August 2015, organised by the Center for International Law, Conflict and Crisis, Faculty of Law, University of Copenhagen.

1 Often referred to as the principle of consistent interpretation or the "Charming Betsy" doctrine. *See Murray* v. *The Charming Betsy*, 6 U.S. (2 Cranch) 64 (1804).

2 Steering Committee for Human Rights, *Report on the longer-term future of the system of the European Convention on Human Rights*, CDDH(2015)R84 Addendum I. Strasbourg, 11 December 2015, pp. 20–21. *See also* the Brighton-Declaration (High Level Conference on the Future of the European Court of Human Rights 19 and 20 April 2012). Point 7 states: "National courts and tribunals should take into account the Convention and the case law of the Court. Collectively, these measures should reduce the number of violations of the Convention. Collectively, these measures should reduce the number of violations of the Convention".

 | DOI 10.1163/9789004343597_009

and thereby also as a means to limit the number of applications brought to the European Court.[3]

At the forefront in this chapter is the status of the principle of *res interpretata* in Iceland in relation to the ECHR, and in particular the case law of the ECtHR. For comparison the situation in Denmark and Norway is examined as well.

2 The Status of the *Res Interpretata* within the ECHR System

The cited words of the CDDH report would seem to suggest that the *res interpretata* principle is somehow embedded in the ECHR, mainly as an offspring of the above-mentioned provisions. This attempt to build into the ECHR an obligation to abide by the *res interpretata* principle with regard to the case law of the ECtHR is unconvincing from a purely legal perspective. Another possible approach has been suggested, namely to look at the status of *res interpretata* principle in public international law. The principle is so widely accepted by the countries of the world, both in common law and civil law systems, that it is a legitimate question whether it should be considered a general principle of international law that states should interpret national law in line with international obligations.[4] This is also a controversial view. Although asserting *res interpretata* as a binding legal principle for states is problematic, it is at the same time difficult to disagree with it as a matter of sound judicial policy on the national level.

The ECtHR has expressed itself on this topic and tried to expand the effect of judgments beyond *inter partes* by asserting what may be termed as *de facto erga omnes* effect.[5] In the case of *Opuz* v. *Turkey* the Court states:

---

3 A. Bodnar, 'Res Interpretata : Legal Effect of the European Court of Human Rights' Judgments for other States Than Those Which Were Party to the Proceedings', in Y. Haeck and E. Brems, *Human Rights and Civil Liberties in the 21st Century* (Springer Verlag, Heidelberg, 2013) p. 223.

4 *See also* A. Nollkaemper, *National Courts and the International Rule of Law* (Oxford University Press, Oxford 2011) p. 149. It is to be added that international law in a certain fields may dictate that contracting states are under the obligation to interpret national law consistent with the state's obligations. This is the case for example in EU law as well as EEA law. *See for example* the EFTA Court judgment in Case E-4/01 – *Karl K. Karlsson hf.* v. *The Icelandic State.* Judgment 30 May 2002 (par. 28) EFTA Ct. Rep. 2002, p. 240. *See also* C. Baudenbacher, 'Methods of Interpretation', *The EFTA Court in Action* (German Law Publishers, Stuttgart, 2010) pp. 30–36.

5 J.-P. Costa, 'Foreword', *2008 Annual Report of the European Court on Human Rights. See also* H.-J. Papier, 'Execution and Effect of the Judgements of the European Court of Human Rights

> In carrying out this scrutiny, and bearing in mind that the Court provides final authoritative interpretation of the rights and freedoms defined in Section I of the Convention, the Court will consider whether the national authorities have sufficiently taken into account the principles flowing from its judgments on similar issues, even when they concern other States.[6]

The *res interpretata* principle is induced from two sides so to speak; namely the duty of states under international law to abide by their obligations and the readiness of most states, when relevant, to streamline their integration and application of national law with regard to such obligations in order to avoid possible conflicts.[7] It is relevant in different situations. The most obvious is when a national provision is ambiguous or unclear and international law is used to compensate for that. There are also situations where legislation or an explanatory report refers to an international treaty or individual provisions thereof. This is an invitation on behalf of the legislature to the courts to resort to international law to strive for interpretation consistent with the international provisions referred to. Consistent interpretation may also be used to give effect to international obligations in reviewing the exercise of discretion on the part of the authorities. In these situations, international law may add additional relevant consideration, mainly to limit the discretion.

There are further reasons for applying *res interpretata*. National courts often resort to legislative intent, which is an accepted canon of interpretation. The idea is that that the legislature did not intend to legislate in breach of an international legal obligation. This is sometimes referred to as the rule of presumption. The narrower version of this rule is confined to incorporated treaties and the presumption that the legislature intended to make domestic law conform to a treaty. The broader version relates to any laws adopted after a particular international obligation entered into force. In this situation the presumption is that the legislature did not intend to legislate contrary to international obligations. In many countries this broader version also accommodates domestic legislation already in force when a particular international obligation came into force.[8] The rationale is that the legislature did not intend to keep in force

---

from the Perspective of German National Courts', 27:1–4 *Human Rights Law Journal* (2006) p. 1 *et seq*.

6 Case of *Opuz* v. *Turkey* (Application no. 33401/02), judgment 9 June 2009, para. 163.

7 D. Feldman, 'Monism, Dualism and Constitutional Legitimacy', 20 *Australian Yearbook of International Law* (1999) p. 106.

8 Nollkaemper, *supra* note 5, pp. 154–155.

an existing national provision which is contrary to or incompatible with the international obligations of the state.[9]

An additional ground for applying *res interpretata* is the persuasive authority of international law. This ground does not relate to the binding nature of an international norm and the presumption of a legislative intent to treaty compliance, but rather to the substantive content of the norm itself.[10] In its broadest sense it can entail incorporated international obligations, unincorporated obligations binding for the forum state and even international norms not binding for the state.

A highly relevant issue in this context is the pervasive authority of case law from international courts, soft law, non-binding international instruments, as for example the Council of Europe recommendations and the like.[11]

Despite forceful arguments in favour of consistent interpretation, it is hardly possible to construe such a legal obligation for national courts, whose powers are defined by national legislation but not by international law. At least, it weakens the claim that, although the practice is generally accepted by states across the globe, there are differences in the conditions under which the principle operates and can be applied.[12]

3 Denmark

The European Convention on Human Rights was ratified in Denmark in 1953 and was incorporated *en bloc* by law No. 285 of 29 April 1992. It is the only human rights treaty incorporated in Danish law to date. Incorporation means that the ECHR is a part of Danish law and has the status of statutory law.[13]

9 O. Spiermann, *Moderne folkeret*, 3rd edition (DJØF Publishers, Copenhagen, 2004) pp. 160–161.

10 *See for example* C. Flanders, 'Towards a Theory of Persuasive Authority', *Oklahoma L Rev.* 55 (2009) p. 62.

11 F. Morgenstern, 'Judicial Practice and the Supremacy of International Law', *27th British Yearbook of International Law* XXVII (Royal Institute of International Affairs, Oxford University Press, Oxford, 1950) p. 85.

12 Nollkaemper, *supra* note 5, pp. 147–151.

13 It is to be noted that this was done although there is no obligation under the ECHR to implement it as statutory law. *See for example* the case of *James and Others* v. *United Kingdom* (Application no. 8793/79) of 21 February 1986 (para. 84) where the Court made it clear that the Convention does not require its domestic incorporation. However, no state can refer to its domestic legislation in order to escape obligations under the Convention. *See also* R. Bernhardt, 'The Convention and Domestic Law', in R. St. J. Macdonald,

The purpose of incorporation was to increase awareness of the Convention among judges, the prosecution, the police and lawyers, as well as of society in general.

The legislation does not contain a specific provision on the status of the Convention or the case law of the ECtHR *vis-a-vis* other legislation or the Constitution, as for example in Norway and Iceland. One scholarly view is that, due to its incorporation, the ECHR takes primacy over other statutory legislation contradicting it, unless there exists a clear legislative intention to the contrary.[14] However, it does not override the Danish Constitution.[15] Moreover, on the same note the view is also that the Convention became a part of Danish national law "with the content" it had in 1992; in other terms, as it had been interpreted by the Council of Europe institutions, *inter alia* the ECtHR, until 1992. On the other hand, due to the dualist approach to international law in Denmark, the practice (including judgements and decisions from the ECtHR) after 1992 is not incorporated. Therefore, it must be applied in line with the principle of consistent interpretation and the rule of presumption.[16] Rytter argues that this distinction is formalistic, unattainable and unrealistic. Moreover, he argues that this approach is incompatible with the intention of the legislature when the text of the Convention was incorporated, where the aim was *inter alia* to create a firmer ground for the Danish courts to fulfil the obligations under the Convention when the Danish legislator has not reacted to new practices by amendments to the law.[17] Rytter certainly may have a point here since in the explanatory report to the Danish legislation it was stated that one of the effects of the incorporation was that Danish courts and others responsible for interpreting and applying the Convention would have a firmer basis for taking note of the newest decisions from the Council of Europe institutions, which the legislature had lesser possibility and flexibility to take into consideration.[18]

Scholarly views on the status of the decisions of the ECtHR in Danish law differ somewhat. Others have emphasised that that ECtHR case law after 1992 finds its application only through traditional principles of consistent interpretation (and rule of presumption) and is not to be considered a binding source

---

F. Matscher and H. Petzold (eds.), *The European System for the Protection of Human Rights* (Martinus Nijhoff, Dordrecht, 1993) p. 26. This also follows from Article 46 of the Vienna Convention on the Law of Treaties.

14 J.E. Rytter, *Individets grundlæggende rettigheder* (Karnov group, Copenhagen, 2016) p. 55.

15 *Ibid.*, p. 53; *see also Den europæiske Menneskerettighedskonvention og dansk ret*, Betænkning No. 1220 1991, p. 149 *et seq.*

16 Rytter, *supra* note 15, p. 54.

17 *Ibid.*, pp. 54–55. *Also* Betænkning No. 1220, *supra* note 16, p. 196.

18 Betænkning No. 1220, *supra* note 16, pp. 113–114.

of law in Denmark. It must be considered an ordinary obligation under public international law and should be treated within the traditional concept of the relationship between Danish law and international law. If ECtHR case law were to be considered a binding legal source, it would involve serious constitutional problems.[19]

Study of the case law of the Supreme Court of Denmark before the incorporation of the Convention has shown that it was inclined to follow the interpretation of the ECtHR and to avoid independent interpretation, in particular where it might have widespread consequences.[20] A similar study on the application of the Convention in Danish legal practice after the incorporation shows a clear increase in references to the Convention and the case law of the ECtHR. Cases concerning freedom of expression and right to a fair trial are mentioned in particular. There are also indications that the Convention and the case law of the ECtHR have such a weight that Danish courts are prepared to set aside what may be seen as the intentions of the legislator, if not doing so would lead to a breach of the Convention. Moreover, the Danish courts would seem to be prepared to set aside established legal administrative practice if it is considered contrary to the Convention.[21] On the other hand, on the basis of the existing practice, it would seem difficult to assess as to whether Danish courts would be ready to set aside a legal provision if it is considered contrary to the Convention. Furthermore, Danish courts will also be inclined to use the principle of consistent interpretation in order to avoid violating the Convention. How far they are willing to go, however, depends on the clarity of the Convention obligations. In areas where there are precedents from the ECtHR, Danish courts would take note of them and assess whether their decisions would be contrary to the relevant judgments from the ECtHR.[22]

4 Norway

By Act No. 30 of 21 May 1999, relating to the strengthening of the status of human rights in Norwegian law (The Human Rights Act), three international

19 M.G. Jørgensen, 'Den Europæiske Menneskerettighedsdomstols praksis og betydningen for dansk ret', p. 1, available at: <law.au.dk/fileadmin/Jura/dokumenter/forskning/rettid/2012/afh8-2012.pdf>, visited 24 August 2016.

20 *See* Betænkning No. 1220, *supra* note 16, p. 80 *et seq.*

21 *Betænkning om inkorporering mv. inden for menneskeretsområdet*, Betænkning No. 1546 (2014), Chapter 4.

22 *Ibid.*

human rights conventions were made part of Norwegian national law, *i.e.* the ECHR, including further specified protocols, the International Covenant on Economic, Social and Cultural Rights (ICESCR) and the International Covenant on Civil and Political Rights (ICCPR), including further specified protocols. Article 3 of the Act states that the conventions and protocols mentioned shall take precedence over any other legislative provisions that conflict with them. Moreover, it was believed that enactment would increase awareness and knowledge about these conventions among the legal practitioners and the public at large and their importance in Norwegian society in general.[23]

Article 3 of the Act is interesting as it relates to the status of the aforementioned conventions *vis-à-vis* other statutory legislation, to the extent they are enacted in the national system. This rule has been called a semi-constitutional rule of primacy (*semikonstitusjonell forrangsregel*) as it provides that the conventions referred to shall prevail over other Norwegian laws, although they shall not prevail over the Constitution itself.[24] Although the wording of Article 3 seems rather clear, certain reservations are expressed in the explanatory report to the legislation. It is submitted, among other things, that primacy is first and foremost meant to secure supremacy of the respective international convention over internal law that provides less protection than the relevant convention provisions. Normally, under such circumstances it may be assumed that the convention provisions should have primacy unless it is clear that it was the will of the legislature to set aside the convention provisions. Further reservations were submitted, for example that the relevant convention provisions must be clear and precise (judgment Rt. 1994, 610) and be relevant to the dispute at hand. In Rt. 2000 p. 996 some of the main principles relating to the interpretation of Article 3 are presented. It is stated that conflict cannot be resolved by a general rule of primacy but rather by harmonisation through *interpretation*. From Article 3 of the Human Rights Act it follows that if the result of interpretation of a provision of the ECHR appears to be reasonably clear, the Norwegian courts are obliged to apply the Convention rule notwithstanding that the application of the rule would set aside established principles of Norwegian legislation or legal practice.[25]

---

23 S.E. Jebens, *Menneskerettigheder í straffeprosessen* (Cappelen Akademisk, Oslo, 2004) p. 76.

24 *Ibid.*, p. 77.

25 Rt. (the Norwegian *Supreme Court Reports*) 2000 p. 996 – plenary, mapping out the principles which Norwegian courts shall apply. This judgment has been followed in subsequent case law. *See also* M. Matningsdal, 'The Influence of the European Convention for the Protection of Human Rights and Fundamental Freedoms on Norwegian Criminal Procedure'

Similar requirements are made as regards the decisions of international bodies which are competent to interpret and apply the relevant conventions. Originally it was proposed in the explanatory report that a similar limitation should apply to Article 3 of the Human Rights Act. However, during the parliamentary proceedings these ideas met with opposition, including from the Norwegian Bar Association, which argued that this would restrain the application of the conventions in the domestic system. This was to some extent accepted under the further proceedings. As a consequence, the explanatory report does not provide a clear guidance as to the interpretation and application of Article 3 of the Human Rights Act.[26] In Rt. 2000 p. 996 it is also stated that the task of developing the Convention lies first and foremost with the ECtHR and that Norwegian courts must respect the wording and the objectives of the Convention and the decisions of the Convention organs. It is the role of the courts in Norway to further define the content of Article 3. In as much as primacy of the ECHR over statutory legislation is accepted, its significance for constitutional interpretation is subject to different scholarly views in Norway.[27]

It is further debated as to which status these instruments have *vis-a-vis* the Norwegian Constitution and their effect for constitutional interpretation. As regards the judgments of the ECtHR, there are several judgments from the Supreme Court of Norway where such judgments have been referred to. Some of these judgments would indicate that the Supreme Court opts for what has been termed autonomous interpretation of the Constitution.[28] Other judgments would show a clearer influence of the ECHR for constitutional interpretation.[29] All in all the case law of the Supreme Court of Norway indicates that the ECHR and case law of the ECtHR is relevant for the interpretation

Scandinavian Studies in Law (2007). *See also i.a.* the plenary judgment in Rt. 2002 p. 557 (565).

26 Jebens, *supra* note 24, pp. 77–78.

27 A. Kierulf, 'International Human Rights in Constitutional Interpretation – The Case of Norway', *Legal Studies Research Paper*, Series No. 2011–19, University of Oslo Faculty of Law, p. 27.

28 *Ibid.*, pp. 40–41. The author mentions for example Rt. 2007, 1281 (Tomtefeste) regarding Article 97 of the Constitution (property rights) and Article 1, Protocol 1 of the ECHR; Rt. 2007, 404 (Brennepunkt) and Rt. 2004, 1737 both concerning Article 100 of the Constitution (freedom of expression) and Article 10 ECHR. The author states that these cases, and more, have in common that the Constitution and the ECHR are dealt with separately in the premises.

29 *Ibid.* Among judgments mentioned are: Rt. 2009, 1412 regarding Article 97 of the Constitution and Article 7 ECHR (prohibition of retroactive effect of criminal provisions); Rt. 2009,1537 (Bokhandlesaken).

of the Norwegian Constitution, the question being rather how much weight should be given. In any case, the case law shows at least that the ECHR and the case law from the ECtHR weighs at least heavily in cases concerning freedom of expression, where the Supreme Court considers carefully the ECtHR case law and shows clear willingness to adopt the main principles developed in Strasbourg.[30]

5 Iceland

5.1 *Introduction*

The ECHR was incorporated and given force as statutory law in Iceland by Act No. 62/1994. The explanatory report for the Act offers several arguments in favour of enactment.[31] The fundamental aim was to strengthen the protection of human rights and to make individuals able to invoke the provisions of the ECHR directly before the national courts and authorities. In addition, it was argued that that incorporation would have an effect on constitutional interpretation and there would be a tendency to apply a broader interpretation of the Icelandic Constitution in accordance with the rules of the ECHR, where appropriate. It was moreover emphasised that the Convention was to be given the force of statutory law, but not a force parallel to the Constitution.[32]

5.2 *Status of the Case Law of the ECtHR in the Icelandic Domestic System*

5.2.1 Article 2 of the ECHR Act

The Icelandic ECtHR Act No. 62/1994 contains a separate provision pertaining directly to the status of the case law of the ECtHR in the domestic system. Thus Article 2 of the ECHR provides that the decisions of the European Commission of Human Rights, European Court of Human Rights and the Committee of Ministers of the Council of Europe are not binding in Icelandic domestic law.[33] Although it would seem that the provision is straightforward and clear, many

30 *See also* J.E. Skoghøy, 'De nordiske domstolene og Den europeiske menneskerettskonvensjon', *SvJT* 2013, available at <svjt.se/svjt/2013/397>, visited on 24 August 2016.

31 *Parliamentary Reports* A 1992–1993, doc. no. 1160, pp. 5847–5939 (pp. 5891–5892).

32 *Ibid.*, p. 5890.

33 Due to the changes in the institutional set-up by Protocol 11, this is now mostly relevant as regards the decisions and judgments of the ECtHR, although many of the decisions of the European Commission still have relevance as precedents for the interpretation and application of the ECHR.

ambiguities remain as regards its actual meaning. Comments in the explanatory report attached to the bill do not offer satisfactory explanations.

The explanatory report states that the incorporation of the Convention as statutory law does not automatically change the status of the decisions of the above-mentioned institutions in the domestic system since these decisions only concern the question as to whether the Icelandic state has breached its obligations under the Convention.[34] The decisions are thus only binding under public international law, and they cannot therefore overturn or invalidate domestic legislation or judgments of the national courts. This is a manifestation of the principle of *dualism*, which applies as regards the decisions of these institutions. It is further reiterated that the incorporation does not involve any transfer of judicial power. Moreover, it is for the Icelandic authorities, which operate on the basis of Icelandic law, to enforce the obligations established by the decisions of the ECtHR and other institutions. It is provided in particular that the power given to the Court to award damages does not automatically create the right for an individual to have it enforced in Iceland and a separate judgment on the national level must be acquired from the Icelandic courts.[35]

Relying on these comments of the explanatory report, it would seem that Article 2 of the ECHR Act means at least two things: *First*, that a judgment against Iceland where a violation is found does not invalidate the final judgment on the national level nor the legislation upon which the national judgments rests, although the problem may be rooted in that legislation. Second, these comments may mean that the judgments and decisions of the ECtHR, whether against Iceland or other contracting states, do not have any binding effect on the national level as precedents. In other words, Article 2 of the ECtHR Act prevents any possible *erga omnes* effect of these decisions. According to the explanatory report, this flows from the principle of dualism, the sovereignty principle embedded in the Icelandic Constitution and its provisions on the independence of the judiciary.

Another set of comments in the explanatory report relate to the possible *res interpretata* effect of these judgments and decisions where it is stated that it is up to the national courts and authorities to interpret the provisions of the Convention *independently*, among others, those provisions where there are no judicial precedents. It is, however, reiterated that it is hardly likely that an independent interpretation of ECHR provisions would in reality be based on considerations and interpretations which are not at the same time based on precedents or academic literature, although the Icelandic courts

34 *Parliamentary Reports, supra* note 32, pp. 5880 and 5895.

35 *Ibid.*, p. 5895.

would be empowered to do that.[36] It must be assumed that the Icelandic courts and administrative authorities will take these decisions into consideration when interpreting and applying the provisions of the Convention, although these decisions are not binding. In the explanatory report it is noted in particular that there were already examples of Icelandic court judgments referring to judgments of the Court and decisions of the Commission when applying the Convention provisions.[37]

The set of comments relating to the significance of the decisions of the ECtHR for interpretative purposes strongly suggests that Article 2 of the ECHR Act should also be read as rejecting a binding *res interpretata* effect of these decisions for the national courts, who are free to interpret the provisions of the ECHR regardless of the case law of the ECtHR.

The comments in the explanatory report show a certain degree of reluctance to fully embrace the Convention and the way in which it has been interpreted and applied by the Council of Europe organs. They may be understood as a manifestation of the dualist approach as a constitutional and political theory, underlining the independence of the national courts from outside influence, and as an assertion of the full sovereignty of the state as such in the international community. It is moreover interesting to relate these considerations to the theory of incorporation on the one hand and the theory of transformation on the other. In this regard, it would seem that these considerations sit well with the dualist theory of *transformation*. From the idea of *transformation,* it flows that the domestic courts may do with the rules as they see fit, as long as it is compatible with accepted *internal* legal standards and methods, regardless of what may otherwise follow from the international law character of the rules.

The Supreme Court of Iceland has expressed itself on Article 2.[38] One of the most relevant one is Case no. 371/2010 of 22 September 2010.

> The State Prosecutor appealed to the Supreme Court the decision of the District Court in a case brought against A, B, C and the company D, where the case was partly dismissed. A, B, C and D submitted that they had already been punished in the form of extra charges on their taxes and by prosecuting them in addition, the state had violated their rights under

36 *Ibid.*, pp. 5890–5891.

37 *Ibid.*, p 5890.

38 *See also* Case no. 248/2005 of 21 September 2005 where general reference is made to the case law of the ECtHR on Article 6(3)(c) ECHR, "although these judgments are not binding under Icelandic law", as stated in the judgment.

> Article 4 of Protocol 7 to the ECHR, *cf.* Act no 62/1994 (*ne bis in idem*). In its judgment the Supreme Court rehearsed that by Article 2 of the Act the legislature had reiterated that, despite the incorporation of the Convention as statutory law, Icelandic law was still based on the principle of dualism as regards the relevance of the decisions of the institutions established on the basis of the Convention. Although Icelandic courts would take note of the decisions of these institutions when interpreting the Convention when applied as a part of Icelandic domestic law, it would be the role of the legislature to make the necessary amendments to Icelandic law to respect the obligations of the Icelandic State under the Convention. The law in Iceland provided that in the field of tax law it was presumed that the tax administration could be organised such that the decision on an extra charge on taxes was separate from criminal prosecution for tax fraud, although they were rooted in the same occurrence. If the claims of A, B, C and D were to be accepted it would amount to finding that the organisation of these matters could not be sustained. In addition the case law of the ECtHR was found to be misguiding regarding the issue at stake in the case when examining whether the decision concerned the same violation in the former and the latter procedures.[39] To find that this arrangement was contrary to the Convention it had to be shown clearly that it was incompatible with the Convention, and, as the case may be, the case law of the ECtHR. Since this was not found to be the situation, already for this reason, the decision of the District Court was quashed, and the District Court was ordered to decide on the substance of the case.

The judgment is interesting for several reasons. It shows that the Supreme Court first and foremost understands Article 2 of Act No. 62/1994 as referring to the binding nature of the ECtHR's decisions as precedents when applying

39 The judgment refers to several judgments and decisions of the ECtHR. They are: case of *Engel and others* v. *the Netherlands* (Applications no. 5100/71 5101/71 5102/71 and 5354/72), judgment of 8 June 1976; case of *Rosenquist* v. *Sweden* (Application no. 60619/00), decision of 14 September 2004; case of *Storbråten* v. *Norway* (Application no. 12277/04) decision of 1 February 2007; case of *Mjelde* v. *Norway* (Application no. 11143/04), decision of 1 February 2007: case of *Haarvig* v. *Norway* (Application no. 11187/05), decision of 11 December 2007; case of *Ponsetti and Chesnel* v. *France* (Applications no. 36855/97 and 41731/98), decision of 14 September 1999; case of *Zolotukhin* v. *Russia* (Application no. 14939/03), judgment of 10 February 2009; case of *Ruotsalainen* v. *Finland* (Application no.13079/03), judgment of 16 June 2009; case of *Maresti* v. *Croatia* (Application no. 55759/07), judgment of 25 June 2009; and case of *Tsonyo* v. *Bulgaria* (Application no. 2376/03), judgment of 14 January 2010.

the Convention on the domestic level, instead of referring to the binding effect of judgments against the Icelandic state on the domestic level, but these two are somewhat mixed together in the explanatory report.[40] Moreover, it bears witness to the limits of *res interpretata*, namely that the Convention, or the case law of the Court, will not be used to directly "amend" Icelandic legislation, and ultimately if it is not possible to put Icelandic legislation in line with the ECHR requirements by way of consistent interpretation, then it is up to the legislature to react and make necessary legislative amendments.

In this regard, it should be noted that the traditional approach in Icelandic law is that precedents in general are not considered a binding source of law. The same would in any case apply to case law from the ECtHR. Scholars use different verbiage to describe this, but this, in general terms, correctly presents their common view. However, in spite of this, it is also generally accepted that it must be presumed that Icelandic courts follow precedents, especially the precedents from the Supreme Court in a similar case, unless there are good grounds for not doing so and thus to depart from an earlier precedent. The difference between scholars lies in the presentation of the factors that may justify departure from a precedent of the Supreme Court. The stricter the requirements to justify departure are, the closer the precedents are to being binding in reality, although they are not so from a formal point of view. The more lenient one becomes concerning the conditions for departing from precedents, the further away they are from being binding.[41] It is asserted here that these considerations also apply *mutatis mutandis* in relation to judgments of the ECHR. To the extent that additional or different considerations come into play they should possibly lead to the conclusion that there is less leeway for the Icelandic courts to depart from the judgments of the ECtHR than from their own judgments. In support of this it is noted that recent precedents from the ECtHR are more likely to have the effect that the domestic courts depart from

40 *See also* judgment of the Supreme Court in Case no. 604/2008 of 18 June 2009, which seems to be based on the same understanding as the explanatory report. This is, however, not entirely clear from the judgment.

41 A. Snævarr, *Almenn lögfræði* (Bókaútgáfa Orators, Reykjavik, 1989) pp. 216–218; S. Líndal, *Um lög og lögfræði* (Hið íslenska bókmenntafélag, Reykjavik, 2003) pp. 288–294; S. Magnússon, *Hin lagalega aðferð og réttarheimildirnar* (Háskólaútgáfan, Reykjavík, Reykjavik, 2003) p. 154; *see also* J.S. Gunnlaugsson, *Um fordæmi og valdmörk dómstóla dómstóla* (Reykjavik University, 2003) pp. 79–83. Gunnlaugsson comes close to asserting the binding effect of judgments when he suggests that departure is only justified if an earlier judgment is wrong or if the legal sources upon which it is based have changed.

their own precedents which are not compatible with the former.[42] This not only applies in cases before the domestic courts which directly relate to the interpretation of Convention provisions as incorporated by Act No. 62/1994, but also in relation to cases concerning the interpretation of other domestic law, including the constitutional provisions on human rights. This has particular bearing in relation to Iceland after the constitutional amendments made in 1995 by Act No. 97/1995, since the aim of these amendments *i.a.* included bringing the protection of human rights in Iceland in line with the Convention requirements, as well as other international human rights instruments. There are thus, in addition to traditional arguments relating to foreseeability, consistency and legal certainty, at least two important reasons for domestic courts to follow precedents from the ECtHR. In the first place, since after incorporation of the provisions as statutory law it is unavoidable to apply them in the domestic system when applicable. At the same time, it is also reasonable to expect them to follow the precedents as otherwise the state will be in breach of its international obligations under the ECHR, and, in the second place, because of the significance of the ECHR and the case law of the Court for constitutional interpretation.

The remarks made in the above judgment concerning the role of the legislature are open to criticism. The fact remains that the Convention is part of Icelandic law. It is indeed the role of the courts to strive to solve any possible conflict between the national norms, of which the ECHR is a part. If the case law of the ECtHR on the matter of the case had been clear, nothing would have prevented the Supreme Court from giving primacy to the Convention provision (if needed) to uphold the ECHR standards. The problem was rather, as the Supreme Court saw it, the lack of clear case law, which allowed the Court to say that it *has not been shown* that the arrangement under Icelandic law was contrary to the Convention. However, this has no direct bearing on the relationship with Article 2 of Act No. 62/1994 or on the importance of ECtHR decisions as precedents when the Convention is applied by domestic courts.[43]

---

42 *See for example* judgment of the Supreme Court in Case no. 120/1989 of 9 January 1990. In this case the Supreme Court clearly deviates from its own case law following instead a decision of the European Commission on Human Rights, *see* the case of *Jón Kristinsson* v. *Iceland* (Application no. 12170/86) Decision of 22 February 1990.

43 It is further noted that in Case no. 371/2010 the Supreme Court states that it "has not been shown (by the parties) that the asserted right is protected under the Convention and that the Court should enforce it". It may be argued that this contravenes the judgment of the Supreme Court in Case. no. 512/2008 of 29 September 2008, where the Supreme Court found that it is for the Court to examine *ex officio* if Article 39, par. 3, of the Code on Criminal Procedure no. 19/1991 contravenes the provisions of Article 70 of the Constitution, Article 6 (3) (c) of the ECHR or Article 14 (3) (b) and (c) ICCPR. For comparison it is the

Further arguments speak in favour of the importance of the decisions of the ECtHR. One is that it is mainly the case law of the Court which generates the adjustment of the Convention "to the developing social and political context of Europe".[44] Full understanding of the meaning and scope of the substantive provisions of the Convention will not be achieved without consulting the most important precedents. Moreover, the ECtHR has to some extent developed its own legal methods and canons of interpretation, which are relevant for demarcation, interpretation and application of the individual substantive provisions.

The reference to the dualism in the explanatory report and the judgments referred to above would seem to represent an attempt to give it practical legal significance. However, a closer look suggests that this dualist approach is first and foremost a theoretical construction of rather limited practical relevance when viewing whether a state has complied with its obligations under the Convention, and for the assessment of the width and depth of such obligations.[45] It in fact represents a certain political aversion against international law governance and thus first and foremost asserts this principle as a constitutional and political theory together with the sovereignty principle embedded in the Constitution. This is, however, a rather typical approach in dualist countries, including Norway and Denmark.

In spite of such reservations, the Supreme Court of Iceland regularly cites decisions and judgments of the ECtHR. First to mention is the judgment of the Supreme Court in Case no. 120/1989 of 9 January 1990, which points out that since Iceland became a contracting party many of the Convention provisions have been further interpreted and developed in the case law of the Commission and the Court. From the context it is clear that even though at the time of Iceland's ratification of the Convention Icelandic law was found to be in conformity with the Convention, this may need to be re-evaluated in the light of the case law of these institutions. Moreover, the judgment contains direct reference to the decisions of the Commission, which held unanimously that the domestic proceedings in the case of *Jón Kristinsson* were in breach of Article

view in the UK, that unless legislation clearly stipulates a private right it is the party asserting such a right that has the burden of proof that a treaty creates it and that the courts should enforce it. *See for example* A. Aust, 'United Kingdom', in D. Sloss (ed.), *The Role of Domestic Courts in Treaty Enforcement. A Comparative Study* (Cambridge University Press, Cambridge, 2009) p. 476 *et seq.*

44 L. Garlicki, 'Some Observations on Relations between the ECtHR and Domestic Jurisdictions', in J. Iliopoulos-Strangas (ed.), *Cours suprêmes nationales et cours européennes: concurrence ou collaboration?* (Bruylant, Brussels, 2007) p. 305.

45 I. Detter, *The International Legal Order* (Aldershot, Dartmouth Publishing, Dartmouth, 1994) pp. 166–167.

6(1)1 of the ECHR.[46] These words clearly corroborate the importance of taking the decisions of these institutions into consideration when interpreting and applying the Convention provisions in the Icelandic domestic system.

Another example of a reference to the case law of the ECHR is the judgment in Case no. 31/1990 from 2 February 1990 which refers to the *Hauschildt* case.[47] In Case no. 103/1994 of 18 May 1995, there is a reference to the *Langborger* case.[48] In this same judgment there is a further general reference to the way in which the Commission and the Court have interpreted the requirements of an impartial court in Article 6(1) of the ECHR. One may also mention the judgment in Case no. 167/2002 of 14 November 2002 (ASÍ), which referred generally to the case law of the ECtHR on Article 11 of the Convention and stressed that when interpreting the ECHR inspiration has been sought, among other sources, from the European Social Charter. Later on, the judgment refers to the "recognised interpretation" of Article 11(1) and (2) of the ECHR without referring to the relevant judgments or decisions of the ECtHR.[49] From this citation it can be deduced that the judgments of the ECHR are of direct value as precedents for the interpretation of Article 74 of the Constitution on freedom of association. See also the judgment of the Supreme Court in Case no. 520/2004 of 19 May 2005. In this case, the Court stated that the ECtHR had interpreted Article 6(3)(d) of the ECHR in a certain way without referring to particular judgments to support that view.

It is also worth mentioning the judgment of the Supreme Court in Case no. 231/2005 of 9 June 2005. In this case, the plaintiff referred to the judgments of the ECtHR in the *Kellermann* case in support of his arguments.[50] However, the Supreme Court did not refer to it in its reasoning. In Case no. 248/2005 of 21 September 2005 a general reference was made to the case law of the ECtHR on Article 6(3)(c) of the ECHR, "although these judgments were not binding

46 *See* the case of *Jón Kristinsson* v. *Iceland* (Application no. 12170/86) Decision 22 February 1990. The reason for the case before the ECtHR is the judgment of the Supreme Court in Case no. 77/1985 of 25 November 1985.

47 *See* judgment in the case of *Hauschildt* v. *Denmark* (Application no. 10486/83), judgment 24 May 1989.

48 *See* judgment in case of *Langborger* v *Sweden* (Application no. 11179/84), judgment 22 June 1989.

49 It is noted that the judgment also contains references to Article 20(2) of the UDHR; Article 22 of the ICCPR; Article 6 of the ICESCR; Article 2 of the ILO Convention (No. 87) concerning Freedom of Association and Protection of the Right to Organize; and Article 11 of the ECHR.

50 Case of *AB Kurt Kellermann* v. *Sweden* (Application no. 41579/98), judgment 26 October 2004.

under Icelandic law". In Case no. 248/2006 of 8 June 2006, the Supreme Court referred to the case law on Article 4, Protocol 7 of the ECHR. In Case no. 179/2008 of 28 April 2008 the Supreme Court referred to the case of *Achour* v. *France*, in support of its interpretation of Article 7 of the ECHR.[51] In Case no. 304/2009 of 26 November 2009, the District Court judge referred to the decision of the ECtHR in the case of *Tirado Ortiz*;[52] and Case no. 178/2007 of 30 March 2007 (dissenting opinion of Judge Jón Steinar Gunnlaugsson), referring to the judgments of the ECtHR in the cases of *Letellier* and *Tomasi* v. *France*.[53] Several other judgments can be referred to where the case law of the ECtHR is cited, including by the parties.[54]

Due to lack of firm criteria to measure against, it is difficult to assess whether these references are more or less frequent than should be expected. Moreover, it cannot be excluded that the case law of the ECtHR plays a more important role than the exact numbers of citations indicate and that it has been consulted although individual cases are not directly referred to. For practical purposes, adapting national jurisprudence to the interpretation furnished by the ECtHR is a natural step to pre-empt future violations.[55]

6 Conclusions

The subtitle for this chapter poses the question whether a Nordic approach can be identified in relation to the status of decisions and judgments of the ECtHR before national courts. In a short article like this one, a complete comparison

---

51 Case of *Achour* v. *France* (Application no. 67335/01) of 29 March 2006.

52 Case of *Tirado Ortiz and others* v. *Spain* (Application no. 43486/98), Decision 15 June 1999.

53 Case of *Letellier* v. *France* (Application no. 12369/86), judgment 26 June 1991; and case of *Tomasi* v. *France* (Application no. 12850/87), judgment 27 August 1992. *See also* the dissenting opinion of Judge Gunnlaugsson, Jón Steinar, in Case no. 255/2007 of 11 May 2007 referring in general to the ECtHR's case law on Article 5(3) ECHR.

54 *See* judgment of the Supreme Court in Case no. 192/2002 of 24 April 2002 referring to *Letellier* v. *France* of 26 June 1991 (the district court judgment); Case no. 328/2002 of 12 December 2002 (the dissenting opinion) it says that Article 95 of the Penal Code no. 19/1940 will not be interpreted properly without taking note of *i.a.* Article 10 of the ECHR. Moreover, when interpreting these provisions one must unavoidably take note of the case law of ECtHR; Case no. 661/2006 of 23 January 2007 where the parties referred to the case of *Ribemont* v. *France* (Application no. 15175/89), judgment 10 February 1995.

55 G. Ress, 'The Effect of Judgments and Decisions in Domestic Law', in R. St. J. Macdonald, F. Matshcer and H. Petzold (eds.), *The European System for the Protection of Human Rights* (Martinus Nijhoff, Dordrecht, 1993) p. 810.

cannot be made. However, on the basis of the material presented here some common features would seem to be evident.

The first thing to mention is the dualist approach under which a binding *erga omnes* effect is rejected. This at the same time relates to sovereignty concerns and the independence of the judiciary in the countries covered.

Secondly, the right to autonomous interpretation of the ECHR is reserved, as well as autonomous interpretation of human rights provisions of the national constitutions, regardless of the case law of the ECtHR. In all the countries under review (Denmark, Norway and Iceland), the ECHR has been incorporated as statutory law, which means that it can never take primacy over the national constitutions. Thus, at least from a formal point of view the constitution enjoys the highest status in the hierarchy of legal norms. This is not altered by the fact that the case law of the ECtHR may affect the interpretation of the constitution. Moreover, in order to override a national provision in in the three countries, the Convention and the case law of the ECtHR must be clear and consistent. This is *i.a.* supported by case law from Norway and Iceland.

It is to be noted that the explanatory report to the Danish legislation incorporating the Convention refers to possible effects of the incorporation of the Convention into Danish law. It is stated in particular that Danish courts and others responsible for interpreting and applying the Convention would have a firmer basis for taking note of the newest decisions from the Council of Europe institutions, which the legislature had lesser chance and flexibility to take into consideration.[56] A similar position was taken in Norway. It would seem that this approach is more receptive of the ECtHR case law when applying the Convention at the domestic level than the Icelandic position. The situation in the UK presents a similar receptiveness: Section 2(1) of the Human Rights Act requires courts to "take into account any judgement of the ECHR in determining any question to which such judgment is relevant". It has been stated that UK courts generally follow the judgments of the ECHR, in particular Grand Chamber judgments involving the UK.[57]

Despite such reservations and concerns in practical terms, the national courts of all three countries regularly (although maybe inconsistently) consult the case law of the ECtHR – not as binding *per se*, but within the framework of *res interpretata* and the rule of presumption.

---

56 Betænkning No. 1220, *supra* note 16, pp. 113–114.

57 D. Spielmann, 'Jurisprudence of the European Court of Human Rights and the Constitutional Systems of Europe', *The Oxford Handbook of Comparative Constitutional Law* (Oxford University Press, Oxford, 2012) p. 1245. *See also* Ress, *supra* note 56, p. 813 *et seq.*

The Implementation of the Rome Statute of the International Criminal Court in the Nordic Countries: A New Comprehensive Criminalization of Serious Crimes

Thordis Ingadóttir

1 Introduction

In the international arena, the Nordic countries have been among the principal supporters of the International Criminal Court (ICC) and effective enforcement of international criminal law. They were active in the drafting of the Rome Statute and played an important role in its adoption and entry into force.[1] Their continued support of the ICC is well reflected in their joint yearly statement to the General Assembly of the United Nations, in which they have renewed their pledge to remain principal supporters of the Court.[2] The Nordic countries have also supported effective enforcement of international humanitarian law at the national level. It was at the request of Denmark, Finland, Norway, and Sweden that the Status of the Protocols additional to the Geneva Conventions of 1949

---

* Thordis Ingadóttir is also the Co-Director of the Project on International Courts and Tribunals (PICT). The author thanks the late Håkan Friman, Harmen van der Wilt and Rolf Einar Fife for their valuable comments. Any errors are entirely the author's own.

1 Denmark, Finland, Norway and Sweden were members of the so-called Like-Minded Group that was influential in the drafting process. Some delegates of the Nordic countries served as key officials in the drafting process of the Rome Statute, as well as in the later work of the Preparatory Commission. In general on the role of various actors in the negotiations process, *see* F. Benedetti, K. Bonneuau and J. Washburn, *Negotiating the International Criminal Court, New York to Rome, 1994–1998* (Martinus Nijhoff Publishers, Leiden, 2014); R. Lee (ed.), *The International Criminal Court, The Making of the Rome Statute, Issues, Negotiations, Results* (Kluwer Law International, The Hague, 1999).

2 Statement on behalf of the Nordic Countries by H.E. Ambassador A. Rönquist, Director General for Legal Affairs Ministry for Foreign Affairs Sweden, in the United Nations General Assembly on the Report of the ICC Agenda item 75, 31 October 2013. *See* also Statement on behalf of the Nordic Countries by H.E. Ambassador A. Rönquist, Director General for Legal Affairs Ministry for Foreign Affairs Sweden, in the United Nations General Assembly on the Report of the ICC, Agenda item 73, 30 October 2014.

 | DOI 10.1163/9789004343597_010

was included in the agenda of the General Assembly of the United Nations during the years 1982–2008, resulting in national reporting on the relevant implementation by the member states of the United Nations.[3] Effective implementation of the European Union Guide-lines on promoting compliance with international humanitarian law was also one of Finland's priorities during its presidency of the EU in 2006. According to the Guidelines, the EU countries are to ensure that those responsible for war crimes are brought before their respective domestic courts, the courts of another State, or the ICC.[4]

A key condition for effective implementation of international criminal law at the national level is proper national legislation. Absence of – or flaws in implementing – legislation can delay or even prevent prosecution of those accused of serious crimes.[5] Importantly, implementation of international criminal law and criminalization of serious crimes at the national level have undergone a major reinforcement in recent years. The entry into force of the Rome Statute in 2002 was the key catalyst for this change. States stepped up their efforts to fight impunity, and ensured that they would be able to exercise jurisdiction in accordance with the complementarity principle of the ICC. These efforts have led to a significant development with respect to quantity and nature of national legislation on international humanitarian law and gross violations of human rights.

The Nordic countries have been part of this phenomenon. In the last few years, most of them have adopted major new items of domestic legislation on genocide, crimes against humanity and war crimes. This is reflected in the Norwegian act of 7 March 2008, incorporating a new substantive chapter in the general national criminal code (*LOV-2008-03-07-4, Lov om straff, Kapittel 16. Folkemord, forbrytelse mot menneskeheten og krigsforbrytelse,* taking effect the same day); a Finnish act similarly inserting a new substantive chapter in Finland's national criminal code (*Law 212/2008, Strafflag 19.12.1889/39, 11 kap. Om krigsförbrytelser och brott mot mänskligheten,* taking effect on 1 May 2008); and most recently a Swedish act of 2014 on the criminalization of genocide, crimes against humanity and war crimes (*Lag 2014:406 om straff för folkmord, brott mot mänskligheten och krigsförbrytelser,* taking effect on 1 July 2014).

3 Status of the Protocols Additional to the Geneva Conventions of 1949 and relating to the protection of victims of armed conflicts, UN Doc (A/37/142).

4 *See* Updated European Union Guidelines on promoting compliance with international humanitarian law (IHL), OJ 2009/C 303/06, OJ C 303/12, 15 December 2009.

5 J.K. Kleffner, *Complementarity in the Rome Statute and National Criminal Jurisdictions* (Oxford University Press, New York, 2008) p. 38.

In Iceland, a committee was established by the government on the drafting of an act on the implementation of the Convention on the Prevention and Punishment of the Crime of Genocide (Genocide Convention), the Geneva Conventions of 1949 and their additional protocols of 1977, and the Rome Statute of the ICC. The committee has submitted its draft to the government and new legislation on the subject is expected this year.[6]

Unlike its Nordic neighbours, Denmark is not in the process of reviewing and enacting new legislation on these serious crimes. Instead, Denmark relies on older legislation on genocide and a military penal code.

This chapter explores the new Nordic legislation and analyses whether the Nordic countries have taken a common approach in the implementation of the crimes within the jurisdiction of the ICC: the crime of genocide, crimes against humanity, war crimes and crime of aggression.[7] The comparison is limited to criminalization (*actus reus*) of these crimes. In all the countries, one of the primary purpose of new legislation was to ensure that the relevant state

---

6 The draft is available at the website of the Ministry of Interior, https://www.innanrikisraduneyti.is/media/frettir-2017/Lagafrv.-um-refsingar-fyrir-hopmord-og-fleira.pdf.

7 In this chapter these crimes will be referred to as serious crimes and international crimes. On international crimes in Nordic legislation, *see* e.g., regarding Denmark: A. Laursen, *Internationale forbrydelser i dansk ret* (Jurist- og Økonomforbundets Forlag, Copenhagen, 2011); and A. Laursen, 'A Danish Paradox? A Brief Review of the Status of International Crimes in Danish Law', 10:4 *J Int Criminal Justice* (2012) pp. 997–1016. Regarding Finland: Ari-Matti Nuutila, 'Implementation of the Rome Statute in Finnish Law', in Matthias Neuner (ed.), *National Legislation Incorporating International Crimes: Approaches of Civil and Common Law Countries* (BWV – Berliner Wissenschafts-Verlag GmbH, Berlin, 2003), pp. 85–104; D. Frände, 'Finnland', in A. Eser and H. Kreicker (eds.), *Nationale Strafverfolgung völkerrechtlicher Verbrechen – National Prosecution of International Crimes* (edition iuscrim Max-Planck-Institut für ausländisches und internationals Strafrecht, Freiburg i.Br., 2003), pp. 21–75. Regarding Iceland: Þ. Ingadóttir, 'Innleiðing helstu sáttmála á sviði alþjóðlegs refsiréttar í íslenskan rétt', in R. Bragadóttir et al. (eds.), *Afmælisrit: Jónatan Þórmundsson sjötugur* (CODEX, Reykjavík, 2007), pp. 619–647. Regarding Norway: S. Eskeland, *De mest alvorlige forbrytelser* (Cappelen Damm As, 2011); Rolf Einar Fife and Kristian Jervell, 'Elements of Nordic Practice 2000: Norway', 70 *Nordic Journal of International Law* (2001) pp. 531–546; Karin Cornils, 'Om kriminalisering av folkmord, brott mot mänskligheten och krigförbrytelser', 44:3 *Lov og rett* (2005), pp. 131–146. Regarding Sweden: O. Bring, S. Mahmoudi and P. Wrange, *Sverige och folkrätten* (5th edn, Norstedts Juridik, Stockholm, 2014), pp. 257–273; H. Friman, 'Political and legal considerations in Sweden relating to the Rome Statute for the International Criminal Court', in R.S. Lee (ed.), *States' Responses to Issues Arising from the ICC Statute: Constitutional, Sovereignty, Judical Cooperation and Criminal Law* (Brill, Leiden, 2005), pp. 121–145; I. Cameron, M.T. Schunke, K.P. Bartes, C. Wong and P. Asp, *International Criminal Law from a Swedish Perspective* (Intersentia, Antwerp, 2011).

would meet the principle of complementary of the ICC. At the same time, the legislation was also to cover some crimes which the states had undertaken in various treaties to criminalize and which they considered part of customary international law. To reach this goal, they undertook major studies on the content of the crimes, as is reflected in their extensive preparatory documents.

2 Individual Criminal Responsibility for Serious Crimes at the International and National Level

Individual criminal responsibility for international crimes is a well-known principle of international law. It entails that individuals are direct addressees of international rules and will be held responsible directly under international law.[8] The principle places the individual directly in international law, eroding traditional definitions of international law as law binding only on states.[9] As to enforcement, the principle has bearing with respect to criminalization and prosecution of these crimes both at the international and the national level. Individuals can be prosecuted for international crimes before international courts, irrespective of national legislation. They can also be prosecuted for international crimes before national courts, even though the relevant crimes had not been implemented in the relevant domestic legislation when committed. Furthermore, individuals can face prosecution for international crimes before national courts worldwide, based on universal jurisdiction.

The jurisdiction of the ICC reflects the enforcement of individual criminal responsibility for international crimes. Its jurisdiction extends to the conduct of individuals in territories of all member states, as well as that of citizens of member states, wherever they are committed. Irrespective of any domestic legislation, the Court may prosecute the conduct of these individuals. ICC's

8 *See* e.g. Articles 227–229 of the Treaty of Versailles, signed 28 June 1919; IMT, judgment of 1 October 1946, in The Trial of German Major War Criminals. Proceedings of the International Military Tribunal sitting at Nuremberg Germany, Part. 22 (22 August, 1946 to 1 October 1946), pp. 446–447. This position of the individual in international law is claiming a separate coverage in any general textbook of international law: e.g., M.N. Shaw, *International Law* (Cambridge University Press, Cambridge, 2008, 6th ed.), Chapter 8; A. Cassese, *International Law* (Oxford University Press, Oxford, 2005, 2nd ed.), Chapter 21; J. Klabbers, *International Law* (Cambridge University Press, Cambridge, 2013), p. 226.

9 On the individual as a participant in the international system, *see* R. Higgins, 'Conceptual Thinking about the Individual in International Law', *in Themes and Theories* (Oxford University Press, Oxford, 2009), p. 77; and A.A.C. Trindade, *The Access of Individuals to International Justice* (Oxford University Press, Oxford, 2011).

predecessors, the ICTY and ICTR, were established to enforce individual criminal responsibility for international crimes at the international level. Both tribunals came into being following serious crimes in the former Yugoslavia and Rwanda and over 250 individuals were prosecuted at these ad hoc tribunals. Establishing the courts, the Security Council underscored the responsibility of individuals for genocide, grave breaches of the Geneva conventions and other violations of international humanitarian law.[10]

Individual criminal responsibility for international crimes is also enforced at the national level. States have in various treaties undertaken the obligation to investigate and prosecute certain serious international crimes before their national courts. The key example is to be found in the Geneva Conventions of 1949 and their First Additional Protocol.[11] According to Article 146 of the Fourth Geneva Convention and Article 85 of the Additional Protocol I each contracting party is under an obligation to search for persons who have committed grave breaches of the convention and bring such persons, regardless of their nationality, before its own courts. These provisions entail an obligation for states to investigate and prosecute crimes committed on their territory and by their nationals abroad. Importantly, however, it also entails an obligation to exercise universal jurisdiction if a suspected perpetrator is found on their territory.

Enforcement of individual criminal responsibility for international crimes at the national level tests the relationship between international law and domestic law. The fundamental principle of international law is that treaties are binding upon states parties to them and they must be performed in good

---

10 Security Council, Resolution 808 (1993), 22 February 1993, UN Doc S/RES/808 (1993); Security Council Resolution 955 (1994), 8 November 1994, UN Doc S/RES/955 (1994).

11 The Geneva Conventions and Protocols were among the first international instruments to stipulate members' state obligation to prosecute crimes falling under the treaty. This was a major development in enforcement of international obligations, as until that time it was up to states how to implement international treaties at the national level; J.S. Pictetet al., *Commentary on the Geneva Conventions of 12 August 1949, Vol I: Geneva Convention for the Amelioration of the Condition of the Wounded and Sick in Armed Forces in the Field* (International Committee of the Red Cross, 1952) p. 353. Furthermore, the new obligation underscored prosecution of war criminals by the state to which the perpetrators belongs. Prior to this the prosecution of war crimes had largely be confined to prosecution through the injured state, *see* R. Wolfrum, 'Enforcement of International Humanitarian Law', in Dieter Fleck (ed.), *The Handbook of Humanitarian Law in Armed Conflicts* (Clarendon Press, Oxford, 1995) pp. 517, 523. The specific articles stipulating the obligation to prosecute are Geneva Convention I Art. 49, Geneva Convention II Art. 50, Geneva Convention III Art. 129, Geneva Convention IV Art. 146, Additional Protocol I Art. 85.

faith – *pacta sunt servanda.*[12] A corollary of the principle is that a state party may not invoke the provisions of its internal law as a justification for its failure to perform a treaty.[13] A state party has to ensure that its domestic legislation is coherent with the international obligation and when a state has a treaty obligation to prosecute a crime, in failing to comply with its obligation the state party has engaged its international responsibility.[14]

States have implemented their international obligation with respect to prosecutions of international crimes in various ways. Indeed, international law is indifferent in what manner states implement their international obligation at the national level. The choice of legislative technique is the reserved domain of the domestic legislature and it depends on the constitutional law of each state. States are often described as followers of one of two theories, dualism or monism. Dualism distinguishes between international and national laws and views them as separate independent legal systems, the only existing rules are those that are part of the system. Monism, in contrast, is described as a system where national and international law are part of one and the same legal system.[15] Following these doctrines, the former group of states needs to adopt implementing legislation, while other can rely on upon direct application of international law in their domestic system.

Individual criminal responsibility for any crime, national or international, is also dependent on adherence to the principle of legality. To respect the principle of legality, the crime and the applicable punishment must be set out in clear terms before its commission – *nullum crimen sine lege* and *nulla poena sine lege*. The principle is underscored both at the international and national level, in numerous international conventions and most national constitutions.[16] As to criminalization of international crimes at the national level this has various implication, e.g., with respect to definitions of the crimes, retroactive application of national legislation, and universal jurisdiction. The nature of individual criminal responsibility for international crimes is well reflected

12 Article 26 of the Vienna Convention on the Law of Treaties, 1155 U.N.T.S 331.

13 *Ibid.*, Article 27. *See* also *Questions Relating to the Obligation to Prosecute or Extradite (Belgium* v. *Senegal)*, Judgment, I.C.J. Reports 2012, p. 422, paras. 111–117.

14 *Ibid.*, paras. 119–121.

15 G. Gaja, 'Dualism – a Review', in J. Nijman and A. Nollkaemper (eds.), *New Perspectives on the Divide Between National & International Law* (Oxford University Press, Oxford, 2007), p. 52; Sir G. Fitzmaurice, 'The General Principles of International Law Considered from the Standpoint of the Rule of Law', *Collected Courses of the Hague Academy of International Law* (Brill/Nijhoff, Leiden, 1957), pp. 70–74.

16 M.C Bassiouni, *Crimes Against Humanity in International Criminal Law* (2nd ed., Kluwer Law International, The Hague, 1999), pp. 123–176.

in how international law defines the principle of legality with respect to prosecution of the crimes. The Geneva Conventions of 1949 and their additional Protocols of 1977 define the principle of *nullum crimen sine lege* and *nulla poena sine lege* as no one should be tried or sentenced for an act which was not forbidden by *national or international law* when committed.[17] Article 11, paragraph 2, of the Universal Declaration of Human Rights, Article 7 of the European Convention on Human Rights and Article 15 of the Convention of Civil and Political Rights stipulate the same principle. While setting forth the fundamental principle of no punishment without law, it makes clear that that there is no requirement of domestic criminalization when it comes to criminal responsibility for international crimes. To date, the European Court of Human Rights has firmly supported this unique applicability of international criminal law at the national level. In *Van Anraat* v. *the Netherlands* the Court considered a Dutch criminal act criminalizing 'a violation of the laws and customs of war' to meet the standards and the elements of rule of law in Article 7, as the act was a violation of customary international law at the time when it was committed.[18] Furthermore, in *Kononov* v. *Latvia* the Grand Chamber of the European Court on Human Rights considered that Latvia had not violated Article 7 of the Convention by convicting the applicant in 2004, for war crimes allegedly committed in 1944, pursuant to Latvian Criminal Code from 1961, a provision inserted in 1993 on war crimes, with blanket reference to international law ('war crime as defined in the relevant legal conventions'), permitting the retrospective application of the provision, and exempting war crimes from limitation.[19]

The international principle of legality with respect to international crimes does not have to be the same at the national level. Some states regard it as a minimal standard that differs from stricter standards set in some national law. A differentiation in the standards of the principle of legality for ordinary crimes and international crimes has also be adopted by various national

---

17 Geneva Convention relative to the Treatment of Prisoners of War, 75 U.N.T.S 13[4], Art. 99, Protocol Additional to the Geneva Convention of 12 August 1949, and relating to the Protection of Victims of International Armed Conflicts (Protocol I), Art. 75, paragraph 4, sub-paragraph (c), 1125 U.N.T.S 2, and Protocol Additional to the Geneva Conventions of 12 August 1949, and relating to the Protection of Victims of Non-International Armed Conflicts (Protocol II), Art. 6, paragraph 2, sub-paragraph (c), 1125 U.N.T.S 608.

18 *Van Anraat* v. *the Netherlands* (App. No. 65389/09), 6 July 2010, paras. 80–92.

19 *Kononov* v. *Latvia* (App. No. 36376/04), 17 May 2010. For a critic of some parts of the judgement, *see* Harmen van der Wilt, '*Nullum Crimen* and International Criminal Law: The Relevance of the Foreseeability Test', 84:3 *Nordic Journal of International Law* (2015) p. 515.

courts.[20] All this has to be taken into account, when a state decides on the extent and manner of its implementing legislation on international crimes. International criminal law has been charged of lacking the degree of precision required in domestic criminal law.[21] However, individual criminal responsibility for serious crimes has also developed greatly in recent years. The jurisprudence of the ad hoc international criminal tribunals and the Rome Statute, and its Elements of Crimes, has refined this area of law and these developments have been aimed towards individual criminal responsibility and prosecutions while respecting the principle of legality.

3 The Complementarity Principle of the International Criminal Court and the Obligation to Prosecute Serious Crimes at the National Level

The complementarity principle of the Rome Statute has transformed the domestic legislation. In fact, few international treaties have led to such extensive national legislative implementation. Member states undertook a comprehensive review of their domestic legislation in order to ensure that the principle of complementary set out in Article 17 of the Rome Statute would be met. No one wanted their legislation to result in their being considered “unwilling or unable genuinely to carry out the investigation or prosecution”, and hence lose its jurisdiction to the ICC. This major undertaking at the national level is interesting for various reasons, one of the more intriguing ones being that the Rome Statute itself does not obligate member states to carry out this implementation, as it does not obligate them to prosecute crimes that lie within the jurisdiction of the Court. Its preamble only refers to the obligation in general, by recalling that it is the duty of every state to exercise its criminal jurisdiction over those responsible for international crimes.[22] Nevertheless, member states ensured that their domestic legislation was up to the task, in order retain jurisdiction.

Thus, the Rome Statute has had a major impact on the national enforcement regime of international criminal law.[23] It has truly empowered the

20 Ward N. Ferdinandusse, *Direct Application of International Criminal Law in National Courts* (T.M.C Asser Press, The Hague, 2006), pp. 224–232.

21 van der Wilt, *supra* note 19, p. 515.

22 The Rome Statute of the ICC, Preamble, para 6. The preamble also affirms that the most serious crimes of concern to the international community as a whole must not go unpunished and that their effective prosecution must be ensured by taking measures at the national level and by enhancing international cooperation, *ibid*, para 4.

23 P. Seils, 'Putting Complementarity in its Place', in C. Stahn (ed.), *The Law and Practice of the International Criminal Court* (Oxford University Press, Oxford, 2015), p. 305.

prior regime, which lacked the enforcement mechanisms. Under older treaties, states had undertaken the obligation to investigate and prosecute certain serious international crimes at the national level. The primary examples are obligations under the Genocide Convention of 1948, with respect to the crime of genocide, and the Geneva Conventions of 1949, with respect to grave breaches of the conventions. However, that was as far it went, which illustrates the weakness of the treaties of that period. Unlike later universal human rights treaties, neither the Genocide Convention nor the Geneva Conventions contained any oversight mechanism on whether states implemented them properly at the national level. Hence, enforcement of these obligations has always been very weak. The Rome Statute, the jurisdiction of which includes the crime of genocide and grave breaches of the Geneva Conventions, has not only given these older treaties an enforcement regime at the international level, but – through its complementarity principle – also at the national level.

4 The Nordic Countries and Implementation of International Crimes in Domestic Legislation

Regarding the relationship between international and domestic law, the Nordic countries have traditionally been described as following a dualistic approach. Following that doctrine, application of international law at the domestic level would require implementing legislation. Surely, the new legislations reflect this by incorporating international crimes into the domestic legislation. At the same time, an examination of practice in the Nordic countries with respect to the implementation of crimes within the jurisdiction of the ICC reveals a much more varied relationship between international and domestic law than is accounted for by the dualistic approach.[24]

Prior to the ratification of the Rome Statute, the Nordic countries had undertaken the obligation to investigate and prosecute international crimes.

---

24 Studies on other areas of law have come to a similar conclusion. For instance, with respect to human rights treaties, there remain examples within the Nordic countries in which those treaties were given preference over conflicting national provisions, despite having not been implemented, *see* Betænkning nr. 1407/2001 pp. 126–127; *Betænkning om inkorporering mv. inden for menneskeretsområdet*, Betækning nr. 1546 (Justitsministeriet, København, 2014) pp. 91–93. *See also*, Bring et al., *supra* note 7, pp. 54–65; J. Klabbers, 'Coming in from the Cold: Treaties in Finland's Legal Order', in T. Koivurova (ed.), *Kansainvälistyvä Oikeus: Juhlakirja Professori Kari Hakapää* (Rovaniemi: University of Lapland, 2005), pp. 143–152; D.T. Björgvinsson, *The Intersection of International Law and Domestic Law: A Theoretical and Practical Analysis* (Edward Elgar Publishing, Cheltenham, 2015).

This tested the relationship between international and domestic law within the countries. Regarding the crime of genocide, Denmark, Finland, and Sweden adopted legislation defining and criminalizing the crime.[25] No such legislation existed in Norway and Iceland but these countries maintained that they could prosecute the crime by relying on general provision of murder in the penal code. As to war crimes, some war crimes were criminalized in military codes, though only applying to certain individuals; this was the case in Denmark, Norway, Finland, and Sweden. Furthermore, the Danish military code is broad, criminalizing war crimes via a very general reference to international law.[26] Similarly, Sweden criminalized serious international crimes by means of a general reference to international law.[27] The Finnish penal code also criminalized specific conduct in war through very general references to international law.[28] Iceland had no penal provisions regarding war crimes.

All this legislation was put to the test with the entry into force of the Rome Statute. With the ratification of the treaty, all the Nordic countries carried out the necessary review of their domestic legislation. That review was twofold. First, all of the countries quickly implemented provisions so as to be able to cooperate with the ICC in accordance with Part 9 of the Rome Statute.[29] That legislation largely built upon existing legislation in the countries on cooperation with the *ad hoc* criminal tribunals of the United Nations, the International Criminal Tribunal for the former Yugoslavia, and the International Criminal Tribunal for Rwanda. Second, in most of the countries, a comprehensive study of the substantive part of the Rome Statute and relevant domestic legislation was undertaken, in order to ensure that the principle of complementary could

25 Denmark, Lov nr. 132 af 29. April 1955 om folkedrab; Finland, Strafflag 19.12.1889/39, Chapter 11, Sections 6–8; Sweden, Lagen 1964:169 om straff för folkmord.

26 Lov om straff for krigsforbrytelser, lov 12. juli 1946, Article 25. *See* also Status of the Protocols Additional to the Geneva Conventions of 1949 and relating to the protection of victims of armed conflicts, Report of the Secretary-General, U.N. Doc. A/61/222, 4 August 2006, p. 9.

27 Brottsbalken, SFS 1962:700, Article 22, para. 6.

28 Strafflag 19.12.1889/39, Chapter 11, Section 1, para. 3.

29 Denmark, Lov nr. 342 af 16/05/2001 om Den Internationale Straffedomstol; Finland, Lag nr. 1284/2000 om ikraftträdande av de bestämmelser som hör till området för lagstiftningen i Romstadgan för Internationella brottmålsdomstolen och om tillämpning av stadgan; Iceland, Lög nr. 43/2001 um framkvæmd Rómarsamþykktar um Alþjóðlega sakamáladómstólinn; Norway, Lov om gjennomføring i norsk rett av Den internasjonale straffedomstols vedtekter 17. juli 1998 (Roma-vedtektene), LOV-2001-06-15-65; Sweden, Lag om samarbete med Internationella brottmålsdomstolen, SFS 2002:329.

be met. Norway took the lead in adopting a new chapter on genocide, crimes against humanity, and war crimes in its general penal code in March 2008.[30] Finland adopted a new chapter on war crimes and crimes against humanity in its general penal code in April 2008 (Chapter 11).[31] In 2002 a comprehensive study on the implementation of the Rome Statute and draft legislation was prepared and presented in Sweden, but adoption was postponed.[32] A new bill was presented in February 2014, followed by the adoption of a separate act on genocide, crimes against humanity, and war crimes.[33] Unlike its neighbouring countries, Denmark has not undertaken a similar reform of its criminal law with respect to definitions of crimes in the Rome Statute.[34] Denmark maintains that it can prosecute those crimes either under its military penal code or provisions of the ordinary penal code on murder, assault, rape, etc.[35] Iceland is in the final phase of preparing legislation on crimes within the jurisdiction of ICC, in a separate act. This will be the first time that the crime of genocide, crimes against humanity and war crimes are defined and criminalized in its national legislation. Only Finland has implemented provisions on the crime

---

30 *See* Lov 7 mars 2008 nr. 4 om endringer i straffeloven 20. Mai 2005 nr. 28 mv., entry into force the same day. As for preparation documents see the government bill, O.t.prp.nr.8 (2007–2008), Om lov om endringer i straffeloven 20. mai 2005 nr. 28 mv. (skjerpende og formildende omstendigheter, folkemord, rikets selvstendighet, terrorhandlinger, ro, orden og sikkerhet, og offentlig myndighet), and Justis- og politidepartemented, *Høringsnotat*-straffebestemmelser om folkemord, forbrytelser mot menneskeheten og krigforbrytelser, Lovavdelingen April 2007, Saksnr. 200701831 EO HI/TRR. In its proposition of ratification submitted to parliament, the government prepared also a comprehensive analysis of the Rome Statute and of its implication, including an analyses of constitutional issues, *see* Det Kongelige Utenriksdepartement, St.prp. nr. 24 (1999–2000).

31 *See* the Finnish government bill RP 55/2007 rd and Law 11.4.2008/212, entering into force 1 May 2008.

32 Internationella brott och svensk jurisdiktion, SOU 2002:98.

33 Lag (2014:406) om straff för folkmord, brott mot mänskligheten och krigsförbrytelser, entering into force 1 July 2014. *See* the government bill, Regeringens proposition 2013/14:146, Straffansvar för folkmord, brott mot mänskligheten och krigsförbrytelser.

34 On criticism of this approach and lack implementing legislation, *see* Laursen, 'A Danish Paradox?', *supra* note 7, pp. 997–1016. *See also* a paper prepared by the Danish Justice Ministry on Danish Criminal Jurisdiction, which included recommendation that would make it easier for Danish courts to prosecute crimes committed abroad, in particular international crimes, Justitsministeret, Dansk straffemyndighed, Betænkning nr. 1488, June 2007.

35 Laursen, "A Danish Paradox?", *supra* note 7, at 1001; *see* also Militær straffelov nr. 530 from 24/06/2005, Lov om Straf for Krigsforbrydelser nr. 395 af 12/07/1946.

of aggression.[36] Iceland includes definition and criminalization of that crime in its draft bill.

The new legislation in Finland, Norway, Denmark, and Sweden on genocide, crimes against humanity, and war crimes is extensive and detailed. Citing the principle of legality, the commentaries to the various bills highlight the importance of having precise provisions. Sweden has altogether abandoned its earlier approach of relying on criminalization via general reference to international crimes, citing criticism of following a monistic approach in otherwise dualist system.[37] Facing the difficulties posed by rapid developments in international criminal law, some flexibility is allowed for in certain provisions of most of the countries, as is done in similar provisions in the Rome Statute. Iceland adheres most closely to the definitions and structure of the Rome Statute, following an approach taken by many members of the ICC. One of its key arguments for such an approach is the harmonization with existing international law and practice. Regarding war crimes, Finland, Norway, and Sweden simplify and reorganize the definitions of the Rome Statute. Finland still retains a provision on criminalization via a very general reference to violations of law of war under international law.

The relevance of the applicability of international law at the national level and individual responsibility for international crimes was also tested in other aspects of the implementing legislation. Citing the international nature of the crimes, Norway had its legislation apply to crimes committed before the entry into force of the legislation. Later, it abandoned this approach due to a decision by the Norwegian Supreme Court. The draft bill in Iceland proposes to have the legislation apply to prior crimes, provided that they were international crimes when committed and could have been prosecuted under the provisions of the general penal code. All the states adopted a provision on the non-applicability of statute of limitations, covering previous crimes, as long as they were not already subject to the statute of limitations when the new legislation took effect. As the states have universal jurisdiction in their penal codes, due care had to be taken that crimes covered by that jurisdiction were also crimes under customary international law.

36 *See* the Finnish government bill, 289/2014 rd, and law 1718/2015 (Lag om ändring av strafflagen, adopted 30 December 2015).

37 Regeringens proposition 2013/14:146, *supra* note 33, p. 68. Interestingly, the argument for Swedish approach when implementing obligations under international humanitarian law in the fifties, was that the obligations in this area were so enormous that it was not possible to spell them out and therefor a general reference was needed, proposition 1948:144, p. 167 and proposition 1953:142, p. 26 f., cited in proposition 2013/14:146, *supra* note 33, p. 68.

5 The Crime of Genocide

For a long time, the implementation of provisions covering genocide in the Nordic countries was not harmonious. All the Nordic countries ratified the Genocide Convention before or soon after its entry into force in 1951.[38] Soon afterwards Denmark and Sweden adopted special laws on the crime of genocide, while Finland incorporated the crime into its penal code in 1974.[39] In all instances the legislation defined and criminalized genocide. Prior to their bills implementing the Rome Statute, Norway and Iceland had no provisions in their domestic legislation criminalizing genocide and the crime was not *delictum sui generis* in their law, though Norway provided for universal jurisdiction over the crime.[40] Iceland's view on the matter is unclear as no commentaries were published on it at the time of ratification of the Genocide Convention or the Rome Statute.[41] At the time of ratification of the Rome Statute, Norway contended that implementation of a definition of the crime was not necessary as the crime could be prosecuted as an ordinary crime of murder. One of the factors that led to later criminalization of the crime in Norway was the decision of the Appeal Chamber of the International Criminal Tribunal for Rwanda in the case of *Bagaragaza*.[42] In this case the tribunal rejected the argument of Norway that genocide could be sufficiently prosecuted under a general penal provision on murder. The case was a major setback to the approach adopted by Norway with respect to implementation of the Genocide Convention, and was an important consideration that led to legislative review and changes in the criminalization of serious crimes.[43]

---

38 Denmark 15 June 1951, Finland 18 December 1959, Iceland 29 August 1949, Norway 22 July 1949, and Sweden 27 May 1952.

39 *See* in Sweden Lagen 1964:169 om straff för folkmord, in Denmark Lov nr. 132 af 29. April 1955 om folkedrab, and in Finland Code 987/1974, later in the general Penal Code, Chapter 11, Sections 6–8.

40 Article 12, para. 4(a) of the Norwegian penal code.

41 In the case of *Eðvald Hinriksson* from 1992, regarding alleged crimes in the Second World War, it was contented that the alleged criminal could be prosecuted for the crime of genocide, based on provisions in the Icelandic penal code on murder. The case did not go to trial, as the Mr. Hinriksson died during the investigation.

42 International Criminal Tribunal for Rwanda, The Appeal Chamber, *The Prosecutor v. Michel Bagaragaza*, Case No. ictr-2005-86-PT, Decision on Rule 11bis Appeal of 30 August 2006. The ICTR assessment was made against rule 11bis of the Court's Rules of Procedure and Evidence, which regarded transfer of proceedings from the Court to national criminal jurisdiction.

43 *See* e.g., Justis- og Politidepartementet, *Høringsnotat* – straffebestemmelser om folkemord, forbrytelser mot menneskeheten og krigforbrytelser, Lovafdelingen April 2007, *supra* note 30, pp. 7–8.

The definition of the crime of genocide in Article 6 of the Rome Statute is materially identical to that in Article II of the Genocide Convention of 1948. It was considered that the definition reflected customary international law and there was reluctance among states to tamper with the definition.[44] However, the list of groups protected by the definition of genocide has been debated and criticized by some as being too rigid.[45] Both during the drafting of Genocide Convention and the Rome Statute, unsuccessful attempts were made to enlarge the list of protected groups.[46] It is also questionable whether other groups now fall within the scope of genocide by virtue of customary international law, or by interpretation.[47]

Denmark's legislation on genocide incorporates the definition as set out in Article II of the Genocide Convention. Sweden adopted the same definition in its legislation of 1964 and adheres to the same in its new legislation. The Norwegian legislation now criminalizes the genocide and defines it in the same way as the Genocide Convention and the Rome Statute. So does the Icelandic draft bill. In its older legislation on genocide, Finland adopted a broader definition of genocide than was stipulated in the Genocide Convention. The groups protected by the Genocide Convention are listed in a closed manner as "national, ethnical, racial and religious" groups. Finland enlarged this list by adding the term "or another comparable group". In its new bill of 2008, Finland still adheres to this broader definition.

Following the new legislative amendments, all the Nordic countries have now criminalized genocide. Finland is the only one that has adopted a broader definition than that stipulated in the Rome Statute, hence enlarging the list of groups protected by the definition.[48] In general, therefore Nordic implementing

44 H. von Hebel and D. Robinsson, 'Crimes within the Jurisdiction of the Court', in Lee (ed.), *supra* note 1, p. 89.

45 *See* A. Cassese, 'Genocide', in A. Cassese, P. Gaeta, and J.R.W.D. Jones (eds.), *The Rome Statute of the International Criminal Court: A Commentary* (Oxford University Press, Oxford, 2002), p. 336.

46 R. Cryer, H. Friman, D. Robinson, E. Wilmshurst, *An Introduction to International Criminal Law and Procedure* (Cambridge University Press, Cambridge, 3rd ed., 2014), p. 210; W.A. Schabas, *Genocide in International Law, The Crime of Crimes* (Cambridge University Press, Cambridge, 2nd ed., 2009) p. 109. Debated missing groups have included social and political groups, and cultural genocide. Recently, some other groups have surfaced in the debate on who are or should be included in the protected groups, such as individuals with Down-Syndrome.

47 This was the view of the judgment in Akayesu, *see* ICTR T. Ch. I 2.9.1998, para. 516. *See* discussion in Cryer et al., *ibid.*, p. 210.

48 A few states, such as Spain, have followed the same path as Finland and have adopted a wider definition than is stipulated in the Rome Statute.

legislation is not progressive in its definition of genocide.[49] However, all the Nordic countries have adopted a provision on universal jurisdiction over crimes of genocide; in doing so, they have opted for a broader jurisdiction than the Genocide Convention requires.

6 Crimes against Humanity

The implementation of provisions on crimes against humanity into the legislation in the Nordic countries raised issues different from those raised by genocide and war crimes. The two latter categories are the subject of international treaties that require states to prevent and punish these crimes. Although crimes against humanity were criminalized in the Nuremberg Charter, and later in the statutes of the international criminal tribunals for the former Yugoslavia and Rwanda, there still exists no international treaty defining these crimes and requiring states to prevent and punish them. At the same time, they are considered as international crimes under customary international law.[50] Still, prior to the implementation of the Rome Statute, none of the Nordic countries had definitions of crimes against humanity, or provisions to punish them, in their legislation.

The Rome Statute's definition of crimes against humanity builds largely on the definitions in the statutes of the international criminal tribunals for the former Yugoslavia and Rwanda, and their case law. Many of the crimes are also listed in the Nuremberg Charter.[51] Nevertheless, negotiation of the definition of the crimes proved difficult. This was the first time that these crimes were defined in a multilateral treaty. Many countries were also concerned that internal violence committed by their officials might fall within the jurisdiction of the court, as crimes against humanity are not required to have a nexus with armed conflict.[52]

49 The preparatory documents of the bills are meager on this point. The Swedish bill had some reservations of using the term 'racial', as it considered it associated with discrimination and racism. It was decided to use the term, given that it would be understood as in the relevant international treaties using it, Regeringens proposition 2013/14:146, *supra* note 33, pp. 79–80.

50 Bassiouni, *supra* note 16. The European Court of Human Rights has also adjudicated on the definition of the crimes against humanity, *Korbely* v. *Hungary* (App. No. 9174/02), 19 September 2008.

51 ICTY Statute, Article 5, ICTR Statute, Article 3.

52 Crimes against humanity have progressed from a crime associated with armed conflict to a crime that can occur whenever there is a widespread and systematic attack directed

Crimes against humanity are defined as serious crimes which are committed *as part of a widespread or systematic attack directed against any civilian population*. They may be committed in a context of conflict or outside it. The bar in the Rome Statute for crimes against humanity is set high. They must not only be committed as part of a widespread or systematic attack against any civilian population, but also *with knowledge of the attack*.[53] This last requirement has been implemented in various ways by state parties to the Rome Statute. None of the Nordic countries has implemented this additional element in the legal text.[54] It is significant that the Nordic countries did not incorporate the definition of "attack", stipulated in Article 7, paragraph 2 (item a), of the Rome Statute, requiring connection with a state or organizational policy. That requirement is considered to lack support in customary law and has for instance been rejected by the International Criminal Tribunal for the former Yugoslavia.[55]

Article 7, paragraph 1, of the Rome Statute stipulates ten crimes which can qualify as crimes against humanity, including murder, torture, sexual violence and persecution. In addition, the article provides for an "open-ended" provision: "Other inhuman acts of similar character intentionally causing great suffering, or serious injury to body or to mental or physical health" (item k). A similar catchall provision was also included in the statutes of the UN *ad hoc* criminal tribunals.[56] Paragraphs 2 and 3 of Article 7 define further the elements of the crimes enumerated in paragraph 1. These detailed provisions reveal the intensive negotiations that took place on the drafting of the text and the efforts made to limit an overly broad interpretation of the provision.

Iceland and Norway implement Article 7, paragraph 1, more or less "as it is", and with the catchall provision.[57] Finland incorporates two provisions on crimes against humanity in its penal code, one on crimes against humanity and

---

against civilian population by means of certain heinous acts. For a detailed account on crimes against humanity, *see* First report on crimes against humanity, by Sean D. Murphy, Special Rapporteur, UN Doc A/cn.4/680, 17 February 2015.

53 According to Article 30, para. 3, of the Rome Statute, "knowledge" means awareness that a circumstance exists or a consequence will occur in the ordinary course of events. "Know" and "knowingly" shall be construed accordingly.

54 To large extent, it is implemented through the applicable *men rea* requirements.

55 *Prosecutor* v. *Kunarac et al.*, Case No. IT-96-23-A, Judgement, Appeals Chamber, 12 June 2002, para 98.

56 ICTY Statute, Article 5(i), ICTR statute, Article 3(i). *See* also M. Boot, revised by C.K. Hall, 'Article 7 Crimes against Humanity (k) "Other inhuman acts"', in O. Triffterer (ed.), *Commentary on the Rome Statute of the Internatinal Criminal Court – Oberservers´ Notes, Article by Articles* (2nd ed., C.H. Beck, Munich 2008), p. 230.

57 Norway, *see* Article 102, para. k.

other on grave crimes against humanity.[58] While differently organized, the former provisions on substance incorporates Article 7, paragraph 1, of the Rome Statute, with some changes. For instance, it does not include the open-ended provision provided. Sweden incorporates Article 7, paragraph 1, though without the open-ended provision. Also, it did not consider it necessary to have a separate provision on apartheid, as it considered it sufficiently covered by the persecution provision.[59] Denmark has not incorporated a provision on crimes against humanity. In its commentary on the Rome Statute, it maintained that the crimes, when committed by military personnel, could be punished under the Military Penal Code. And failing that, then under the provisions of the ordinary penal code on murder, rape, etc.[60] This statement has been harshly criticized by some, and it has been argued that crimes against humanity could not fall within these provisions.[61]

All the Nordic countries only incorporated paragraph 1 of Article 7 of the Rome Statute, leaving out paragraphs 2 and 3. Norway considered that such a detailed description in the law itself would go against traditional law-making practice at its national level.[62] Some of the definitions in paragraph 2 were taken into account by the countries when formulating the provisions, such as torture. With respect to certain crimes, some countries considered it necessary to broaden the definitions, like Norway with respect to persecution and apartheid.[63] In incorporating crimes against humanity Sweden considered that criminalization should not go further than what customary law provides, due to the country's universal jurisdiction.[64]

A new treaty on crimes against humanity is on the horizon. It has been in the making for years, but in 2013 considerable progress was made when the International Law Commission of the United Nations adopted the topic in its program.[65] The Nordic countries supported this work and in their statement to Sixth Committee of the General Assembly they called for robust inter-state cooperation for the purposes of investigation, prosecution and punishment

58 *See* Strafflag 19.12.1889/39, Chapter 11, Articles 3 and 4.

59 Regeringens proposition 2013/14:146, *supra* note 33, p. 117.

60 Folketingstidende (The Folketing Hansard), 2000–2001, Appendix A, p. 499, cited by Laursen, 'A Danish Paradox?', *supra* note 7, p. 1001.

61 *See* Laursen, *ibid.*, pp. 1003, 1007.

62 Höringsnotat, *supra* note 30, p. 32.

63 Höringsnotat, *ibid.*, pp. 33–36.

64 Regeringens proposition 2013/14:146, *supra* note 33, p. 78.

65 *See* Report of the International Law Commission on the Work of its Sixty-Fifth Session, U.N. GAOR, 68th Sess., Supp. No. 10, U.N. Doc. A/68/10, at 116, para. 170 and Annex B (2013).

of these crimes.[66] The International Law Commission has now prepared the first draft articles of the new treaty.[67] The proposed draft articles adopt the same definition of crimes against humanity as the Rome Statute. The draft articles also require states to prevent these crimes and to prosecute the alleged offenders.

7 War Crimes

7.1 *Legislation Adopted Prior to the Rome Statute*

All the Nordic countries have ratified all major treaties on war crimes. They are bound by the Hague Conventions on the laws and customs of wars and prohibited weapons of 1899 and 1907, either by ratification or customary international law.[68] They are all parties to the four Geneva Conventions of 1949, and their two Additional Protocols of 1977. Furthermore, they are also parties to Additional Protocol III of 2005. The Nordic countries are all parties to other major conventions on methods and means of warfare, including the Convention on the Prohibition of Biological Weapons of 1972, Convention prohibiting Chemical Weapons of 1993, and the Anti-Personnel Mine Ban Convention of 1997. They are parties to the Optional Protocol to the Convention on the Rights of the Child on the involvement of children in armed conflict.

As described earlier, already with the ratification of the Geneva Conventions of 1949, the Nordic countries undertook a sweeping obligation to investigate and prosecute war crimes at the national level. According to the Geneva Conventions, state parties were to enact any legislation necessary to provide effective penal sanctions for persons committing grave breaches of the conventions, to search for such persons, and bring such persons, irrespective of their nationality, before their own courts. The conventions also incorporated the principle of *aut dedere aut judicare*, i.e., states could, if they preferred, hand such persons over for trial to another party concerned, provided that such party had made out a *prima facie* case.[69]

66 Statement to the Sixth Committee by Norway on behalf of the Nordic Countries, at 5 (28 October 2013), available at https://papersmart.unmeetings.org/media2/703463/norway-part-1.pdf.

67 United Nations, UN Doc A/CN.4/680, 17 February 2015.

68 *Legal Consequences of the Construction of a Wall in the Occupied Palestinian Territory*, Advisory Opinion, I.C.J. Reports 2004, p. 136, para. 89.

69 Geneva Convention I, Article 49, Geneva Convention II, Article 50, Geneva Convention III, Article 129, and Geneva Convention IV, Article 146.

Furthermore, prior to the ratification of the Rome Statute all the Nordic countries except Iceland had domestic legislation on war crimes. Interestingly, in all of these instances the relevant provisions criminalizing war crimes were very broadly defined and far reaching. The Danish Military Penal Code described the possibility for military personnel to be punished if, during an armed conflict, they acted in defiance of international conventions ratified by Denmark or in defiance of international customary law.[70] The Norwegian Military Penal Code criminalized violations of the Geneva Conventions of 1949 and its two protocols.[71] In an addition to a military penal code, Sweden had a very broad definition and reference to war crimes. Under the Swedish penal code, Article 22, para 6, a violation of international humanitarian law, whether according to a treaty or customary law, was a crime.[72] The provision was adopted in order to implement Sweden's obligations under the Hague Convention of 1904, the Geneva Conventions of 1949 and their Protocols of 1977.[73] Under the Finnish penal code, anyone who violated treaties on the law on war that Finland had ratified, or customary law relating to war, was to be sentenced.[74] Iceland had no provisions at all on war crimes in its legislation, and it was maintained by the government that the general provisions of the penal code could be used to prosecute war crimes.[75]

With the ratification of the Rome Statute, some of the Nordic countries undertook studies of the need to implement legislation with respect to the

70 Article 25, Lov om straff for krigsforbrytelser, 12 July 1946. *See* also Status of the Protocols Additional to the Geneva Conventions of 1949 and relating to the protection of victims of armed conflicts, *supra* note 26, p. 9.

71 Article 108, Militær Straffelov, LOV-1902-05-22-13. Norway had also a penal code on foreign war criminals, Lov om straff for utlendske krigsbrotsmenn 13 December 1946 nr. 14. Then some general provisions of its penal code were to apply to some of the crimes. *See* Høringsnotat, *supra* note 30, p. 38.

72 Brottsbalken, SFS 1962:700.

73 *See* Friman, *supra* note 7, p. 141.

74 Strafflagen, Chapter 11, Section 1, paragraph 3.

75 It was the view of the Ministry of Foreign Affairs in 2001, that there was no need to implement the Geneva Conventions with respect to protection of citizens, as general provisions of the penal code could be used, *see* Utanríkisráðuneytið, Umsögn um tillögu til þingsályktunar um lagabreytingar til að fullnægja ákvæðum Genfarsáttmálans um vernd óbreyttra borgara á stríðstímum, 7 May 2001. *See* also this view, to some extent, in Status of the Protocols Additional to the Geneva Conventions of 1949 and relating to the protection of victims of armed conflicts, *supra* note 26, p. 10. There is an ambiguous provision in Law 73/2007 on the Icelandic Peacekeeping, according to Icelandic Peace-keepers shall "honour" international law that Iceland is bound of and have legal effects towards individuals, *see* Law 73/2007, Article 6.

criminalization of war crimes. Denmark and Norway considered that no further legislation was needed.[76] Like the older code, a recent Danish military penal code has a very broad reference to violations of international law.[77] On the contrary, Sweden and Finland concluded that changes were indeed needed in order to bring their domestic legislation into line with the Rome Statute. In its later review of legislative amendments, Norway proposed major changes to criminalization of war crimes. With the ratification of the Rome Statute, Iceland did not undertake a review of its legislation with respect to the crimes within the jurisdiction of the ICC. According to information submitted to the Secretary-General of the United Nations in 2006, Iceland considered some war crimes to fulfil the elements of the relevant provisions of its penal code, e.g., those on homicide, bodily injury and sexual offences.[78] In a study done some years later, commissioned by the Ministry of Justice in Iceland, it was concluded that changes were needed to the national legislation in order to comply with the Geneva Conventions and to be able to benefit from the complementary jurisdiction of the ICC.

7.2 *The Content of Article 8 of the Rome Statute*

In general, Article 8 of the Rome Statute on war crimes was to reflect customary international law.[79] It defines 50 types of conduct as war crimes, classifying them according to whether they are committed in international armed conflict (Article 8, paragraphs 2, a and b) or armed conflict not of international character (Article 8, paragraphs 2, c and e). This is in harmony with major treaties on international humanitarian law. It fully incorporated the Hague Conventions and Regulations of 1899 and 1907, and the provisions of the

76 However, in the Norwegian proposition for ratification, it was proposed to that further legislation should be considered at a later stage and in the context of a major revision of the criminal code, *see* Det Kongelige Utenriksdepartement, St.prp. nr. 24 (1999–2000), *supra* note 30.

77 For instance, according to Article 36 of Act 530 of 24/06/2005, anybody who during armed conflict deliberately abuses or does not respect characteristics or designations reserved for people, equipment and materials designated to provide help to people who are wounded or ill shall be punished with imprisonment for life, and anybody who deliberately uses war methods or procedures contrary to an international agreement signed by Denmark or international customary law shall be punished similarly. The Danish military penal code applies to Danish military personnel, international military personnel interned in Denmark, and other people who are, according to international agreements accepted by Denmark, entitled to treatment as military personnel, *see* Article 1.

78 Status of the Protocols Additional to the Geneva Conventions of 1949 and relating to the protection of victims of armed conflicts, *supra* note 26, p. 10.

79 On the drafting of Article 8, *see* von Hebel and Robinsson, *supra* note 44, pp. 103–122.

Geneva Conventions of 1949 on grave breaches, all of which are considered to reflect international customary law. The customary law status of some norms was debated, in particular in relation to war crimes in non-international conflict, e.g. some provisions of Additional Protocol II to the Geneva Conventions. In the end, that protocol did not fully make it into the Rome Statute. However, in some aspects, Article 8 was progressive, i.e., in relation to sexual violence.[80] The horrific experience of victims in the former Yugoslavia and Rwanda, and the case-law of the criminal tribunals of the United Nations, were the driving force behind that development.

One of the highly contentious issue in Rome relating to war crimes was methods of warfare. Particularly controversial was the inclusion or non-inclusion of nuclear weapons on the list of prohibited weapons.[81] In the end, weapons of mass destruction did not make it into the Rome Statute as prohibited weapons. In connection with ratification of the Rome Statute, Sweden included a statement recalling the Advisory Opinion given by the International Court of Justice on the *Legality of the Threat or Use of Nuclear Weapons*,[82] recalling that according to the decision that there can be no doubt as to the applicability of humanitarian law to nuclear weapons.[83] No consensus was reached on the issue at the Review Conference of the Rome Statute in Kampala in 2010. Some other criticism on the convention with respect to war crimes was, however, met in Kampala. There, the state parties adopted amendments to Article 8, with respect to crimes committed in non-international conflict. The weapons which had made it to the list in Rome with respect to international conflict, were included also with respect to prohibited weapons in non-international conflict. Only Finland and Norway have ratified the amendment to Article 8 on war crimes, but ratifications by the other Nordic countries are expected.[84]

7.3 *Legislation Adopted by the Nordic Countries to Implement Article 8 of the Rome Statute*

Today, all the Nordic countries except Denmark have prepared or adopted comprehensive legislation in order to implement Article 8 of the Rome Statute in domestic law. In all instances, the legislation was enacted to implement

80 C. Steains, 'Gender Issues', in Lee (ed.), *supra* note 1, pp. 103–122. *See* also D.M. Koening and K.D. Askin, 'International Criminal Law and the International Criminal Court Statute: Crimes agains Women', in K.D. Askin and D.M. Koening (eds.), *Women and International Human Rights Law*, Volume II (Transnational Publishers, Inc., New York, 2000) p. 3.

81 *See* von Hebel and Robinsson, *supra* note 44, pp. 113–116.

82 *Legality of the Threat or Use of Nuclear Weapons*, 8 July 1996, ICJ, Advisory Opinion.

83 UNTC, Chapter XVIII, 10, Rome Statute of the International Criminal Court, Declarations and Reservations, Sweden.

84 Norway as of 16 June 2013 and Finland as of 30 December 2015.

the substantive part of Article 8, primarily in order to ensure full compliance with the complementary jurisdiction of the ICC. In some instances, all these countries adopted wider definitions of war crimes than stipulated in Article 8, primarily in three aspects. First, all the countries declined to include the phrase in paragraph 1 of Article 8, limiting war crimes to "when committed as part of a plan or policy or as a part of a large-scale commission of such crimes". All the commentaries to the bills noted that this restriction applying to war crimes did not reflect international humanitarian law and was only meant to restrict the jurisdiction of the ICC. Secondly, citing ratification of the Optional Protocol to the Convention on the Rights of the Child on the involvement of children in armed conflict, all the countries raised the age of children covered in the provision on the war crimes of conscripting or enlisting children into armed forces or using them to participate actively in hostilities (Article 8, paragraph 2, (b) (xxvi), and Article 8, paragraph 2, (e) (vii)). The Rome Statute limits this to children under the age of 15, but the Nordic countries raised this age limit to 18. Thirdly, all the countries broadened the definition of prohibited weapons, substantially largely reflecting controversial Article 8, paragraph 2, (b) (xx), which was awaiting determination in Kampala. The countries also considered criminalization of prohibited weapons applicable in a conflict of non-international character. The countries considered this necessary so as to implement their obligations under other international treaties. Furthermore, they considered that the Rome Statute did not reflect customary international law in this matter.[85]

While the provisions on genocide and crimes against humanity in the new legislations are very much alike, the new provisions on war crimes differ immensely. Iceland is the country that follows the Rome Statute to the fullest extent. Its draft provision on war crimes more or less follows the structure and definition of Article 8 of the Rome Statute, with the substantive changes listed above. According to the commentary to the bill this was done in order to ensure full compliance with the Geneva Conventions, and to give full effect to the principle of complementarity contained in the Rome Statute. This method was also considered to facilitate legal harmony with international practice.

The new Article 5 of Chapter 11 of the Finnish penal code defines and criminalizes war crimes. It is much more itemized than the earlier text. The article

85 The concern of the Nordic countries to address war crimes in non-international conflict and sexual violence is reflected in a number of statements during the negotiations, *see* e,g,, Summary records of the meetings of the Committee of the Whole, 6th Plenary meeting, para. 33 (Finland), U.N. Doc. A/CONF.183/SR.6, and 4th meeting, para. 72 (Denmark) and para. 74 (Sweden), U.N. Doc. A/CONF.183/C.1/SR.4.

is a combination of a definition of war crimes and general open references to violations of treaties and customary international law. Under the article, individuals are to be punished for war crimes for acts in violations of the Geneva Conventions and its Protocols or other international law and customs relating to war, armed conflicts and occupations; these acts are then listed in 14 items. In addition, punishment for war crimes for other acts will be imposed if they are in violation of Article 8 of the Rome Statute on war crimes, or of Finland's international obligations relating to war, armed conflict or occupation, or other recognized international law or customary law of war. As with crimes against humanity, the Finnish penal code has a separate provision on serious war crimes (if the crime is directed against a large group of people, the resulting harm is great, etc.), leading to a more severe minimum sentence.

The provisions in Norway and Sweden are similar. They define and list war crimes, but in a very concise manner. At the same time it is noted in the commentaries to the bills that notwithstanding this concise manner, the new provisions are considered to incorporate fully all the war crimes listed in Article 8 of the Rome Statute.[86] The crimes are categorized according to the nature of the crime; whether it is directed against a person or property. The provisions on war crimes do not have any general references to international law. In this way, Sweden has made a substantial departure from its earlier approach, with earlier provisions including broad references to international law. Norway still has a reference to violations of the Geneva Conventions and their Protocols in its military code.[87]

What is truly striking about the new provisions on war crimes in Finland, Norway, and Sweden is that they depart from the traditional distinction between law applicable in international armed conflict and armed conflict that is not of an international character. This distinction is firmly rooted in international humanitarian law, as is illustrated by Article 3 common to the four Geneva Conventions, Protocol II to the Geneva Conventions and Article 8 of the Rome Statute, which closely follow this distinction. However, as can be seen in the Finnish legislation on war crimes, this distinction is blurred. Article 5 of Chapter 11 of the Finnish Penal Code, refers to the Geneva Conventions and their Protocols in general and defines war crimes irrespective of whether they are committed in international armed conflict or armed conflict not of international character. Norway and Sweden erase the distinction

86 Höringsnotat, *supra* note 30, pp. 10–11; Regeringens proposition 2013/14:146, *supra* note 33, p. 77. Sweden notes also that the yardstick for the Swedish legislation is international customary law, rather than the definitions of the Rome Statute.

87 Article 108, Militær Straffelov, LOV-1902-05-22-13.

fully and define war crimes as acts in armed conflicts, and do not make any references to whether they are committed in an international armed conflict or a domestic one.[88] Certainly, the normative gap between the two types of armed conflict has decreased in the last decades, as is illustrated by Article 8 of the Rome Statute. However, full abandonment of the distinction has not yet happened at the international level, and these three Nordic countries are taking a very progressive step at the national level in this respect.[89]

8 Aggression

The crime of aggression comes under the jurisdiction of the ICC, *cf.* Article 5, paragraph 1(d), of the Rome Statute. The inclusion of the crime was highly debated, both among governments, UN officials, and non-governmental organizations.[90] In the final days of the negotiations in Rome it was agreed that

88 Sweden notes, while there is no distinction in the law, a distinction shall be made only if international customary law does not allow application to a non-international armed conflict or the crime is such that it can be committed only in an international armed conflict or during occupation; Regeringens proposition 2013/14:146, *supra* note 33, pp. 125–128.

89 One of the arguments made by Norway for this approach is the decision of the International Criminal Tribunal of the former Yugoslavia in the *Tadić* case. The government bill included the often cited quote in the case: "What is inhumane and consequently proscribed, in international wars, cannot but be inhumane and inadmissible in civil strife", *see* O.t.prp.nr.8 (2007–2008), p. 88, and Höringsnotat, *supra* note 30, p. 42. The Swedish government bill also cited the case as illustrating the development of the law, *see* Regeringens proposition 2013/14:146, *supra* note 33, p. 127. *See* ICTY, *The Prosecutor* v. *Duško Tadić aka "Dule"*, Decision on the Defence Motion for Interlocutory Appeal on Jurisdiction, Appeals Chamber, 2 October 1995, Case No. it-94-1-AR72, para. 119. For criticism of the approach of suppressing the dichotomy between norms of international armed conflict and non-international armed conflict, *see* C. Hellestveit, 'The Geneva Conventions and the dichotomy between international and non-international armed conflict: curse or blessing for the 'Geneva Co of humanity'?', in K.M. Larsen, C.G. Cooper, and G. Nystuen (eds.), *Searching for a 'Principle of Humanity' in International Humanitarian Law* (Cambridge University Press, Cambridge, 2012) p. 86.

90 Some states supportive of the establishment of the ICC, and even some major NGOs, thought that the crime should not be included at all in the statute as it risked the credibility and operation of Court. Their concern was that the definition of the crime was too contentious, too political and would involve delicate questions of national security and defense, which should be left outside of the Court. The Court should rather focus on the other remaining crimes of genocide, war crimes and crimes against humanity, *see* C. Kress and L. Holtzendorff, 'The Kampala Compromise on the Crime of Aggression', 8 *Journal of International Criminal Justice* (2010) p. 1179.

aggression should be covered by the statute, but delegates were not able to agree on the definition of the crime or the relationship between the jurisdiction of the Court and the authority and mandate of the Security Council with respect to determining threats to peace and security under Chapter VII of the Charter of the United Nations. That task was deferred to the Review Conference in Kampala, where it was successfully brought to a conclusion with the adoption of amendments on aggression.[91]

The definition adopted reflects the international condemnation of the crime and the prohibition of the use of force as one of the key principle rules of international law, enshrined in Article 2, para 4, of the Charter of the United Nations. The state act of aggression is defined using the core element of the 1974 General Assembly definition of aggression (Article 8 *bis*). A threshold clause was added; the act of aggression must constitute "by its character, gravity and scale" a "manifest violation of the Charter of the United Nations".[92] The definition sets forth the criminal act of the individual and limits the criminal responsibility to leaders. The mechanism adopted for the exercise of the jurisdiction of the Court illustrates well the compromises that had to be made. Unlike the situation with the other crimes within the jurisdiction of the Court, jurisdiction here is narrowly limited to states parties and the act must both take place on state territory and be committed by a national of the state party. Furthermore, states parties can even opt out of the jurisdiction. Regarding the relationship to the Security Council, the Court is not dependent on a determination by the Security Council of an act of aggression committed by the state concerned, but a notification period is added. As was already provided in Article 16 of the Rome Statute, the Security Council can defer an investigation or prosecution for a period of 12 months. Thirty states need to ratify the amendments on the crime of aggression in order for it to take effect. However, exercise of jurisdiction is still subject to a decision to be taken after 1 January 2017 by the same majority of states parties as is required for adoption of an amendment to the Rome Statute.

---

91 Rome Statute of the International Criminal Court, Rome 17 July 1998, Amendments to the Rome Statute of the International Criminal Court, Kampala, 11 June 2010, Adoption of amendments on the crime of aggression, Reference: C.N.651.2010.TREATIES-8. On the history of the negotiations, see P. Wrange, *Aggressionsbrottet och Internationella brottmålsdomstolen* (Totalförsvarets folkrättsråd, Försvarsdepartementet, 2011).

92 *Handbook, Ratification and Implementation of the Kampala Amendments to the Rome Statute of the ICC: Crime of Aggression, War Crimes* (Liechtenstein Institute on Self-Determination, Woodrow Wilson School of Public and International Affairs, Princeton, 2012).

The divergence among states on crime of aggression is illustrated by the fact that the Nordic countries do not yet see eye to eye on the issue. Finland was keen from the outset to include the crime of aggression in the Rome Statute. During the negotiations in Rome, Denmark, Norway and Sweden all supported its inclusion, although their enthusiasm varied.[93] The subtle approach taken by Norway is well reflected in the personal view of Ambassador Rolf Fife of Norway, commenting that *jus ad bellum* should not be developed through the back door of international criminal law.[94] During the negotiations in Kampala the states seem to have had different view on some key issues.[95] The different path taken is also reflected in the ratification of the amendment and so far only Finland and Iceland of the Nordic countries are on board. On 30 December 2015, Finland ratified the amendments on the crime of aggression and at the same time implemented it in its domestic legislation. Iceland ratified the amendments on the crime of aggression on 17 June 2016.[96] Norway only ratified the Kampala amendment with respect to war crimes and not the

93 Norway favoured limited list of crimes, *see* Summary records of the plenary meetings, 2nd plenary meeting, U.N. Doc. A/conf.183/SR.2, para. 20. Norway appreciated the efforts made by Germany to include the crime, but had doubts if agreement could be reached on the definition of the crime and jurisdiction with respect to relation with the Security Council of the United Nations, *see* Summary records of the meetings of the Committee of the Whole, 6th meeting, U.N. Doc. A/CONF.183/C.1/SR.6, para. 33. Sweden favored the inclusion of the crime of aggression, provided that it was properly defined and treated in a way that it respected the role of the Security Council, Summary records of the plenary meetings, 2nd plenary meeting, U.N. Doc. A/CONF.183/SR.2, para. 60. Denmark was very supportive of the inclusion, stating that "it would be a most unfortunate signal to the world public if the primary crime of aggression could not be included in the Statute. The Charter of the United Nations was based on the need to save succeeding generations from the scourge of war. To claim that aggression could not be included in the Statute because it had not been defined was unacceptable", *see* Summary records of the meetings of the Committee of the Whole, 27th meeting, A/CONF.183/C.1/SR.27, para. 47.

94 R. Fife, 'Criminalizing Individuals for Acts of Aggression committed by States', in M. Bergsmo (ed.), *Human Rights and Criminal Justice for the Downtrodden* (Martinus Nijhoff Publishing, Leiden, 2003) pp. 53, 70–73; *see* also this concern raised by him in Chatham House, Meeting Summary, The International Criminal Court and its Review Conference, 29 April 2010.

95 The permanent members of the Security Council insisted that the Court could not exercise its jurisdiction of the crime unless the Security Council had declared an aggression, cf. Article 39 of the Charter of the United Nations. Few states backed this position, but notable both Denmark and Norway, *see* Wrange, *supra* note 91, p. 28.

96 For the proposition for ratification, *see* Tillaga til þingsályktunar um fullgildingu breytinga á Rómarsamþykktinni um Alþjóðlega sakamáladómstólinn viðvíkjandi glæpum gegn friði, Þingskjal 1115–687. mál, Alþingi 145 löggjafarþing 2015–2016.

one on aggression. Its royal resolution on ratification notes that ratification of the later amendment will be considered when the jurisdiction of the Court has finally been decided in 2017.[97] Sweden does not foresee ratification in the near future. The 600-page Swedish bill from 2014 simply states that the ratification of the amendment with respect to aggression is under review by the ministry.[98] Similarly, Denmark has not begun on the process of ratification. At the time of writing, 30 states have ratified the amendment on the crime of aggression, including several European states such as Austria, Belgium, Croatia, Cyprus, Czech Republic, Estonia, Germany, Latvia, Liechtenstein, Luxembourg, Malta, Poland, Slovakia, Spain and Switzerland.[99]

In its implementation of provisions covering the crime of aggression, Finland followed the approach taken in Kampala. Its penal code now defines and criminalizes aggression (*cf.* Article 4a, Chapter 11, of the Finnish Penal Code). The definition of the crime is the same as in Article 8 *bis* of the Rome Statute. It defines the criminal act of the individual and limits criminal responsibility to leaders. The state act of aggression is defined using the core element of the 1974 General Assembly definition of aggression. A threshold clause is added, under which the act of aggression must constitute "by its character, gravity and scale" a "manifest violation of the Charter of the United Nations".[100] Iceland is following the same approach as Finland with respect to the implementation of provisions on the crime of aggression. As in Finland, the crime is defined exactly the same way as in the Rome Statute.

9 Entry into Force and the Question of Retroactive Applicability

One of the key questions that had to be decided in the new implementing legislations was the commencement of the application of the new provisions.

---

97 Kongelig resolusjon, Ratifikasjon af endring af 10. Juni 2010 i Artikkel 8 nr. 2 bokstav e) i Roma-vedtektene om den Internasjonale straffedomstol av 17. July 1998, 7 May, para. 3.

98 Regeringens proposition 2013/14:146, *supra* note 33, p. 54.

99 Numerous other states are in active process of ratification, *see* R.S. Clark, 'The Crime of Aggression', in C. Stahn (ed.), *The Law and Practice of the International Criminal Court* (Oxford University Press, Oxford, 2015). The European Parliament has adopted a resolution on the crime of aggression in which they reiterate its full support for the ICC and call on member states to ratify the Kampala amendment with respect to the crime of aggression, and to swiftly align national legislation with the Kampala amendments definitions, European Parliament resolution of 17 July 2014 on the crime of aggression (2014/2724(RSP)), P8 TA(2014)0013.

100 *Handbook, Ratification and Implementation of the Kampala Amendments*, *supra* note 92.

For the two countries that did not have any prior legislation on the international crimes, Norway and Iceland, this was a particularly tricky question. Would crimes such as genocide and war crimes, committed prior to the commencement of the legislation, be prosecuted under the new legislation? Both states are parties to the Geneva Conventions and are accordingly obligated to investigate and prosecute the grave breaches of the conventions. Of course, as originally intended by the states, they could prosecute some crimes under the general provisions of their criminal codes, and Norway had also a provision in its Military Code covering some war crimes. However, both states became parties to the Rome Statute of the ICC prior to enactment of the new legislation and therefore the jurisdiction of the court was active prior to that date. Also, it was perhaps a matter of more practical concern for the states, that they could prosecute individuals who were already in their own countries, escaping justice elsewhere, and even the risk of becoming safe havens for such individuals, due to weak legislation.

The legislations in Sweden and Finland took effect from the day they were adopted. Crimes committed prior to the commencement of the new provisions are to be prosecuted under the older provisions on international crimes. In both countries, a new provision on a statute of limitation should apply retroactively, although it should not apply to actions which were already covered by the statute of limitation according to the older law.

The Norwegian implementing legislation of 2008 contained a provision on retroactive applicability, *cf.* Article 3, paragraph 2, provided that the act committed was criminal according to the criminal code at the time of commission and constituted genocide, crime against humanity or war crimes according to international law. However, the penalty applied could not exceed that provided for in the general penal code at the time of commission.[101] Interestingly, this retroactive application was not considered or proposed in the first draft bill. During the legislative process, however, several actors proposed such a retroactive application, including non-governmental organizations such as the Norwegian Center for Human Rights and Norwegian Red Cross, and governmental offices like the Ministry of Foreign Affairs, the Norwegian Prosecution Authority, the National Criminal Investigation Service (Kripos), and the National Police Authority. The key arguments for retroactive application were that these acts were international crimes at the times of commission. It could be expected that prosecutions and jurisdiction in Norway would primarily consist of cases covered by universal jurisdiction. For instance,

101 As an example it is illustrated that individuals participating in the genocide in Rwanda in 1994, will be prosecuted for genocide according to the new law, but the sentencing will follow the frame provided the general penal code on murder.

there were already dozens of war criminals from the Balkan war hiding in the country. It would not be consistent to prosecute such crimes as ordinary crimes in Norway, as they would be prosecuted as international crimes before International Criminal Tribunals for the former Yugoslavia, or under other national jurisdictions. According to legal analyses by the government, retroactive application would not be in violation of Article 97 of the Norwegian Constitution stipulating the principle of non-retroactivity.[102] A precedent from the Norwegian Supreme Court was also considered to confirm this interpretation.[103] These were international crimes that Norway had long been under an obligation to prosecute, and they would otherwise have been prosecuted under general provisions of the penal code. To comply with the principle of legality the sentencing would follow parameters of relevant provisions of the general penal code, which would have applied to the conduct. This approach was also considered to be in accordance with the principle of legality and non-retroactivity as stipulated in Article 7 of the European Convention on Human rights and Article 15 of the Convention on Civil and Political Rights.

Under a legislative amendment in 2015 the retroactive application of the Norwegian law was abandoned.[104] The reason for this turnaround was a decision by the Supreme Court of Norway, which determined that the retroactivity of the law was in violation of Article 97 of the Norwegian Constitution.[105] The majority of the Court (11 judges against 6) considered that it was a violation of Article 97 of the Constitution to apply the new provisions on crimes against humanity and war crimes for conduct committed prior to the adoption of the law. According to this decision it would also be more onerous for the accused to be sentenced according to a provision describing conduct as genocide, crimes against humanity or a war crime, rather than under the general provision of the penal code.[106]

---

102 O.t.prp.nr.8 (2007–2008), Om lov om endringer i straffeloven 20. mai 2005 nr. 28 mv. (skjerpende og formildende omstendigheter, folkemord, rikets selvstendighet, terrorhandlinger, ro, orden og sikkerhet, og offentlig myndighet), *supra* note 30, pp. 62–63.

103 *Klinge-saken*, Rt. 1946, p. 198.

104 LOV-2015-06-19-65. 19 June 2015.

105 Norges Høyestrett, 03.12.2010 i sak HR-2010-2057-P – Rt-2010-1445. The case regarded prosecution of crimes committed in Bosnia-Hercegovina in 1992, prosecuted and sentenced as war crimes and crimes against humanity under the new provisions of Chapter 16 of the penal code of 2005.

106 Norges Høyestrett, 03.12.2010, HR-2010-2057-P – Rt-2010-1445, para. 106. For a critique of the judgment, *see* S. O'Connor, *War Crimes before the Norwegian Supreme Court: The Obligation to Prosecute and the Principle of Legality – An Incumbrance or Opportunity?* (Oxford Institute for Ethics, Law and Armed Conflict, 2013).

The Icelandic draft bill proposes retroactive application of the law. The legal arguments for such an effect are similar to those advanced in Norway. The offences in question could have been prosecuted under the provisions of the general penal code and were considered as international crimes at the time of commission. They constituted serious international crimes, as defined under the Genocide Convention, the Geneva Conventions and the Rome Statute, and their criminalization is foreseeable. For instance, Icelandic citizens can already be prosecuted for these crimes before international courts and various national jurisdictions. It is argued that this application of law would be in accordance with Article 69 of the Icelandic Constitution, which allows punishment for conduct if it is totally analogous to a criminal offence according to the law at the time when it was committed.[107] The application would be in accordance with Article 7 of the European Convention on Human Rights and Article 15 of the Convention on Civil and Political Rights. As in Norway, sentencing would follow the parameters of the provisions which would otherwise have been used.

10 Conclusion

The Nordic countries are keen supporters of the ICC and enforcement of international criminal law. Effective implementation is dependent on proper legislation at the national level, providing for the prosecution of serious crimes. While they were states parties to all major treaties on serious crimes prior to the commencement of the Rome Statute, the Nordic countries' legislation was fragmented, and in some cases not even in compliance with the international obligations undertaken to prosecute serious crimes. It is perhaps somewhat ironic, as the Rome Statute does not oblige its states parties to prosecute the crimes that lie within the jurisdiction of the Court, that its principle of complementarity has truly transformed legislation in the Nordic countries, as it has in many others. Today, it can be stated that the Nordic countries' legal frameworks give their national authorities the legal tools to fight impunity and to honour international commitments to do so.

The new legislations in the Nordic countries reflect a new approach to criminalization of serious crimes within the countries. The countries, apart from Denmark, now have in place comprehensive criminalization of serious crimes, whether in a separate law or a separate chapter in the domestic penal code.

107 In this sense the provision of the Icelandic Constitution is different from the Norwegian one.

Furthermore, the states chose to adopt much more clearly defined provisions than before, some even departing entirely from older provisions that relied on general references to violations of international law. Iceland and Norway abandoned their earlier approach of relying on general penal provisions. The Rome Statute and the jurisprudence of the ad hoc international criminal tribunals facilitated this development, providing more refined area of the law than before.

The Nordic states' legislations reveal how flexible their domestic systems need to be to be able to implement complex and fast-developing area of international law. Moving beyond a definition of adhering to a dualistic system, with their new implementing legislations the Nordic countries are embracing new international norms and principles into their domestic penal systems, inspired by the international criminal jurisdictions. In all systems, international terminology has been used, which calls for interpretation against other references than what would otherwise be used in the domestic system. Some provisions refer also to customary international law, reflecting how varied the relationship between international and domestic law can be in these countries.

This major undertaking within the Nordic countries contributes to a common position and strong footing in their shared international pledge for effective enforcement of international law. While remaining true to the Rome Statute in their implementing legislation, they all avoided the compromises made in Rome and strove to have their legislation reflect their international obligations and customary international law. Their broader provisions on weapons of mass destruction and child soldiers reflect that approach. And in some matters they pushed the boundaries of international law from the home front and facilitated progressive development of the law. The departure by the majority of the Nordic countries from the traditional distinction between law applicable in international armed conflict and in armed conflict that is not of international character is remarkable. In other matters, e.g. in defining what groups would be protected from the crime of genocide, they chose to remain mainstream. And the apparent hesitation of some of the Nordic countries to ratify the Kampala amendment with respect to the crime of aggression, the inclusion of which they supported in Rome, is also interesting.

The impact of the new legislations on serious crimes in the Nordic countries remains to be seen. Hopefully will the codification of the crimes at the national level have some deterrent effect. Whether the new legislations will enhance national investigation and prosecutions depends on various factors. Without doubt the relevant legal professions will need thorough education of this new domestic crimes, in order to be able to investigate them, and to successfully prosecute and adjudicate them. That expertise may also lead to more effective collaboration and cooperation with other states exercising jurisdiction over serious crimes. States' view on the need of the legislation may have changed in the fifteen years since the Rome Statute entered into force. Their concern to be able to exercise complementary jurisdiction of the Rome Statute has faded as the limited reach of the Court has dawned, it will only focus on few situations and will only focus on few primary perpetrators. At the same time, recent large-scale conflicts and atrocities have made enforcement by the states pertinent and will activate the jurisdiction of the Nordic states in various ways.

In the Line of Fire: Denmark and Law and Legitimacy in 21st Century War of Choice

Anders Henriksen

1 Introduction

After the terrorist attacks on New York and Washington, DC in September 2001, Denmark embarked upon a new foreign policy activism that included the contribution of Danish troops to a series of primarily U.S.-led operations in the Middle East, Asia and North Africa. While Danish politicians were also willing to participate militarily in international military operations in the 1990s, particularly in the Balkans, the post-9/11 military activism has been of a much more potent character. Starting with the deployment of Special Operations Forces (SOF) to Afghanistan in the weeks immediately after the 2001 attacks, Denmark sent troops to the U.S.-led invasion of Iraq and to the UN-led International Security Assistance Force (ISAF) in Helmand Province in Afghanistan. In addition, Danish F-16 fighter jets have been engaged in aerial bombardments in Afghanistan and in the UN-sanctioned "humanitarian intervention" in Libya in 2011, and since 2009 Danish frigates have been extensively involved in counter piracy operations off the Coast of Aden in East Africa. By March 2017, Denmark contributed to the UN led mission in Mali, and Danish F-16's and SOF's were deployed on a rotating basis to the counter-ISIL campaign in Iraq and Syria.[1]

Contemporary theories within the field of international relations (IR) hold that public support for participation in war are conditioned by a set of variables that often include adherence to certain norms and values.[2] Adherence to legal norms will often be among such variables and one of the characteristics of the post-9/11 Danish military activism has been the manner in which perceptions of abidance by international law has taken centre stage in the public debate. In many cases, the legitimacy required to ensure public and political support

1 For an updated overview, *see* online at http://www.fmn.dk/videnom/Pages/Internationale-operationer.aspx.

2 See, *inter alia*, the discussion in P.V. Jakobsen and J. Ringsmose, 'In Denmark, Afghanistan is worth dying for: How public support for the war was maintained in the face of mounting casualties and elusive success', 50:2 *Cooperation and Conflict* (2015) pp. 211–227.

 | DOI 10.1163/9789004343597_011

for Danish participation in war has been tied to an understanding that both the initial decision to go to war as well as the actual war fighting comply with the relevant norms in international law. The purpose of the present chapter is to explore the link between international law and legitimacy and to discuss how Denmark has coped with the increasing significance of perceptions about international law compliance. To be more precise, the chapter seeks to answer the following questions: Why has legitimacy become so intertwined with law in the armed conflicts that Denmark engages in? What are the implications for the politicians who send Danish military contributions to contemporary armed conflicts and for the armed forces whose job it is to fight the war? How have the relevant institutions dealt with the new reality?

The chapter proceeds as follows. Section 2 provides an overview of the increasing legalization of contemporary war and of the ensuing 'instrumentalization' of the law. Section 3 notes the change in the justifications for modern war and lists some of the most important implications that are associated with the tighter link between law and legitimacy. Section 4 examines how Denmark has dealt with the new reality of law and legitimacy, and Section 5 contains the conclusions.

2 The Legalization of War and the Instrumentalization of Law

The first step to understanding the contemporary link between law and legitimacy in war is to realize that international law is now a well-ingrained element in any armed conflict. Historically, of course, this has not always been the case and most people are familiar with the famous Latin saying that *inter armas silent leges* – often translated into "in times of war, the law falls silent".[3] Even after the emergence of early limitations on the conduct of war, legal norms were deemed to be of negligent importance. The most illustrative example is how international law is simply brushed aside as an abstraction in Carl von Clausewitz's seminal 1832 book *Vom Kriege* ("On War"). To the famous Prussian general, war was an act of force designed to "compel our enemy to do our will" and legal impediments were referred to as "certain self-imposed, imperceptible limitations hardly worth mentioning".[4] Today, however, as David Kennedy has demonstrated, even war is a tightly regulated affair and legal arguments

3 The phrase originates from Cicero's *Pro Milone* speech from 52 BC. More recently, Judge Antonin Scalia of the US Supreme Court referred to the phrase in his Dissenting Opinion in *Hamdi v. Rumsfeld*, 542, U.S. 597 (2004), *see Section* V of the Opinion.

4 C. von Clausewitz, in M. Howard and P. Paret, *On War* (Princeton University Press, Princeton, 1976) p. 75.

feature prominently in our political debates about war.[5] The current political discourse that surrounds both the initiation of war and the tactical decisions made in the course of the war often revolves around questions of legality.[6] This, of course, also helps to explain the extensive political attention aimed at the legality of the U.S.-led invasion of Iraq and the lawfulness of the use of force for humanitarian purposes in the absence of a mandate from the UN Security Council as well as the intense political focus on what is contained within the principle of proportionality in attack and the legal definition of 'collateral damage' in targeting.

The more we regulate war and the more our politicians talk about the law, the more we look towards law to provide the answers to the questions war raises. One of the implications has been an extensive 'instrumentalization' of law and legal arguments. Especially in American literature, the term 'lawfare' describes the use of law as a political and tactical tool in modern warfare.[7] In its current form, that term lawfare was coined in 2001 by U.S. Major General Charles J. Dunlap who adopted it to capture a "strategy of using – or misusing – law as a substitute for traditional military means to achieve a warfighting objective".[8]

5 D. Kennedy, *Of War and Law* (Princeton University Press, Princeton, 2006).

6 *Ibid.*, pp. 5–8.

7 See, *inter alia*, the collection of articles by different authors in 'Lawfare!', 43:1 *Case Western Reserve Journal of International Law* (2010). More recently, the term 'lawfare' has been used to describe what some perceive to be anti-American and anti-Israeli litigations by allegedly 'unpatriotic' human rights lawyers, see D.J.R. Frakt, 'Lawfare and Counterlawfare: The Demonization of the Gitmo Bar and Other Legal Strategies in the War on Terror', 43:1 *Case Western Reserve Journal of International Law* (2010) p. 341. In this context, mention should also be made of 'The Lawfare Project' that seeks to counter what it perceives to be "the abuse of law as a weapon of war against Western democracy", *see* http://thelawfareproject.org/mission-2/. The lawfare blog is dedicated to legal debates about how "actions taken or contemplated to protect the nation interact with the nation's laws and legal institutions". The blog notes that the name Lawfare "refers both to the use of law as a weapon of conflict and, perhaps more importantly, to the depressing reality that America remains at war with itself over the law governing its warfare with others. This latter sense of the word which is admittedly not its normal usage binds together a great deal of our work over the years". *See* https://lawfareblog.com/about-lawfare-brief-history-term-and-site.

8 C.J. Dunlap, Jr., 'Law and Military Interventions: Preserving Humanitarian Values in the 21st Century Conflicts', address at the Humanitarian Challenges in Military Intervention Conference, Carr Center for Human Rights Policy, Kennedy School of Government, Harvard University, 29 November 2001. *See also* the same author in 'Lawfare; A Decisive Element of 21st-Century Conflict?', 54:3 *Joint Forces Quarterly* (2009) p. 35; and 'Lawfare Today ... and Tomorrow', in R.A. "Pete" Pedrozo and D.P. Wollschlager (eds.), *International Law and the Changing Character of War* (Naval War College. Newport, RI, 2011) p. 315.

The most comprehensive treatment of the topic is found in a 2015 book – *Lawfare: Law as a Weapon of War* – authored by Orde F. Kittrie.[9]

According to Kittrie, lawfare has predominantly taken two forms. The first is so-called 'instrumental lawfare' whereby law is used as an instrument to achieve "the same or similar effects as those traditionally sought from conventional kinetic military action".[10] Some of Kittrie's examples of 'instrumental lawfare' include the creation of new laws that seek to curtail the acts of an adversary, such as the imposition of economic sanctions or the freezing of financial assets, the reinterpretation of existing laws to the disadvantage of an adversary, and the initiation of criminal prosecutions against the adversary.[11] Kittrie seems to omit what may well be the best example of the instrumental use of law: The George W. Bush administration's "Global War on Terror" (GWOT). As is well-known, the Bush administration (2001–2009) responded to the 11 September 2001 terrorist attacks by adopting a number of important – and controversial – legal interpretations that facilitated the subsequent American efforts to fight international terrorism.[12] In fact, one of the most important strategic decisions of the entire GWOT was a legal one. Instead of classifying the 9/11 attacks as an ordinary criminal act that triggered a traditional law enforcement approach, the lawyers in the Bush administration considered the attacks as an "act of war" that warranted the application of not just law enforcement tools but also an armed conflict legal paradigm. By so doing, the lawyers opened up a legal toolbox that granted the president immense authority to fight terrorism, including the authority to use deadly force against suspected terrorists, to resort to administrative military detention and to prosecute suspected terrorists before special military commissions.[13] The decision not to grant captured members of the Taliban and al Qaeda protection under the 1949 Geneva Conventions

9 O.F. Kittrie, *Lawfare: Law as a Weapon of War* (Oxford University Press, Oxford, 2015).

10 *Ibid.*, p. 11.

11 *Ibid.*, p. 13. *See also* the discussions and examples provided in chapters 4–6 of the book.

12 For an overview of some of the legal debates within the US administration, *see* J. Goldsmith, *The Terror Presidency: Law and Judgment Inside the Bush Administration* (W.W. Norton & Company, New York, 2009); C. Savage, *Takeover: The Return of the Imperial Presidency and the Subversion of American Democracy* (Back Bay Books, New York, 2008); J. Yoo, *War by Other Means: An Insider's Account of the War on Terror* (Atlantic Monthly Press, New York, 2006). *See also* the overview in Anders Henriksen, *Arven efter Bush, Præsidentembedet og krigen mod terror* (Gyldendal, Copenhagen, 2009).

13 One of the most important legal documents of the GWOT remains George W. Bush's *Military Order – Detention, Treatment, and Trial of Certain Non-Citizens in the War against Terrorism* (13 November 2001).

and to detain them at Guantanamo Bay and elsewhere away from American territory – and thus far from the jurisdictional reach of U.S. courts – was also an example of 'instrumental lawfare'.[14]

The second form of lawfare that Kittrie discusses is what he terms 'compliance-leverage disparity lawfare' which is "designed to gain advantage from the greater influence that law, typically the law of armed conflict, and its processes exerts over an adversary" – usually on a kinetic battlefield.[15] In practice, this form of lawfare is a sort of asymmetric warfare waged by actors against adversaries who feel more compelled to comply with the relevant laws. One of the examples provided by Kittrie is that of battlefield tactics whereby an actor, such as the Taliban in Afghanistan, makes it appear that the adversary (usually a Western state) wages war in violation of the laws of armed conflict. A more or less similar example is that of Hamas in Gaza.[16] The purpose of 'compliance-leverage disparity' tactics is two-fold. First, it seeks to cause the armed forces of the adversary to "self-impose restraint that would render them less effective", such as refraining from conducting air strikes. Secondly, 'compliance-leverage disparity' lawfare aims to erode the "public's will to fight" by creating the appearance that the war is fought in violation of the relevant international laws.[17]

The two forms of lawfare that Kittrie describes help illuminate how law may interact with politics and strategy in times of war. The concept of 'compliance-leverage disparity' lawfare is particularly relevant because it revolves around the understanding that the public will be uncomfortable with wars that are not fought in accordance with international law. Where Kittrie's work falls short, however, is in explaining *why* adherence to international law has become so important to the public's will to fight. To answer that question, we need to tie the increasing legalization of armed conflict to theories of IR and a more recent shift in strategic narratives and the justifications offered for going to war.

---

14 On the domestic scene, the Bush administration relied upon his powers as Commander in Chief under the American Constitution to initiate a number of controversial counterterrorism policies, including the surveillance of U.S. nationals, *see* the overview in Goldsmith, *supra* note 12.

15 Kittrie, *supra* note 9, p. 11.

16 *Ibid.*, pp. 283–295. *See also* S. Bilsborough, "Counterlawfare in Counterinsurgency", *Small Wars Journal* (14 December 2011), online at <http://smallwarsjournal.com/jrnl/art/why-the-counterinsurgent-cannot-follow-counterlawfare-in-counterinsurgency>.

17 Kittrie, *supra* note 9, p. 18; *see also* Dunlap, *supra* note 8, pp. 36–37; J.M. Beard, "Law and War in the Virtual Era", 103:3 *American Journal of International Law* (2009) p. 424.

3 Legitimacy in Contemporary Wars of Choice

It is a topic of debate within the study of IR how states build and maintain broad domestic support for participation in war, in particular when confronted with casualties on the battlefield.[18] The key seems to be the strategic narrative that governments design to justify and explain their decisions to initiate and continue war. For most Western states, this narrative and thus the political rationale for participating in war has undergone a fundamental change since the end of the Cold War. The traditional narrative was tied to a 'Clausewitzian' understanding of war by and large linked to that of the total war that was fought to ensure the survival of the state. In such a 'war of necessity', it is never really about *whether* you go to war but rather *how* your state survives it. Post-Cold War conflicts, however, have for the most part been 'wars of choice' where the participating states do not go to war to ensure the survival of the state but rather to promote certain greater goods. In the 21st century, war has (so far) been optional for the West. The shift from wars of necessity to wars of choice is important because it means that the strategic narrative must change accordingly. In a war of necessity, legitimacy revolves around the need to ensure the survival of the state. In a war of choice, however, the legitimacy must be derived from somewhere else and it is for that reason that values and legal norms have become increasingly important.

In many cases, in a war of choice, a successful strategic narrative takes account of both the national interest of the state as well as the values and conceptions of role already held by the elites of the state and the overall

18 The relationship between international law and international relations is a matter of increased attention in the literature, *see, inter alia*, D. Armstrong, T. Farrell and H. Lambert, *International Law and International Relations*, 2nd ed. (Cambridge University Press, Cambridge, 2012); and M. Byers (ed.), *The Role of Law in International Politics; Essays in International Relations and International Law* (Oxford University Press, Oxford, 2000). Much has been written about how legitimacy may pull states toward general compliance with their international legal obligations. For a classic work on the latter, *see* T.M. Franck, *The Power of Legitimacy among Nations* (Oxford University Press, Oxford, 1990); *see also* A. Guzman, *How International Law Works, A Rational Choice Theory* (Oxford University Press, Oxford, 2008) pp. 33–71; C. Reus-Smit, 'Politics and the international legal obligation', 9 *European Journal of International Relations* (2003) p. 591; H.H. Koh, 'Why Do Nations Obey International Law?', 1:1 *The Yale Law Journal* (1997) p. 2599. The critical view on the ability of international law to influence politics is reflected in J.L. Goldsmith and E. Posner, *The Limits of International Law* (Oxford University Press, Oxford, 2006). There has so far been little theoretical focus on what effects, if any, the adherence to international law has on political legitimacy in times of war.

population.[19] Western states – like Denmark – tend to go to war in places like Kosovo, Iraq, Afghanistan or Libya, to serve national interests and to further or uphold respect for certain international norms and values, such as the spread of democracy or the protection of fundamental human rights or the rule of law. Since there is a natural presumption that wars are fought in accordance with the norms and values that justify them, the legitimacy of contemporary wars of choice is therefore also tied to a perception that the war is 'just' and fought with due regard for moral and legal norms. In wars of choice, then, our acts are not merely judged on the basis of their functionality but also on what they say about us.

When it matters not only how the military of the Western states reaches its military objective, but also that it does so in a manner that is true to the noble cause of the war, the states become vulnerable to allegations of ill-treatment of prisoners and civilian casualties. As Jack M. Beard has noted about the latter "incidental civilian casualties ... threaten the legitimacy of these military operations on a fundamental level, especially when humanitarian motives are invoked as a basis for ... intervention".[20] The legality and morality of warfare is particularly important in wars that involve elements of so-called 'counter-insurgency' where the participating state seeks to persuade a local civilian population that what it has to offer is more appealing than that of the enemy. The war in Afghanistan, for example, gradually developed into a counterinsurgency campaign and a fight for the now infamous "hearts and minds" of the Afghan population. In such a war, to quote the 2007 U.S. Army Field Manual: "loose moral legitimacy, lose the war".[21]

We saw earlier that the Bush administration relied upon 'instrumental lawfare' and utilized law and legal interpretation as a tool in its efforts to fight international terrorism. What the Bush administration neglected to pay sufficient attention to, however, was how harmful many of the policies were to the strategic narrative and overall legitimacy of the entire counterterrorism campaign. The Abu Ghraib prisoner abuse scandal was particularly harmful

19 Jakobsen and Ringsmose, *supra* note 2, pp. 216–217.

20 Beard, *supra* note 17, p. 423.

21 U.S. Army Field Manual No. 3–24, 2007, p. 252. For classical works on counterinsurgency, *see* D. Kilcullen, *The Accidental Guerrilla: Fighting Small Wars in the Midst of a Big One* (Oxford University Press, Oxford, 2011); D. Kilcullen, *Counterinsurgency* (Hurst & Company, London, 2010); J.A. Nagl, *Learning to Eat Soup with a Knife* (University of Chicago Press, Chicago, 2002); D. Galula, *Counterinsurgency Warfare, Theory and Practice* (Praeger Security International, Santa Barbara, 1964). *See also* T.X. Hammes, *The Sling and the Stone, on War in the 21st Century* (Zenith Press, Minneapolis, 2004).

and Charles Dunlap has called the scandal the "U.S. military's most serious setback since 9/11". To Dunlap, Abu Ghraib was a "strategic military disaster" that indicated "how law has evolved to become a decisive element and – sometimes the decisive element – of contemporary conflicts".[22] He cites two well-known American scholars and notes how public support in modern popular democracies "can erode or even reverse itself rapidly, no matter how worthy the political objective, if people believe that the war is being conducted in an unfair, inhumane, or iniquitous way".[23] Following the release of the Abu Ghraib pictures, two of the editors of the American Journal of International Law similarly observed that unless U.S. counterterrorism policies "are seen by its own citizens and other nations as legitimate and in compliance with broadly accepted legal and moral standards, they will fail to gain domestic and international support".[24] In terms of military strategy, the modern emphasis on perceptions of legality and morality is about understanding the true political nature of the war and the shift in what is the primary source of strength – what Clausewitz referred to as the "center of gravity".[25] The vulnerability to accusations – whether right or wrong – that the conduct of war is illegal and immoral has in many ways become one of the centres of gravity for Western states and where the enemy will focus its effort.[26]

The Obama administration (2009–2017) had a much better understanding of how important perceptions about legality and morality are to the legitimacy of modern warfare and counterterrorism. In one of his first decisions as president, Barack Obama issued an executive order for the closure of the controversial detention center at Guantanamo Bay, Cuba. He accompanied his decision with the following statement:

> There is no question that Guantanamo set back the moral authority that is America's strongest currency in the world. Instead of building a durable framework for the struggle with al Qaeda that drew upon our deeply

22 Dunlap, *supra* note 8, p. 34.

23 *See* the citation of W.M. Reisman and C.T. Antoniou, *The Laws of War: A Comprehensive Collection of Primary Documents on International Laws Governing Armed Conflict* (Vintage Books, New York, 1994), Chapter xxiv.

24 R.B. Bilder and D.F. Vagts, 'Speaking Law to Power: Lawyers and Torture', 98:4 *American Journal of International Law* (October 2004) p. 695.

25 *See, for instance,* the reference to center of gravity in von Clausewitz, *supra* note 4, pp. 485–486.

26 *See also* W.G. Eckhardt, 'Lawyering for Uncle Sam When He Draws His Sword', 4 *Chicago Journal of International Law* (2003) p. 441; *see also* Bilsborough, *supra* note 16.

> held values and traditions, our Government was defending positions that undermined the rule of law ...[27]

Although the Obama Administration also relied upon 'instrumental lawfare' in its counterterrorism policies (most notably the program of targeted killings of suspected terrorists far from a conventional battlefield), President Obama took great strides in conveying the message that legality and legal process were core concerns to his administration.[28]

One of the best examples of how perception of adherence to law and legitimacy have become intertwined is the role law plays in Israel's decades long 'on and off' wars with its Palestinian neighbours, particularly Hamas in Gaza. The actions of the Israeli Defence Forces (IDF) are closely scrutinized by the international community, and it is clear that both Palestinians and Israelis are highly conscious of the negative effects that allegations of Israeli war crimes have on the legitimacy of Israel's wars. So while the Palestinians will go to great lengths to portray the Israelis as war criminals that show little regard for the well-being of the Palestinian civilian population, the Israelis will do their utmost to try to counter that narrative. As a former Israeli legal adviser notes:

> Obtaining the support of world public opinion is a major political objective of any state involved in an armed conflict. For tiny Israel, which sees itself as part of the democratic Western world, it can be crucial. If a state action is seen to be illegal, the state involved will invariably lose public support in the democratic world.[29]

The link between law and legitimacy in the Middle East conflict is reflected in the massive international political interest dedicated to the international legal assessments by the UN Human Rights Council (UNHRC) of alleged violations of international law by the IDF, such as the 2009 UNHRC 'Goldstone Report',[30]

---

27 The White House, *Executive Order – Review and Disposition of Individuals Detained at Guantanamo Bay Naval Base and Closure of Detention Facilities*, 22 January 2009.

28 For an insight into some of the Obama counterterrorism policies, *see* Charlie Savage, *Power Wars, Inside Obama's Post-9/11 Presidency* (Little Brown and Company, New York, 2015); D. Klaidman, *Kill of Capture: The War on Terror and the Soul of the Obama Presidency* (Houghton, Mifflin, Harcourt, New York, 2012); D.E. Sanger, *Confront and Conceal, Obama's Secret Wars and Suprising Use of American Power* (Crown Publishers, New York, 2012).

29 R. Sabel, 'The Gaza Legal Battle', *The Jerusalem Post* (8 September 2014).

30 Human Rights Council, *Report of the United Nations Fact Finding Mission on the Gaza Conflict*, A/HRC/12/48, 15 September 2009. A few years after the release of his report, Richard

the 2010 report on the 'Flotilla Incident',[31] and the report on the 2014 Gaza conflict.[32] The wars against the Palestinians have consistently degraded Israel's legitimacy in international media.[33] The realization that Israel's superior conventional military capabilities are not in themselves sufficient to secure long-term Israeli victory in the conflict against the Palestinians is reflected in Israeli political circles. As Tzipi Hotovely of the Likud Party noted in 2010:

> The stronger army is not in the best position anymore. Our strength has become a burden. Israel cannot beat the Palestinians militarily, because the world won't accept the inevitable pictures of dead children.[34]

The link between law and legitimacy has a number of important implications for Western states that participate in international military operations. As Dunlap notes, they need to conduct an effective "legal preparation of the battlespace".[35] First of all, the new reality requires that the political branches and the armed forces can deal effectively with the many legal challenges that are associated with contemporary warfare. Professional and capable legal counsel must be readily available to politicians as well as the armed services on the battlefield, and there is no way around the fact that lawyers become increasingly important. In theory, of course, the legal preparation must begin with the presentation of a convincing legal case for the intended armed action.[36] Troops and pilots must also be sufficiently educated and trained in the application of the laws of armed conflict before they are deployed.[37]

Equally important is the ability of the state to skilfully communicate with the public and constantly be able to leave a credible impression that it takes its

---

Goldstone apparently felt the need to offer some more nuance to his conclusions, *see* R. Goldstone, 'Reconsidering the Goldstone Report on Israel and war crimes', *The Washington Post* (2 April 2011).

31 Human Rights Council, *Report of the International Fact-Finding Mission to Investigate Violations of International Law, Including Humanitarian Law and Human Rights Law, Resulting from the Israeli Attack on the Flotilla of Ships Carrying Humanitarian Assistance*, A/HRC/15/21, 27 September 2010.

32 Human Rights Council, *Report of the Detailed Findings of the Independent Commission of Inquiry Established Pursuant to Human Rights Council Resolution S-21/1*, A/HRC/29/52, 24 June 2015.

33 *See also* Bilsborough, *supra* note 16.

34 G. Hoffmann, 'Meanwhile, On the Right ...', *The Jerusalem Post* (3 September 2010).

35 Dunlap, *supra* note 8, p. 37.

36 *See also* Bilsborough, *supra* note 16.

37 Dunlap, *supra* note 8, p. 37.

legal responsibilities seriously. It is not enough that the public hears politicians say that legal commitments are important. It must see it. The public must be reassured that the armed forces do their utmost to avoid breaches of international law, and that any credible suspicion of foul play or immoral behaviour on the part of the members of the armed forces is dutifully investigated. An example of skilful communication was the decision by President Obama to be very public about the decision-making processes in the American drone program for targeted killings of suspected terrorists. The President was well aware that the program was controversial and posed a potential threat to the legitimacy of his counterterrorism policies. He therefore made a significant effort to inform the public of the elaborate procedure for authorizing drone strikes which included that he personally approve of all individual strikes.[38] In July 2016, Obama also published an Executive Order laying out the different pre- and post-strike measures that the U.S. takes to avoid excessive civilian casualties in U.S. operations.[39]

The policies adopted by the Israeli government in response to the widespread criticism of its military operations provide another example of effective public communication. Since the war in Gaza in 2008–09, the Israeli government seems to have taken a number of initiatives intended to both minimize civilian casualties and to show to the outside world that Israel does its utmost to comply with its international legal obligations. Aside from the establishment of a special office for handling all proceedings against Israel and Israeli soldiers or officials,[40] the IDF claims that it tries to avoid excessive civilian casualties by warning civilians who may find themselves in harm's way ahead of a planned military strike. These apparent warnings take the form of leaflets, phone calls or text messages to members of the civilian population. Another tactic seems to be the so-called 'knocking on the roof' tactic whereby the IDF fires blank ammunition on a house in an attempt to warn the inhabitants that it is about to be targeted by live ammunition.[41] In the current counter-ISIL campaign, the U.S. military has tried to replicate this technique in air strikes in Iraq.[42] The Israelis have also sought to engage with the public in an effort to explain what

38 J. Becker and S. Shane, 'Secret 'Kill List' Test Obama's Principles', *The New York Times* (29 May 2012).

39 The White House, *Executive Order – United States Policy on Pre- and Post-Strike Measures to Address Civilian Casualties in U.S. Operations Involving the Use of Force*, 1 July 2016.

40 *See* the overview in Kittrie, *supra* note 9, pp. 269–270.

41 Kittrie, *supra* note 9, p. 297; *see also* A. Whitnall, 'Israel-Gaza conflict: Israeli 'knock on roof' missile warning revealed in remarkable video', *Independent.co.uk* (13 July 2014).

42 A. Taylor, 'Israel's controversial 'roof knocking' tactic appears in Iraq. And this time, it's the U.S. doing it', *The Washington Post* (27 April 2016).

they perceive to be the correct interpretation of international law. In addition, Israel has expanded the role legal advisors play in the targeting process in the military, improved the investigations of alleged violations by Israeli soldiers of the laws of armed conflict, and embarked upon a major media campaign to explain how the IDF makes its decisions to target a military objective. To that end, the individual units now document – through the use of photographers or cameras mounted on fighter jets, helicopters or gunships – the circumstances surrounding each strike.[43]

The Israeli policies illustrate how perceptions about law compliance are not just something the enemy can use against a militarily superior state, but something that all parties to a conflict can resort to, in particular in wars where it is important to remain legitimate in the eyes of the local population.[44] It is, in other words, "a resource that democratic militaries can – and should – employ affirmatively".[45]

An additional requirement brought about by the increasing link between the legitimacy of the war and the manner in which it is conducted is tight civil/ political control over the military. When operational decisions about whether or not to move forward with a potential strike on a target can impact the legitimacy of the entire war, politicians must ensure that the conduct of the armed forces remains within the boundaries of what is not only legally, but also politically acceptable. If, for instance, civilian casualties are deemed to be very harmful to the strategic narrative and the legitimacy of the war – as was the case in Afghanistan – the politicians must ensure that this is reflected in the relevant Rules of Engagement (RoE). The 1 July 2016 Executive Order by President Obama on measures to address civilian casualties in U.S. operations opens up by noting how the

> protection of civilians is fundamentally consistent with the effective, efficient, and decisive use of force in pursuit of U.S. national interests. Minimizing civilian casualties can further mission objectives; help maintain the support of partner governments and vulnerable populations, especially in the conduct of counterterrorism and counterinsurgency operations; and enhance the legitimacy and sustainability of U.S. operations critical to our national security. As a matter of policy, the United States therefore routinely imposes certain heightened policy standards that are

43 *See* the overview in Kittrie, *supra* note 9, pp. 298–305.

44 Dunlap, *supra* note 8, p. 38.

45 *See also* Bilsborough, *supra* note 16.

> more protective than the requirements of the law of armed conflict that relate to the protection of civilians.[46]

In the counter-ISIL campaign in Iraq and Syria, the Obama-administration introduced very strict guidelines for when air strikes could be conducted. When explaining the operational limitations, a spokesman for the U.S. Joint Chiefs of Staff in 2015 noted: "How we conduct ourselves in warfare against a terrorist enemy intermingled within the society that they have infiltrated will have profound impacts on the way in which the U.S. is viewed in the Middle East and in this campaign".[47] While strict RoE's may be a cause of frustration for members of the armed forces,[48] the military needs to understand the different strategic landscape and how consequential their conduct – lawful as it may be – can be on the overall legitimacy of the war.

At the time of writing (March 2017), it is too early to tell what effect (if any) the election of Donald J. Trump as the 45th President of the United States of America will have on the legitimacy and thus public support for the war against ISIL and potential future wars the United States may become involved in. During his presidential campaign, Trump indicated a willingness to allow for more civilian casualties in the military campaign against ISIL[49] and to consider the use of torture against suspected terrorists.[50] If introduced, such policies are likely to have a substantial negative effect on the overall legitimacy of the American counter-terrorism campaign.

4 The Danish Experience

The link between legitimacy and legality is particularly relevant to a small state like Denmark that has historically sought to strengthen international respect for international norms. Peter Viggo Jacobsen and Jens Ringsmose have argued that public support for a costly war, such as the war in Afghanistan, requires that the Danish government creates a coherent narrative that link Denmark's

46 The White House, *Executive Order*, 1 July 2016, *supra* note 39.

47 K. Wong, 'US aim for 'zero civilian casualties' draws criticism', *The Hill* (24 June 2015).

48 *Ibid. See also* E. Schmitt, 'U.S. Caution in Strikes Gives ISIS an Edge, Many Iraqis Say', *The New York Times* (26 May 2015).

49 *See, for example*, A. Ross, 'Donald Trump Says He'd 'Take Out' Terrorists' Families', *Time Magazine* (2 December 2015).

50 *See, inter alia*, A. Server, 'Can Trump Bring Back Torture?', *The Atlantic* (26 January 2017), online at <https://www.theatlantic.com/politics/archive/2017/01/trump-torture/514463/>.

national interests with its commonly accepted ideas and values. Clearly, then, adherence to legal norms is also of importance to maintaining public support for wars in Denmark. In the remainder of the chapter we shall see how Denmark approached the ever-closer link between international law and legitimacy in the post-9/11 wars.

The first observation is that the new military activism clearly challenged the existing institutions and their capabilities to deliver the legal advice that was required almost overnight. As the head of legal affairs in the Danish Ministry of Foreign Affairs noted in 2016, the post-9/11 military activism required a fair bit of 'catching up' on parts of international law – most notably the laws of armed conflict – that had up until that point been fairly underdeveloped in Denmark.[51] But things improved as time passed. The relevant institutions learned from their experiences, and Denmark began to actively try to move the development of the law in a direction that was deemed to be in accordance with longer-term Danish interests.[52] By so doing, the Danish government not only signalled that the fulfilment of international obligations was a core priority; it also sought to preempt any harm that would be done to the strategic narrative that had been built to justify Denmark's wars.

The best example of how Denmark sought to engage with international law in a strategic manner may be the so-called 'Copenhagen Process on the Handling of Detainees in International Military Operations' that was initiated in 2007 in an effort to reach agreement on a set of non-binding criteria for the treatment of individuals detained in 'internationalized' non-international armed conflicts and in peace operations.[53] Reference must also be made to the efforts Denmark has made to work towards the establishment of a *right* to humanitarian intervention in the absence of a resolution from the United Nations Security Council. The Danish government has apparently reached the conclusion that Denmark's long term strategic interests are served by the

---

51 T.E. Rehfeldt, 'Dansk udenrigspolitisk aktivisme og udviklingen af den humanitære folkeret – danske strategier på det folkeretlige område', in P.V. Kessing and A. Laursen (eds.), *Robust Mandat – juridiske udfordringer ved danske militære missioner i det 21. århundrede* (Jurist- og Økonomforbundets Forlag, Copenhagen, 2016) p. 47.

52 For an overview, *see ibid.*, p. 52–57; *see also* T. Winkler, 'Udenrigsministeriets folkeretsrådgiver: aktuelle spørgsmål – med danske fingeraftryk', in Jens Hartig Danielsen (ed.), *Max Sørensen 100 år* (Jurist- og Økonomforbundets Forlag, Copenhagen, 2013) pp. 179–199.

53 *See*, 'The Copenhagen Process on the Handling of Detainess in International Military Operations' (2013). <http://um.dk/en/politics-and-diplomacy/copenhagen-process-on-the-handling-of-detainees-in-international-military-operations/>; *see also* T. Winkler, 'The Copenhagen Process on Detainees: A Necessity', 78 *Nordic Journal on International Law* (2010) pp. 489–498.

introduction of another exception to the overall ban on the use of force in Article 2(4) of the UN Charter. Hence, Denmark is one of only three states which have publicly argued for the existence of a right to humanitarian intervention without a UN mandate.[54] Other examples of a 'pro-active' Danish effort to influence the creation of relevant parts of international law include the consistent work done in relation to counter-piracy[55] and the operationalization of the Responsibility to Protect (R2P) doctrine.[56]

But while Denmark's efforts to influence the future direction of the law have been noteworthy for a country of its size, it is also fair to say that it took some time for the responsible institutions, and in particular for the armed forces, to understand how the legitimacy of the political decision to contribute to international military operations interacts with the perception that the military did their utmost to ensure that Denmark complied with its international legal obligations. The point here is *not* that Danish soldiers in Iraq or Afghanistan generally disregarded their international obligations. In fact, it is highly commendable that after more than 15 years of more or less constant deployment to very complicated battlefields there has yet to be case where a Danish soldier has been found guilty of violating Denmark's obligations under international law, including the laws of armed conflict. This is more than the U.S. and U.K. can claim. Instead, the problem appears to have been a lack of preparation for the many novel legal questions that arose in the course of the military operations to which Danish forces were deployed. The insufficient preparation in turn led to a stream of cases questioning the extent to which the relevant decision makers took Denmark's international obligations seriously. As a result, the overall legitimacy of the Danish military activism was damaged, at least in some circles.

As it turned out, the biggest challenge was the proper handling of detainees captured in the course of military operations. Like other participating states, Denmark struggled to ascertain what legal rights detainees were entitled to in the armed conflicts in states like Iraq and Afghanistan.[57] Detention issues

54 Danish Ministry of Foreign Affairs, 'General Principled Considerations on the Legal Basis for a Possible Military Operation in Syria' (my translation), (UPN, Alm.del. Bilag 298, 30 August 2013).

55 For a brief overview, *see* Winkler, *supra* note 52, pp. 194–198.

56 See Rehfeldt, *supra* note 51, pp. 54–56.

57 The task was not made easier by the simultaneous developments in the case-law of the European Court of Human Rights in the 2000s and the early part of the 2010s relating to the extraterritorial application of the European Convention on Human Rights. For relevant practice, *see* from ECtHR, Strasbourg: *Bankovic and Others* v. *Belgium and Others*, Case No. 52207/99 paras. 67–81; *Issa* v. *Turkey*, Case No. 31821/96, 16 November 2004, paras.

were a cause of concern from the very beginning of the post-9/11 Danish military activism. In 2006, a Danish documentary alleged that Danish SOF's deployed to Afghanistan in the winter of 2001/2002 had handed over a group of Afghan detainees to U.S. forces even though the Danish government was aware that there was a risk that the Afghans would be abused and ill-treated in U.S. custody.[58] In January 2002, the Danish Government had received information that the American Government was not willing to grant protection under the 1949 Geneva Conventions to individuals in detention.[59] This posed a problem because Denmark was required by the Third Geneva Convention on the protection of prisoners of war to only transfer detainees to another state after it "has satisfied itself of the willingness and ability" of the receiving state "to apply the Convention".[60] In 2013, the Danish Supreme Court concluded that the Danish Government neither could have known nor ought to have known that the transfer of the Afghanis to the U.S. in 2002 was associated with a risk of ill-treatment in custody.[61] What is of interest for present purposes was that

---

71, 74–75; *Ocalan* v *Turkey*, Case No. 64221/99 12 March 2003, para. 93; *Pad and Others* v. *Turkey*, Case No. 60167/00 28 June 2007, paras. 53–54; *Medvedyev and Others* v. *France*, Case No. 3394/03 10 July 2008, paras. 64–67; *Al-Skeini et al.* v. *the United Kingdom*, Appl. No. 55721/07, 7 July 2011; *Jaloud* v. *the Netherlands*, Appl. No. *47708/08*, 20 November 2014; and *Hassan* v. *the United Kingdom*, Appl. No. 29750/09, 16 September 2014. For the contentious issue of attribution of conduct to international organizations, *see Behrami and Behrami* v. *France*, Appl. No. 71412/01; and *Saramati* v. *France, Germany and Norway*, application No. 78166/01, GC – admissibility, 2 May 2007, paras. 57–61; and *Case of Al-Jedda* v. *The United Kingdom*, Appl. 27021/08, Judgment (GC), 7 July 2011, paras. 83–84.

58 The documentary 'Den Hemmelige Krig' ('The Secret War') was directed by C. Guldbrandsen and aired on 4 December 2006. The response from the Danish Ministry of Defense is available at Forsvarsministeriet, 'Redegørelse for faktuelle og retlige spørgsmål i tilknytning til danske styrkers tilbageholdelse og overladelse af personer i Afghanistan i 1. halvår 2002', 13 December 2006. A critical assessment of the Danish military contribution to the US-led war in Afghanistan is available in J.E. Rytter, 'With eyes shut, Denmark alongside of the US fights terrorism in Afghanistan', in R.F. Jørgensen and K. Slavensky (eds.), *Implementing Human Rights, Essays in Honour of Morten Kjærum* (The Danish Institute for Human Rights, Copenhagen, 2007) pp. 405–432.

59 *See, inter alia*, The White House, *Military Order – Detention, Treatment, and Trial of Certain Non-Citizens in the War Against Terrorism*, 13 November 2001; and The White House, *Memorandum for: The Vice President et al., SUBJECT: Human Treatment of Taliban and al Qaeda Detainees*, 7 February 2002.

60 GC III, Art. 12. A decision to transfer a detainee to another state may also raise issues under international human rights law, in particular under Art. 3 of the European Convention on Human Rights, *see, inter alia*, the analysis in A. Henriksen, *Refoulement in Afghanistan* (Danish Institute for Military Studies, Copenhagen, 2008).

61 *See* the decision by the Supreme Court in case 180/2011, 27 June 2013.

the court proceedings showed that the Danish Armed Forces and the Ministry of Defence were not at the time certain if the transfer of detainees to the Americans was in compliance with Denmark's international obligations, and that they therefore did not know what guidance they should give to the SOF in the field. When the detainees were brought into Danish custody, no one had considered what to do with them, and when the commander of the SOF brought his concerns about the manner detainees were treated in U.S. custody to his superiors in Copenhagen, he did not receive any useful legal guidance.

A somewhat similar situation arose in Iraq where Denmark had deployed a battalion of soldiers to the U.K. controlled area around Basra. In the summer of 2004, the Danish Minister of Defence withdrew the top officers of the Danish battalion due to a suspicion that an intelligence officer – Annemette Hommel – had subjected Iraqi detainees to humiliating interrogations. Although Hommel was later acquitted of charges of violating the Geneva Conventions, the case was another example of insufficient legal preparation. Like in Afghanistan in 2002, the soldiers and officers in the field were left without proper legal instructions on how to treat detainees.[62] The allegations of inhuman treatment of detainees in the *Hommel* case arose a few months after the Abu Ghraib scandal, and the Danish politicians were well aware of how vulnerable the legitimacy of the war was to allegations of war crimes, and how important it was for them to send the message that they took allegations of ill-treatment very seriously. The legitimacy of the Danish participation in the war in Iraq was already very strained due to strong political opposition to the war in the Danish Parliament. The Hommel-case made the politicians so concerned with potential allegations of ill-treatment of detainees that they did everything in their power to distance themselves from the issue. The result was that the relevant institutions began to adopt 'instrumental lawfare' to avoid any allegations of ill-treatment.[63] One of the 'legal tools' was the introduction of a policy in Iraq whereby Danish forces were ordered to completely desist from taking individuals into their physical custody when they were on joint operations with British and/or Iraqi forces. By adopting a creative interpretation of the international rules on state responsibility, the armed forces concluded that Denmark could avoid legal responsibility if they ensured that Iraqi or British servicemen and not Danish soldiers carried out the physical act of arresting and handcuffing individuals. This so-called 'British trick' ensured that Danish

62 *See also* the overview in A. Henriksen, 'Jura som strategi og Danmark i krig', in K.S. Kristensen (ed.), *Danmark i krig; Demokrati, politik og strategi i den militære aktivisme* (Jurist- og Økonomforbundets Forlag, Copenhagen, 2013) p. 145.

63 *See also* A. Henriksen, 'Fanger, folkeret og brite-finter', 1 *Økonomi & Politik* (2014) pp. 9–11.

soldiers could participate in military operations without ending up with the legal responsibility for the treatment of individuals brought into detention.[64]

In Afghanistan, the Danish government also introduced 'diplomatic assurances' to enable the transfer of detainees to the local Afghan authorities without violating Denmark's international obligations. The transfer of detainees to a state like Afghanistan may raise issues under the prohibition on the transfer to a risk of ill-treatment contained in human rights law.[65] The Danish government sought to avoid concerns about ill-treatment by conditioning the transfer of detainees to the Afghan authorities on the existence of a written agreement between the Danish government and Afghanistan on the minimum treatment of any individuals that would be transferred from the Danish forces to the Afghan authorities.[66] In a 2005 Memorandum of Understanding (MoU) between Denmark and Afghanistan, the latter promises to "observe applicable national law … and international law pertaining to the treatment and transfer of persons from the military forces of Denmark to Afghan authorities"[67] and not to subject any such person to the death penalty.[68] While the MoU did pave the way for the transfer of a number of detainees from Danish to Afghan custody, the Danish government suspended transfers in 2012 after allegations of ill-treatment of detainees in Afghan custody. As a result of the suspension of transfer, the Danish armed forces had to detain an individual for nearly seven months until it was possible to find an Afghan prison to which the detainee could be transferred in compliance with Denmark's human rights obligations.[69]

The military operations in Afghanistan and Iraq tested lawyers and legal advisors in the relevant institutions in Denmark, most notably in the armed services. Over the years, however, progress has been made and it now appears that the most important lessons have been learned. A notable contribution to the future 'preparation of the battlespace' was the release in 2016 in the form of the

64 Letter of 16 December 2011 from the Danish Chief of Defense to Det Udenrigspolitiske Nævn, Forsvarsudvalget, 2011–12, FOU alm del Bilag 43. *See also* the overview in *ibid.*, pp. 9–10.

65 For a discussion, *see* Henriksen, *supra* note 60.

66 *Ibid.*

67 *Memorandum of Understanding between the Ministry of Defense of the Islamic Republic of Afghanistan and the Ministry of Defense of Denmark concerning the transfer of persons between the Danish Contingent of the International Security Assistance force and Afghan authorities*, 8 June 2005. *See also Amendment to the Memorandum of Understanding*, 1 May 2007, *see* Art. 1.

68 *Ibid.*, Art. 7.

69 *See* the overview in Henriksen, *supra* note 63 pp. 10–11.

first ever Danish Military Manual.[70] While the Manual is unlikely to provide all the legal answers to the many questions that will emerge in future armed conflicts, it does set out a basis from which more detailed legal guidance can be made. Another sign of improvement was the decision of the Danish Government to establish a special high-level inter-governmental "task force" to offer legal guidance to the Danish SOF currently deployed to the campaign against ISIL in Iraq and Syria.[71] The taskforce has been given the dubious task of issuing legal guidance if and when forces end up taking individuals into custody. The creation of the taskforce is interesting because it illustrates many of the lessons the armed forces have had to learn over the years. First, it illustrates that the relevant authorities now understand the importance of preparing *in advance* for what Danish soldiers may face on the ground in places like Iraq and Syria. Second, it seeks to ensure that potentially very complicated legal issues with important political implications are dealt with by legal advisors close to those politicians who have made the decision to deploy the forces, and not merely by a legal advisor on the ground in Iraq or Syria. Third, and most interesting for present purposes, the establishment of the task force sends an important signal to the public that the relevant decision-makers care about Denmark's international legal obligations and that adherence to international law is a key priority.

There is, however, still room for improvement. Among other things, Denmark is not very engaged in the public relations domain and does very little to try to engage with the perceptions about the extent to which it adheres to international law in times of armed conflict. Accusations of violations of international law are still something the Danish Armed Services defend themselves *against* and not something they leverage against their opponent. Few efforts are made to explain exactly how careful the armed forces actually are to avoid civilian casualties. There is also a shortage of information on how often the enemy – whether the Taliban or ISIL – violates basic legal and moral norms. Since 'playing by the book' is generally an essential part of the strategic narrative for participating in war in Denmark, this is somewhat surprising.

A brief reference must also be made to the prospect of Denmark's participation in future wars under President Trump. As noted previously, we do not yet know how Trump will conduct American wars, but his campaign statements do not bode well for the U.S.' intention to abide by international law under

70 Danish Ministry of Defence, *Militærmanual om folkeret for danske væbnede styrker i internationale militære operationer*, September 2016. The manual is in the process of being translated into English.

71 *See* Folketingsbeslutning B 108, 29 March 2016, *see* p. 3.

his presidency. In practice, the legitimacy costs that will be associated with potential American violations of international law will in all likelihood not just tarnish the U.S. but to some extent also those states that decide to participate in Trump's wars. The election of Donald J. Trump as the 45th President of the United States may therefore also raise profound questions about the continued viability of Denmark's policy of military activism and military contributions to America's wars.

5 Conclusion

Like other Western states participating in 21st century 'wars of choice', Denmark has had to learn the hard way how closely linked law and legitimacy have become in contemporary warfare. The Danish authorities were forced to come to terms with the reality that that the strategic narratives created to ensure public support for war requires that the war is fought with due regard to the norms of international law. Law is (no longer) a mere distraction in war. Law is something that must be managed professionally as well as communicated effectively.

On a final note, a word of caution is in order. The extensive 'legalization' of war and the tendency to link law and legitimacy in the strategic narratives come with a risk that our societal discussions about war become completely dominated by law. The fact remains, however, that war is not just a legal affair. It is also – if not primarily – an ethical, moral, political and strategic affair. When the public discourse about the initiation of war or the acceptance of civilian casualties is almost exclusively focused on the proper legal interpretation of a provision in a resolution from the UN Security Council or the legal determination of what constitutes 'excessive collateral damage' in the Geneva Conventions, less attention will inadvertently be turned to important non-legal considerations. So while our policy-makers must ensure that their lawyers conduct a proper "legal preparation of the battlefield", they must also be aware that law cannot always provide a satisfactory answer to all the tough questions that arise in times of war. Legal analysis is no substitute for strategic and political analysis, and our politicians must ensure that society relates to war in a manner that takes account of all relevant considerations.[72]

72 *See also* Henriksen, *supra* note 62, pp. 147–148.

Communities of Interest in the Nordic Management of International Watercourses

Julie Gjørtz Howden

1 Introduction

An international watercourse is a "system of surface waters and groundwaters constituting by virtue of their physical relationship a unitary whole and normally floating into a common terminus", while crossing the border of two or more states.[1] Today there are 276 such international watercourses in the world, and 148 states have their territory within one or more international basins.[2] Strong and efficient transboundary cooperation over these vulnerable resources is crucial to secure sustainable management and avoid regional water scarcity. In contrast to the popular and media friendly scenario of 'water wars', state practice shows that international watercourses are, in most cases, sources of cooperation rather than conflict and that states continue to adopt bilateral, regional or international instruments to regulate the utilisation and management of their shared resources.

One such regulatory instrument is the EU Water Framework Directive (WFD), of which Article 3–3 compels the member states to "ensure that a river basin covering the territory of more than one Member State is assigned to an international river basin district". To meet this requirement, Norway and Finland created the Finnish-Norwegian River Basin District in 2013.[3] The District is composed by the river basins Tana, Pasvik, Neiden and Munkelv with their respective tributaries, and is administered by the regional authorities on each side of the border, who are in charge of making water management plans for their respective areas and to coordinate their plans in accordance with an

---

1 The United Nations Convention on the Law of the Non-navigational Uses of International Watercourses, 1997, Article 2.

2 United Nations Water Statistics, <www.unwater.org/statistics/thematic-factsheets/en/>, visited on 8 June 2015.

3 The Agreement can be found in Norwegian and Finnish at <www.vannportalen.no/globalassets/vannregioner/norsk-finsk/norsk-finsk---dokumenter/samarbeidsavtale-norge-finland-signert.pdf>, visited on 8 May 2015.

 | DOI 10.1163/9789004343597_012

established procedure.[4] There are, however, ambitions of producing common water management plans at a later stage that will address *inter alia* the issues of "common environmental objectives, significant water management issues [and] coordinated monitoring programmes".[5]

At first glance, the organization in the Finnish-Norwegian River Basin District seems much less committing than the pioneering Finnish Swedish Frontier Rivers Commission (FSFRC), established in 1971.[6] This latter Commission executed a wide range of functions relating to the general management and protection of the two states' frontier waters; it could function both as a judicial and administrative organ, which is quite an extraordinary arrangement for an international organisation in international practice.[7] In 2010, the FSFRC was replaced by a new agreement that brought significant changes to the old regime by removing much of the Commission's decisive power, and reducing it to an advisory committee to assist the governments in matters relating to the frontier waters.[8] Nevertheless, the early FSFRC's work and practice was innovative of its kind, and an important point of reference when examining Nordic approaches to international freshwater cooperation.

The former FSFRC shared several attributes with the community of interest doctrine in international water law. This approach to international water management was introduced by the Permanent Court of International Justice (PCIJ) in the *River Oder* case (1929). The main question before the Court was whether the jurisdiction of the river's administrative organ – the International Joint Commission – covered only the main channel of the river and its *international* tributaries, or also included tributaries that were situated exclusively on the territory of one state. In its reasoning, the Court concluded that the solution had to be sought "not in the idea of a right to passage for upstream

4 "Memorandum of Understanding pursuant to the Agreement on the Norwegian-Finnish River Basin District", <www.vannportalen.no/globalassets/vannregioner/norsk-finsk/norsk-finsk---dokumenter/memorandum-of-understanding-l125281.pdf>, visited on 8 May 2015.

5 *Ibid.*, Article 9; *supra* note 3, Article 4-4.

6 The Frontier Rivers Agreement of 16 September 1971 between Finland and Sweden, <http://gis.nacse.org/tfdd/tfdddocs/340ENG.pdf>, visited on 8 March 2016.

7 M. Fitzmaurice, 'The Sámi People: Current Issues Facing an Indigenous People in the Nordic Region', 8 *The Finnish Yearbook of International Law* (1997) p. 202.

8 J.G. Howden, 'Reconciling Sovereignty with Supranationality: Selected Cooperative Regimes', in T.Tvedt, O. McIntyre, and Tadesse Kassa Woldetsadik (eds.), *A History of Water, Series 3 volume 2: Sovereignty and International Water Law* (I.B. Tauris, London, 2015).

States, but in that of a community of interest of riparian States".[9] The Court explained the community of interest in a navigable river as "the basis of a common legal right, the essential features of which are the perfect equality of all riparian States in the user of the whole course of the river and the exclusion of any preferential privilege of any one riparian State in relation to the others".[10] The International Court of Justice has later endorsed this approach in the *Gabčikovo-Nagymaros* case and in the *Pulp Mills* case,[11] and it has been frequently analysed and debated in legal theory.[12]

In essence, the community of interest approach encourages states to conceive their shared watercourse as one single unit to be managed in common by all the states. The approach builds on a conception of common management, and is given concrete expression in a number of international agreements.[13] Managing an international watercourse in accordance with the principles of the community of interest approach can represent quite a challenge for state sovereignty as it summons the watercourse states to enter into a more committing cooperation with focus on common interests rather than on sovereign entitlements.

Although the community of interest approach is not particularly Nordic per se, its common history and development makes the Nordic region quite suitable for this kind of common management. Moreover, the community of interest approach is constructed of trust, solidarity and sense of community – values that have been characteristic for Nordic water cooperation and the Nordic approach to international law. This chapter will conduct a systematic analysis of some important aspects of the Finnish-Norwegian River Basin District in comparison with the main characteristics of the community of interest approach in order to see if, how and why the Finnish-Norwegian cooperation

9 *Case Relating to the Territorial Jurisdiction of the International Commission of the River Oder*, 10 September 1929, PCIJ, p. 27, <www.icj-cij.org/pcij/serie_A/A_23/74_Commission_internationale_de_l_Oder_Arret.pdf>, visited on 21 March 2016.

10 *Ibid.*

11 *See Case concerning the Gabcikovo-Nagymaros Project*, 25 September 1997, ICJ, </www.icj-cij.org/docket/files/92/7375.pdf>, visited on 21 March 2016; *Case Concerning Pulp Mills on the River Uruguay*, 20 April 2010, ICJ, <www.icj-cij.org/docket/files/135/15877.pdf>, visited on 21 March 2016.

12 *See e.g.* S. McCaffrey, *The Law of International Watercourses* (Oxford University Press, Oxford, 2007); O. McIntyre, *Environmental Protection of International Watercourses under International Law* (Ashgate, Aldershot, 2007); F.R. Loures, 'History and Status of the Community-of-Interest doctrine', in Tvedt *et al.* (eds.), *supra* note 8; L. Boisson de Chazournes, *Freshwater in International Law* (Oxford University Press, Oxford, 2013).

13 McCaffrey, *ibid.*, p.155.

should take steps towards more committing management. The backdrop for this analysis is the earlier Finnish-Swedish Frontier Rivers Cooperation and the value of water cooperation in the Nordic countries.

2 Components of the Finnish-Norwegian River Basin District

2.1 *The Area*

The Finnish-Norwegian River Basin District encapsulates a geographic area of interconnected land and freshwater resources. It covers the catchment areas of the watercourses Tana, Leiden, Munkelv and Pasvik, as well as the upper tributaries to the Tuloma River, a total area of 48,000 km^2 of which approximately two thirds are on Finnish territory.[14] The first three rivers flow on Norwegian and Finnish territory and into the Barents Sea, while the latter two also flow into Russian territory. With the exception of the Russian frontier, the delimitation of the River Basin District follows the natural periphery of the catchment area instead of the political border drawn across them.

In comparison, the area of management for the earlier FSFRC comprised a number of individual rivers and lakes that crossed the border between the two states.[15] The same rules and policy, and the same managing institution were thus governing these areas concurrently. Although many of these watercourses were interconnected, the FSFRC did not operate within one integrated basin district, as is the case in the Finnish-Norwegian cooperation. Nevertheless, application of the same rules and principles to partly interconnected watercourses in the same area secured the stability of management and the predictability for the users and stakeholders.

The unity of the watercourse or watercourses is also one of the characteristics of the community of interest approach. In the *River Oder* case, the PCIJ expressed that the essential features of a community of interest were the perfect equality of all riparian states in "the user of the whole course of the river".[16] In addition to securing the equality of the involved watercourse

14 'Roof Report: Overordnet kapittel for den regionale vannforvaltningsplan for Finnmark vannregion og grensevassdragene', Finnmark Fylkeskommune and Klima- og Miljødepartementet, p. 5, <vannportalen.no/globalassets/vannregioner/finnmark/finnmark---plandokumenter/plandokumenter-2016-2021/forvaltningsplan-og-tiltaksprogram-2016-2021/overordnet-kapittel-til-den-regionale-vannforvaltningsplanen-for-finnmark-vannregion-og-grensevassdragene-2016-2021.pdf>, visited on 14 March 2016.

15 The Frontier Rivers Agreement between Finland and Sweden, *supra* note 6, Article 1.

16 *The River Oder* case, *supra* note 9, p. 27.

states, the famous quote also underlines the wholeness of the watercourse and the importance of managing the whole course of the river as one unit. The main question in the judgment concerned the geographical jurisdiction of the river basin commission and navigation was the main interest at stake. It was important to recognise all watercourse states' interest in free navigation in the whole course of the river, regardless of their geographic position on it. In the *Gabčikovo-Nagymaros* case, the ICJ recognised that the principles from the *River Oder* case had been strengthened for non-navigational uses of international watercourses as well.[17]

The unity of the watercourse is thus a central feature in the community of interest approach. During the last decades, the natural inter-dependency of land and water and the necessity of managing catchment areas or ecosystems as integrated units have gained increased recognition. The community of interest approach is also part of this growing tradition, as it incorporates the narrative of integrated and holistic resource management with emphasis on preservation and sustainable development. If the freedom of navigation was the main interest and motivating factor behind the original doctrine of the community of interests, the modern version of the doctrine for non-navigational uses is motivated by environmental regards and the need to coordinate the utilisation of a precious and vulnerable resource.

By creating the River Basin District in accordance with the natural borders of the catchment area, Finland and Norway have thus taken an important step towards an integrated management of their shared watercourses, and possibly toward a community of interest approach.

2.2 *The Interests*

In the community of interest approach, states seek cooperation to better protect their common interest or interests. The common interest is what incites the parties to enter into cooperation and also what defines them as a community. In general terms one could say that Finland and Norway's cooperation is motivated by their shared interest in the environmentally sound, sustainable and profitable management of the River Basin District in accordance with the purpose of the WFD.[18] However, questions of interest are often more complex than what such general terms suggest, and states' motivation for entering into cooperation can also be dual and unclear. For the sake of more detailed

17 *The Gabcikovo-Nagymaros* case, *supra* note 11, p. 56.

18 The Water Framework Directive, Article 1, <eur-lex.europa.eu/resource.html?uri=cellar:5c835afb-2ec6-4577-bdf8-756d3d694eeb.0004.02/DOC_1&format=PDF>, visited on 14 March 2016.

examination, the interests can be divided into three categories: universal values, concrete goals and individual interests.

Universal values are closely related to Bruno Simma's concept of 'community interests', which he defines as "a consensus according to which respect for certain fundamental values is not to be left to the free disposition of States individually or *inter se* but is recognized and sanctioned by international law as a matter of concern to all States".[19] Amongst these community interests, we find international peace and security, protection of the environment, as well as the 'common heritage' concept. All these interests relate to values that are fundamental to human existence and that transcend the mere bilateral relationship. The common interests can also be identified in peremptory norms and obligations *erga omnes*.[20]

Undoubtedly, Finland and Norway have interests in maintaining peaceful relations both in their cooperation over the shared River Basin District and in other aspects of their co-existence. They also have strong interests in protecting and preserving the environment both in a general and specific meaning. Environmental protection as universal value relates to its general meaning – the protection of human habitat and preservation for future generations, which is the common duty of all states and a strong motivating factor for co-operation. The 'common heritage' concept is also of relevance to Finland and Norway in their management of the shared River Basin District. Although the River Basin District is not an area of common heritage in the same manner as, for example, the ocean floor – to be managed to the benefit of all human kind – the same universal value of respect for nature and future generations still apply. There is a need to regulate the River Basin District beyond the limits of national jurisdictions in order to replace biased regimes of national interests with common interests; this will also take better into account the interests

19 B. Simma, 'From Bilateralism to Interest in International Law', in *Recueil des Cours 250*, Collected Courses of the Hague Academy of International Law (Martinus Nijhoff Publishers, The Hague, 1994) p. 233.

20 *See e.g.* M. Ragazzi, *The Concept of International Obligations* erga omnes (Clarendon Press, Oxford, 1997); P. Wouters and D. Tarlock, 'The Third Wave of Normativity in International Water Law: The Duty to Cooperate in the Peaceful Management of the World's Water Resources: An Emerging Obligation Erga Omnes?', 23 *Journal of Water Law* (2013); C. Tomuschat, 'International Law: ensuring the survival of mankind on the eve of a new century: general course on public international law', in *Recueil des Cours 281*, Collected Courses of the Hague Academy of International Law (Martinus Nijhoff Publishers, The Hague, 1999); P. Weil, 'Towards Relative Normativity in International Law?', 77:3 *The American Journal of International Law* (1983); M. Koskenniemi, 'The Pull of the Mainstream', 88:6 *Michigan Law Review* (1990).

of future generations and the responsibility of managing natural resources on behalf of these. The universal values thus concern the moral aspects of managing the shared River Basin District and guide the two states in their decision-making and cooperation. Universal values have always had a strong presence in Nordic cooperation, as the FSFRC is an example of. While maintaining and developing peaceful relations through the neutral managing commission, the Finnish-Swedish cooperation had the ambition to protect and preserve the environment in the whole area of their frontier rivers.

The concrete goals are interests that relate to the conditions in the specific watercourse and objective environmental goals such as water quality or quantity, preservation of particular species, flood control, reduction or prevention of pollution, or the realisation of specific projects in the waters. The concrete goals for the Finnish-Norwegian River Basin District follow the requirements in the WFD.[21] For instance, the two states have agreed to coordinate the characterisation and risk assessment for the water bodies in the River Basin District including delineation, classification and typification of water bodies; identification of pressure and assessment of extent of pressure and impact on these water bodies; assessment of environmental status; and assessment of which water bodies are at risk of not reaching the environmental objectives of the WFD.[22] Coordinating classification methods is especially important since Finland and Norway today obtain different results from their assessments, and Finland generally classifies the common water bodies to a higher environmental status than Norway does. In order to achieve common environmental goals, it is thus of fundamental importance to operate in accordance with the same methods.[23]

In addition to universal values and concrete goals, Finland and Norway have individual interests in the River Basin District. These interests are generally an expression of each State's particular needs, utilisation, or geographic predisposition, and they can be incompatible, reciprocal or exclusive. One of the matters creating disagreement in the Norwegian-Finnish water cooperation is the use and preservation of the Tana River,[24] a border river that separates Norway and Finland for 256 of its 361 kilometres. The Tana River is known as one of the biggest and most important rivers for salmon fishing in Europe, and since

21 Agreement between Norway and Finland on the Creation of the Norwegian-Finnish Water Region, *supra* note 3, Article 1.

22 Memorandum of Understanding pursuant to the Agreement on the Norwegian-Finnish River Basin District, *supra* note 4, Article 5.

23 Roof Report, *supra* note 14, p. 19.

24 The river is called Tana in Norwegian, Tenon or Tenojoki in Finnish, and Deatnu in Sàmi.

the 1970s yearly catches have varied between 70 and 250 tonnes of salmon.[25] In later years, the salmon stock in the river has been decreasing and overfishing is suspected to be one of the reasons for this. Finland and Norway have tried to negotiate an agreement to replace the now out-dated 1989-agreement that regulated salmon fishing in the river, but so far without result. The salmon conflict arises from the different methods used for evaluating the ecological conditions in the watercourse: according to the Norwegian method, the fish stock in the watercourse is decreasing and Norwegian authorities want stricter fishing regulation, while on the Finnish side, however, the method does not give the same result and there is so far no consensus for stricter regulation.[26]

Individually, both states have fishing interests in the river; on the Norwegian side there is a large Sámi population that fishes for livelihood using traditional methods; on the Finnish side, the fishing is more commercialised and seems less restricted.[27] The tourist industry of salmon fishing is a considerable source of income for the scarcely populated municipalities in northern Finland, and fishing enthusiasts come from all over the world to participate. Here we can observe that the individual fishing interests of the two states are conflicting as the one is a threat to the other. The introduction of stricter fishing regulations in order to preserve the fish stock stands in direct conflict with the economic interests in tourist fishing and free fishing access in the whole course of the river. And yet, both states share the universal value of environmental preservation and the interest of preserving a healthy fish stock in the watercourse. Resolving the disagreement that originates from these conflicting interests would necessitate a compromise where other shared interests – universal values or concrete goals – are given decisive weight.

This complex picture of interests is what incites watercourse states to enter into cooperation – it is the foundation for the community. There is a high level of trust between the two states, especially with regard to promoting common interests. The Nordic tradition of peaceful and democratic cooperation with an increasingly strong environmental orientation creates a good foundation for an interest-based cooperation over natural resources where solutions are

25 G.B. Ween and B.J. Colombi, 'Two Rivers: The Politics of Wild Salmon, Indigenous Rights and Natural Resource Management', 5:2 *Sustainability* (2013).

26 Roof Report, *supra* note 14, pp. 19–21.

27 Finnish Ministry of Agriculture and Forestry *et al.*, 'Information about Teno for Fishing Enthusiasts', pp. 6–8, <www.ely-keskus.fi/documents/10191/57368/Tenoinfo+ENG+vedos.pdf/a6f275cd-85f1-4dba-a43d-f4a0e73b9dc1>, visited on 12 May 2015.

found in the balance between the universal values, concrete goals and individual interests.

2.3 *The Community and Its Participants*

2.3.1 Non-State Participation in International Environmental Issues

In traditional international law, states are actors or subjects of law and individuals are addressees or objects. Traditional cooperation over shared resources is normally carried out by sovereign states who negotiate and adopt agreements on behalf of their respective populations. However, as the modern international community is evolving, this traditional pattern of international law is increasingly being questioned and challenged. A myriad of NGOs, international organisations, lobby groups and other non-state actors now operate on the inter- and transnational levels, and are being granted status as observers or consultants in international negotiations. Several scholars and activists advocate that participation at the international legal arena should not be reserved to states alone, especially in questions concerning the management of common interests.[28] Bruno Simma has also addressed the question of which moral basis states can claim for their monopolisation of the discourse on the definition and pursuit of community interests in international law.[29]

The *community* of interest is an assembly of legal subjects that share common interests. The term 'community' suggests inclusiveness and unity, as well as a sense of common spirit and identity. The community of interest approach recognises that other actors than States can have strong interest in how the water resource is managed, and that a sustainable use and development of the waters requires the inclusion of these actors in the decision-making process. There are good reasons for such an inclusion; firstly, it may enhance the democratic legitimacy of watercourse management. Conflicts over the utilisation of an international watercourse do not necessarily originate from disagreements between states, but in many cases rather "from transnational competition among rival domestic groups or even from collusion between several interest

28 *See e.g.* E. Hey, *Teaching International Law: State-Consent as Consent to a Process of Normative Development snd Ensuing Problems* (Kluwer Law International, The Hague, 2003); E. Benvenisti, *Sharing Transboundary Resources: International Law and Optimal Resource Use* (Cambridge University Press, Cambridge, 2002); A. Peters, 'Membership in the Global Constitutional Society', in J. Klabbers, A. Peters and G. Ulfstein (eds.), *The Constitutionalization of International Law* (Oxford University Press, Oxford, 2009); R. Higgins, 'Conceptual Thinking About the Individual in International Law', in R. Falk, F. Kratochwil and S.H. Mendlovitz (eds.), *International Law: A Contemporary Perspective* (Westview Press, Boulder, CO, 1985).

29 Simma, *supra* note 19, p. 236.

groups, all in an effort to capture a disproportionately larger share and externalize costs at the expense of other interest groups within those states, including future generations".[30] This makes international negotiations a two-level game where states consult both with each other and with their respective domestic actors, without having any guaranteed control over the process or the outcome. Through his transnational conflict paradigm, Eyal Benvenisti suggests that collective action problems are best solved on a transnational level, where groups and institutions are given an individual voice and opportunity to participate in law making and negotiations instead of being represented by their respective governments. The challenge for classic sovereignty rests in the fact that the paradigm redistributes power that is normally reserved states. Domestic pressure groups may thus achieve an individual voice and a possibility to participate directly in the process of managing an international watercourse. This could prevent domestic political constraints from spilling over to the international scene,[31] at the same time as it might ensure closer connection between the decision-makers and the users of the waters. Although the transnational conflict paradigm reduces the total power of the state, it might contribute to an increase in the effective sovereign power in areas other than international resource management. Moreover, the act of opening up for alternatives is itself an act of sovereignty; the power of the state is thus not lost but redistributed.

Secondly, the inclusion of interest groups and stakeholders in the decision-making process can increase compliance with plans and decisions. Proximity to decisions enlarges the feeling of ownership to the process and thereby also the will to comply. Also, stakeholders and local interest groups often have first-hand knowledge of actual utilisation, needs and traditions in the water area, information that may not be as well known to politicians on higher levels. Such knowledge can be of considerable value when creating management plans for the watercourse, since it can secure more sustainable utilisation and preservation accustomed to the water users.

2.3.2 Participation and Management Structure in the Finnish-Norwegian River Basin District

The management structure in the Finnish-Norwegian River Basin District is traditional in the sense that the two states, Norway and Finland, are the only two parties to the agreement. With this in mind, it is necessary to take a closer look at a couple of fundamental issues. The first issue is the absence of

30 Benvenisti, *supra* note 28, p. 49.

31 *Ibid.*, p. 47.

Russian participation in the management of the River Basin District. The natural borders of the River Basin District stretch into Russian territory through the Pasvik watercourse and tributaries to the Tuloma River. In addition to the fact that parts of the River Basin District are situated on Russian territory, pollution from the Russian Norilsk Nickel plant located only 7 km from the Russian-Norwegian border contaminates land and water in the area.[32] The plant releases yearly around 100,000 tons of sulphur dioxide and a large additional amount of heavy metals into the air and water in the north-eastern part of the region.[33] This exemplifies the essence of transboundary watercourse management: utilisation in one area of the watercourse can affect the conditions elsewhere in the basin and thus other states' use of the same waters. Since the Finnish-Norwegian River Basin District is partly situated on Russian territory and parts of the region suffer from Russian industrial pollution, it seems obvious that Russia should be an active part of the cooperation. By means of an example, Botswana is an active party to the cooperation in the Orange-Senqu River Basin, although only a very small, and to a large degree dry, fraction of the River Basin is situated on Botswanian territory.[34] Certainly, being party neither to the European Union nor to the European Economic Community, Russia does not have the same obligations towards the WFD as Norway and Finland have. In addition, both Norway and Finland are engaged in bilateral cooperation with Russia on environmental issues,[35] and there is a tripartite cooperation through the Pasvik Inari Trilateral Park.[36] Yet, the continuity and consistency that is characteristic for holistic management is threatened when natural parts of the watercourse are governed by a different regime. The efficiency of the Norwegian-Finnish management of the River Basin District is also weakened since they have little or no control over Russian pollution or its impact on the conditions in the north-eastern parts of the District. This influences the predictability of decisions and monitoring in the River Basin

32 Roof Report, *supra* note 15, p. 6.

33 *Ibid.*

34 *See* <www.orasecom.com>, visited on 12 May 2015.

35 *See* 'Miljøsamarbeid med Russland', Norges Klima- og Miljødepartement, <www.regjeringen.no/nb/tema/svalbard-og-polaromradene/innsiktsartiklerpolaromradene/miljovernsamarbeid-med-russland-og-i-barentsregionen/id2343387/>, visited on 22 May 2015; 'Nature Conservation Cooperation between Finland and Russia', Finnish Ministry of the Environment, <www.ym.fi/enUS/International_cooperation/Cooperation_with_Russia/Nature_conservation_cooperation_between_Finland_and_Russia>, visited on 22 May 2015.

36 Pasvik Inari Trilateral Park, <www.pasvik-inari.net/neu/eng/main.html>, visited on 22 May 2015.

District, and from an overall perspective it reduces the actual power of the Norwegian-Finnish authorities.

The second fundamental issue is the participation from non-state actors. In the field of natural resource management, and in environmental matters in general, there is broad engagement and involvement from actors other than states. A number of environmental, wildlife and stakeholder organisations are active in the Finnish-Norwegian River Basin District. They have no decision-making power or access to the bilateral negotiations, but play a fundamental role in the preliminary preparations and establishment of domestic plans.

Norway is divided into 11 water regions, in addition to the Finnish-Norwegian River Basin District that counts as a separate region. In accordance with Article 21 of the WFD, the regional management committee of Finnmark acts as regulatory committee on the Norwegian side. This regulatory committee is composed of representatives from regional and local authorities and relevant governmental sub-organs,[37] who assist the commission in its policy-making and monitoring of the water region. The regulatory committee thus ensures participation from regional and governmental authorities, at the same time as these authorities are given the opportunity to fulfil their responsibilities of surveillance and measure-proposals in the water region. The regulatory committee is also assisted by a reference group composed by smaller groups of stakeholders and NGOs such as local fishery organisations and environmental groups.[38] These are invited to information meetings where they are notified about the policy process and encouraged to comment and propose changes to the plans. Although these interest groups are not part of the formal decision-making process, they are given the possibility to influence the policy of the River Basin District, at least domestically.

A similar structure exists on Finnish side, where the ELY centres for development, transport and environment are in charge of the water management. Each ELY centre is responsible for its respective water region, and one of the centres is in charge of coordinating the work in Finland's five water regions.[39] National and regional authorities, organisations and stakeholders are invited to

37 These include the Norwegian Coastal Administration, the Norwegian Food Safety Authority, the Norwegian Public Roads Administration, the Directorate of Fisheries, the Norwegian Water Resources and Energy Directorate; *see* 'Members of Finnmark Water Region', <www.vannportalen.no/globalassets/vannregioner/finnmark/motedokumenter-vru-og-referansegruppe/motedokumenter-vru/oversikt-medlemmer-vru-2014.pdf>, visited on 22 May 2015.

38 'Deltakelse i regional referansegruppe', <www.vannportalen.no/vannregioner/finnmark/organisering/deltagelse-i-regional-referansegruppe/>, visited on 1 June 2015.

39 Roof Report, *supra* note 14, p. 7.

participate through common workshops, and cooperation between authorities, interest groups and citizens is central in the regional water management plans.[40]

The regional organisation of the Finnish-Norwegian River Basin District reflects the strong democratic tradition in the Nordic countries, where public participation enjoys much respect and is strived for in the fields of national as well as international law. Although the Finnish-Norwegian cooperation is traditional in the sense that its formal members are sovereign states, regional and local authorities and interest groups are indirectly parties to the cooperation over the River Basin District; their interests and concerns are taken into consideration by their respective regulatory committees. This can create a good 'community' feeling amongst the involved actors since it reduces the distance between water users, stakeholders and authorities. However, the Finnish-Norwegian model creates communities on each side of the border that care to protect their own interests. Although these interests in most cases will be similar, they may also sometimes be conflicting. The question is thus whether it would be more efficient and easier to ensure consistent and sustainable management of the waters if one single commission managed the whole River Basin District.

2.4 *The Institution*

Amongst the defining features of the community of interest approach is the process of decision-making, which differs from the consent-based, positivist tradition of international law where a legal norm is binding only upon explicit consent. In the community of interest approach, the process of decision-making is closer to Ellen Hey's concept of consent to a process; instead of seeking consensus to every single norm, the involved states agree on a framework of principles and a process of normative development.[41] An example of such consent is the European Court of Human Rights; by contributing to the creation and existence of the court, state parties also contribute and consent to the Court's ability to develop international law.[42]

Another example of process-oriented consent is the FSFRC. The 1971 Frontiers Rivers Agreement between Finland and Sweden was a framework agreement that established the main principles for the management of the shared watercourses, as well as the competence of the Frontiers Rivers Commission. Central values in the treaties' general provisions were the equality of the two

40 *Ibid.*

41 Hey, *supra* note 28.

42 *Ibid.*, p. 13.

states and the interest of nature conservancy.[43] The treaty contained detailed provisions about permitted constructions in the waters, water regulation, fishing, protection against pollution, and compensation for losses due to others' use of the waters. And, as codified in Article 8, the law prevailing in each state was to be applied only in cases where the agreement did not contain special provisions to the contrary. The FSFRC exercised their powers within the limits of this framework agreement, but were accorded considerable authority and freedom.

The Commission's most important competences were its substantial decision-making powers. Any construction in the water (defined in the Agreement as an installation in the water area), diversion of water and regulation of run off, and other measures "which may cause a change of the water level or discharge or of the depth or position of the water",[44] required a permit from the Commission. The same went for projects that could affect the ground water, the building of a bridge or a pipe or other constructions over or under the water area. Hence, permits were required for *all types* of construction in, over, or under water and for projects that could interfere with the water quantity or quality. When receiving an application for a permit, the Commission decided on the permissibility of the undertaking,[45] and could set special conditions for the granting of an eventual permit.[46] Consequently, the Commission decided on virtually all matters concerning the utilisation of the watercourses, and was in full control of the exploitation of the resource and of the potential disadvantages that might occur.[47] The FSFRC could also, *with or without* relation to a permit application, decide on the question of economic compensation by reason of a measure covered by the Frontier Rivers Agreement.[48] This provision established a fundamental matter falling within the judicial competence of the Commission, since it directly affected entitled private parties in the watercourse area.[49]

The Commission was also entitled to act on its own initiative and to the extent itself deemed necessary. As stated in the Frontier Rivers Agreement,

43 The Frontier Rivers Agreement between Finland and Sweden, *supra* note 6, Articles 3 and 5.

44 *Ibid.*, Chapter 3, Article 1.

45 *Ibid.*, Chapter 8, Article 11.

46 *Ibid.*, Chapter 10, Article 13.

47 *See* Howden, *supra* note 9.

48 The Frontier Rivers Agreement between Finland and Sweden, *supra* note 6, Chapter 7, Article 1.

49 M. Fitzmaurice and E. Olufemi, *Watercourses Co-operation in Northern Europe: A Model for the Future* (TMC Asser Press, The Hague, 2004).

the Commission should "itself decide on the examinations and investigations required in order [to] fulfil its obligations".[50] The Commission was not acting upon orders or recommendations from the two member states, but was alone responsible for the management of the frontier waters. Although the member states created the Commission and granted it these competences, the FSFRC was not dependent upon the national authorities' consent before exercising its powers.

This is an example not only of consent to a process but also of an institution with quite considerable power. Within its designated mandate, the Commission was free to act as it deemed right, while quite unrestricted by the sovereign powers of the two states, and was itself responsible for taking any measures necessary to fulfil its obligations according to the agreement. Through the carefully crafted Frontier Rivers Agreement the states relinquished some of their exclusive control over the resources to be exercised by the Commission, but the Agreement would ensure that the Commission made decisions that were in accordance with the states' intent. A breach of the Agreement by the Commission would entitle the authorities of the two states to redefine its competences or to ultimately regain control over the resources. Through the exercise of state sovereignty, Sweden and Finland thus created a sovereignty-free space where the Commission operated on their behalf.[51]

L'Organisation pour la Mise en Valeur du Fleuve Sénégal (OMVS) is a similar international basin organisation created by the watercourse states to the Senegal River: Senegal, Mali, Mauritania and Guinea. The first three parties have been cooperating over the shared River Basin since 1963, while Guinea joined in 2006. The cooperative regime in the Senegal River is one of few describing itself as a community of interest,[52] based on its level of commitment and the member states' will to "relinquish their sovereign control and even their ownership of the land and the river works" to the OMVS.[53] The Bamako Convention, adopted by the riparians in 1963, established a sub-organisation called the 'Inter-State Committee', in charge of promoting and coordinating studies and

50 The Frontier Rivers Agreement between Finland and Sweden, *supra* note 6, Chapter 2, Article 3.

51 Howden, *supra* note 9.

52 M.M. Mbengue, 'A Model for African Shared Water Resources: The Senegal River Legal System', 23:1 *Review of European, Comparative & International Environmental Law* (2014); M.J. Vick, 'The Senegal River Basin: A Retrospective and Prospective Look at the Legal Régime', 46:1 *Natural Resources Journal* (2006).

53 *Ibid.*, p. 215.

activities for the harnessing of the Senegal River.[54] The Convention leaves almost no room for unilateral action in the watercourse and accords any watercourse state some kind of veto right on any project from another state.[55] However, the real step towards a genuine community of interest-regime was taken in 2002, with the adoption of the *Charte des Eaux du Fleuve Sénégal*.[56] The Charter has been called a "constitution" in the legal pyramid of agreements concerning the government of the Senegal River,[57] because it fixes the new spirit of solidarity for the management of the watercourse in accordance with which all other agreements must be interpreted.[58] The organisation is also, through its Council of Ministers, given the ability to create obligations for its member states, for instance the power to fix the financial contributions from its members and the ability to define and decide what projects should be accorded priority.[59]

In the Finnish-Norwegian River Basin District there is no such joint commission and no common management plan. So far, management plans and policies have been created on each side of the border. Plans are created for a period of five years, and as the current plan runs from 2010–2015, the upcoming plan runs from 2016–2021. When the Finnish-Norwegian River Basin District was established, in 2013, the plans for 2016–2021 were already under creation, and differences in methodology and organisation made it too difficult to make a common management plan for the upcoming plan period.[60] The goal is, however, to create one common plan for the whole River Basin District for the plan period of 2021–2027.

Nevertheless, a Finnish-Norwegian Transboundary Water Commission has existed since 1980. This Commission has three members from each state – in

54 Mbengue, *supra* note 52, p. 60.

55 *Ibid.*

56 'Charte des Eaux du Fleuve Sénégal', <www.portail-omvs.org/sites/default/files/fichierspdf/charte_des_eaux_du_fleuve_senegal.pdf>, visited on 8 March 2016. As there is no official English translation of the *Charte*, all translations in the present text are unofficial translations on file with author, or author's own)

57 M.M. Mbengue, 'The Senegal River legal regime and its contribution to the development of the law of international watercourses in Africa', in L. Boisson de Chazournes, C. Leb and M. Tignino (eds.), *International Law and Freshwater: Multiple Challenges* (Edward Elgar, Cheltenham, 2013) p. 231.

58 *Ibid.*

59 Convention portant création de l'organisation pour la mise en valeur du Fleuve Sénégal signée a Nouakchott, le 11 mars 1972, Article 8, <gis.nacse.org/tfdd/tfdddocs/344FRE.pdf>, visited on 8 March 2016.

60 Roof Report, *supra* note 14, p. 3.

essence mayors and local politicians – and its main responsibility is to "put forward proposals, submit initiatives, and issue statements on matters pertaining to the management of the transboundary waters between Finland and Norway, the monitoring and supervision of the condition and quality of the waters, the fishing condition in the waters, construction in the watercourse, and the regulation of the waters".[61] The Commission conducts common surveillance of water quality and quantity in the border region and gives collective advise to the two governments. The Finnish-Norwegian Transboundary Waters Commission does not have authority to accord permits or adopt management measures for the watercourses as the former FSFRC was entitled to. The Finnish-Norwegian Commission has the characteristics of an advisory committee, while the FSFRC was a decision-making and judicial organ.

2.5 *Assessment and Recommendations for Further Development*

From this we can observe that the process of decision-making is still very traditional in the Finnish-Norwegian River Basin District; it is domestic, positivist and consent-based. When comparing with the FSFRC, it can seem like Nordic water cooperation has regressed in terms of holistic and institutional management. A possible explanation for this is that at the time of the adoption of the Finnish-Swedish Frontier Rivers Agreement international law and international cooperation was less comprehensive and regional cooperation had a stronger position. Comprehensive agreements like the Frontier Rivers Agreement strengthened the sense of community and solidarity between Nordic neighbours, and our common history and development had created a level of trust that permitted such close cooperation. Today, however, we operate in a much more globalised environment, where agreements are made on the international scene or in accordance with an ever-growing corpus of international legal principles. It could be that the more reserved attitude states tend to adopt towards international environmental commitments may have influenced our Nordic community and made us more sovereignty-minded and less prone to our community values.

If Finland and Norway want to change this development, they should create a common management institution for their River Basin District. This could better protect the interconnectedness of the resources in the district and its general environmental condition, as well as increase efficiency and reduce bureaucracy in the water management. One possible way to realise this would be

---

61 Agreement between Finland and Norway on a Finnish-Norwegian Transboundary Water Commission, Finland and Norway, Article 1, <http://www.ymparisto.fi/default.asp?contentid=187347&lan=EN>, visited on 12 May 2015.

to expand the competence of the existing Finnish-Norwegian Transboundary Waters Commission. Throughout its 35 years of existence, the Commission has obtained unique knowledge and experience in Finnish-Norwegian water questions. Such expertise is valuable when creating management plans and observing changes in water quality and quantity. Expansion of the Commission's mandate and composition, with members from the local, legal, environmental, technical, political and official arenas, could give the Commission the necessary competence to manage the River Basin District on behalf of its member states. Such a development would however necessitate a more ambitious management ideology from the member states, a detailed agreement creating the required competence for such committee, and – not the least – political will to engage in more committing cooperation over shared water resources.

3 Conclusion

The main objective of this chapter has been to see if, how and why the Finnish-Norwegian cooperation should take steps towards a more holistic and committed management of their River Basin District, by incorporating more of the characteristics from the community of interest doctrine.

Starting with the question *why* the two states should seek a more engaged cooperation in the River Basin District, one of the first reasons is the efficiency of common management. Domestic management plans, although regularly harmonised, will not respect the inter-connected nature of the resources that extends beyond the political border drawn across the area.

Further, both Finland and Norway are parties to the two most prominent international water conventions: the 1992 UNECE Convention on the Protection of Transboundary Watercourses and International Lakes, and the 1997 United Nations Convention on the Non-navigational Uses of International Watercourses. Both instruments contain provisions on the establishment of joint management bodies. Where the UNWC merely encourages watercourse states to enter intro consultations that "may include the establishment of a joint management mechanism",[62] the UNECE Convention is more compelling when it states that bilateral and multilateral cooperation over shared water

62 The United Nations Convention on the Law of the Non-navigational Uses of International Watercourses, Article 24, *see also* Article 28, <treaties.un.org/doc/Treaties/1998/09/19980925%2006-30%20PM/Ch_XXVII_12p.pdf>, visited on 8 May 2015

resources "shall provide for the establishment of joint bodies".[63] Both states thus have international legal obligations to create a joint management structure.

More committed and integrated management would also be in line with the growing focus on holism in international environmental law – exemplified through the ecosystem approach – which, according to its advocates, can result in more sustainable development.[64]

And finally, holistic management of the River Basin District would maintain the peaceful and democratic tradition of Nordic water management, and also take a step towards strengthening the Nordic model on the international stage.

The question of *how* Finland and Norway should cooperate closer in the River Basin District requires solutions to the two main problems this chapter has examined: the parties and the institution. First, the two states should examine the possibility of inviting Russia to take part in the management of the River Basin District and thus create a trilateral cooperation in the district. Public participation in the region could be increased through trilateral meetings and workshops with interest groups and stakeholders to ensure that local and transnational interests are incorporated in the management plans. Second, it is necessary to create a joint commission that would execute decisions made by the governments and operate within a framework of principles and rules drawn up by the national authorities. This commission should have jurisdiction in the whole River Basin District, and should at the minimum be in charge of surveillance and data collection, elaboration of joint monitoring programmes and action programmes.

After the questions of *why* and *how*, and after having examined realities and prospects for future cooperation in the River Basin District throughout the chapter, the last question – *if* Finland and Norway should create a more committing cooperation – appears to have been thoroughly answered. The Nordic

63 Convention on the Protection and Use of Transboundary Watercourses and International Lakes, Article 9(2), <www.unece.org/fileadmin/DAM/env/water/pdf/watercon.pdf>, visited on 12 May 2016.

64 *See e.g.* J. Brunnee and S.J. Toope, 'Environmental Security and Freshwater Resources: Ecosystem Regime Building', 91:1 *The American Journal of International Law* (1997); R.E. Grumbine, 'What Is Ecosystem Management?', 8:1 *Conservation Biology* (1994); O. McIntyre, 'The Protection of Freshwater Ecosystems Revisited: Towards a Common Understanding of the 'Ecosystems Approach' to the Protection of Transboundary Water Resources', 23:1 *Review of European, Comparative & International Environmental Law* (2014); D. Tarlock, 'Ecosystems', in D. Bodansky, J. Brunnée and E. Hey (eds.), *The Oxford Handbook of International Environmental Law* (Oxford University Press, Oxford, 2007).

tradition of peaceful cooperation, the well-established trust between the watercourse states, and the abundance of water in the region create an ideal starting point for community of interest-based management of the River Basin District. Experience from other regions, especially the FSFRC, shows that there are good reasons to go in this direction. It could be an inspiring example of innovative water management for other states seeking similar solutions, as well as a new Nordic pioneer project.

A Nordic Approach to Promoting Women's Rights within International Law: Internal v. External Perspectives

Cecilia M. Bailliet

1 Introduction

The Nordic countries are renowned for leading the world in terms of achieving the highest levels of gender equality. The World Economic Forum produces a Gender Gap Index which measures economic participation and opportunity (salaries, participation and leadership), education (access to basic and higher levels of education), political empowerment (representation in decision-making structures), and health and survival (life expectancy and sex ratio). The top five countries in 2014 were Iceland, Finland, Norway, Sweden and Denmark.[1] Nordic internal promotion of women's rights is linked to women's historical political participation. Nordic women's political engagement led to the breaking of the private/public divide, thereby improving women's access to education and labour participation.[2] At the external level, Nordic states lead in earmarking Gender Marked Aid; according to the Organisation for Economic Co-operation and Development (OECD), in 2015 Sweden and Denmark ranked highest while Finland and Norway were among the top ten donors.[3] One may query whether there is a Nordic approach to women's rights within international law.

This chapter commences by examining the emergence of Nordic legal feminism and the Nordic contribution to the drafting of the Convention on the Elimination of Discrimination against Women (CEDAW). It then presents current challenges to the internal promotion of human rights, such as implementing

1 World Economic Forum, *The Global Gender Gap Report 2014*, available at: <reports.weforum.org/global-gender-gap-report-2014/>, visited on 16 March 2016.

2 A key feature of their remarkable achievements is the guarantee of maternity and paternity leave (which in Norway guarantees 80 per cent salary for the first year), as well as the provision of kindergarten and pre-school programmes. On Norway's parental benefits *see*: </www.nav.no/en/Home/Benefits+and+services/Relatert+informasjon/Parental+benefit.353588.cms>, visited on 16 March 2016.

3 OECD information on aid in support of gender equality and women's empowerment is available at: <www.oecd.org/dac/stats/aidinsupportofgenderequalityandwomensempowerment.htm>, visited on 16 March 2016.

 | DOI 10.1163/9789004343597_013

legislation, low level of knowledge of rights among state actors and civil society, intersecting forms of discrimination, and violence against women. This is followed by a review of the Nordic external dimension of promotion of women's rights through development aid and support for peacebuilding initiatives. The final sections consider dilemmas relating to the possibility of identifying a Nordic feminist foreign policy and promotion of Nordic women as creators of international law.

2 Nordic Legal Feminism and Promotion of Women's Rights

Nordic legal feminism addresses the structural conditions of equality and non-discrimination, examining legislation on the welfare state and the labour market, as well as criminal law pertaining to violence against women.[4] It differs from US feminism because Nordics do not characterise the state as being primarily patriarchal, as it provides the welfare protection that enables women to enjoy greater participation in the workforce and ensures support for the family.[5] As noted by Margaret Davies, "in Sweden feminism has been able to promote its objectives through the mechanism of the state".[6] Further, at the cultural level, although there are differences between the genders within employment and other areas, these differences are not articulated as reflecting power structures.[7] Nordic legal feminism can be described as pluralistic because there are variances among the Nordic scholars pertaining to thematic focus and approach.

Eva-Maria Svensson defines feminist legal studies as pursuing "an emancipatory purpose, a critical, non-dogmatic approach, a rejection of a distinction between theory and practice and a contextual epistemological standpoint".[8] Nordic feminist scholars, such as Tove Stang Dahl, Trine Baumbach, Åsa Gunnarson, Kevät Nousiainen, Ruth Nielsen, Kirsten Ketscher, Christina Tvarnø and Anne Hellum, engaged to promote women's rights. Within Norway, 'women's law' emerged at the University of Oslo in 1975 as an approach which would

4 Å. Gunnarsson, E. Svensson, and M. Davies (eds.), *Exploiting the Limits of Law: Swedish Feminism and the Challenge to Pessimism* (Routledge, Abingdon, 2007) p. 4.

5 *Ibid.*, p. 3.

6 M. Davies, 'Notes Towards an Optimistic Feminism: A Long View', in Gunnarsson *et al.* (eds.), *supra* note 4, p. 219.

7 *Ibid.*

8 E. Svensson, 'Is there a Future for Scandinavian Women's Law?', in R. Nielsen and C. D. Tvarnø (eds.), *Scandinavian Women's Law in the 21st Century* (Djøf, Copenhagen, 2012) p. 28.

take women's reality and values as a point of departure, instead of relying on a gender neutral basis which tended to reflect the life experience of men. It seeks to describe, explain and understand the situation of women in order to improve their status within the law and society.[9] Further, this field constructed other areas of law, such as 'birth law' and 'care work', reflecting women's life experiences.[10] Norwegian feminist theorists at the University of Oslo collaborated with the legal clinic JURK and empirically examined the practical effect of legal rules upon women's lives in order to promote law reform. Nordic feminist scholars emphasised the linkage of equality with non-discrimination, supported legal activism to promote law reforms and underscored the impact of structural discrimination – addressing a range of issues from labour law to criminal law. They also explained the relevance and interaction of different legal regimes, such as human rights and European Union (EU) law, and advocated attention to legal pluralism within increasingly multicultural Nordic societies.[11] It is arguable that Nordic contributions to women's law paved the way for the international promotion of women's rights.

---

9 T. S. Dahl (ed.), 'Innledning til kvinneretten', in *Kvinnerett I* (Universitetsforlaget, Oslo, 1985) p. 15.

10 A. Hellum, 'Continuity and change in women's law scholarship: Perspectives on women, gender and the law from above and below'/ 'Kvinnerettslige utviklingslinjer: Forståelser av kvinner, kjønn og rett – nedenfra og ovenfra', *Tidsskrift for kjønnsforskning* (Idunn 2012), pp. 131–148; *see also* T. Svedrup, 'Folketrygden I kvinneperspektiv', in A. Kjønstad (ed.), *Folketrygden i støpeskjeen* (1984); I. Ikdahl, 'Om rettsvitenskap og internasjonalisering: Fagutvikling ved kvinnerettsmiljøet i Oslo i perioden 1985–2013', (37 1/144) *Rettfærd* (Jurist-og Økonomforbundets Forlag, 2014) p. 101; K. Ketscher, 'Nogle udviklingslinjer i kvinderetten', *Normativa perspektiv: Festskrift til Anna Christensen* (Juristforlaget, Copenhagen, 2000). JURK is available at: <https://jurk.no/>, visited on 17 March 2016. *See also* J. Westerstrand, *Mellan mäns händer. Kvinnors rättssubjektivitet, internationell rätt och diskurser om prostitution och trafficking* (Uppsala University, Uppsala, 2008), presenting Swedish policies on prostitution to be representative of a contextual approach, cited by E. Svensson, 'Is there a Future for Scandinavian Women's Law', in R. Nielsen and C. D. Tvarnø (eds.), *Scandinavian Women's Law in the 21st Century* (Djøf, Copenhagen, 2012) p. 27. *See also* E. M. Svensson *et al.* (eds.), *På Vei: Kjønn og Rett I Norden* (Makadam, 2011); *see also* T. Baumbach, 'Hvor er kønnet i dansk strafferet?', in Nielsen and Tvarnø, *ibid.*, p. 298.

11 T. S. Dahl, 'Taking Women's Lives as a Starting Point: Building Women's Law', 14 *International Journal of the Sociology of Law* (1986) pp. 239–247; T. S. Dahl, *Women's Law: An Introduction to Feminist Jurisprudence* (Norwegian University Press, Oslo, 1987); K. Nousiainen, A. Gunnarsson, K. Lundström, and J. Niemi-Kiesiläinen (eds.), *Responsible Selves: Women in the Nordic Legal Culture* (Ashgate, Aldershot, 2001); E. Svensson, A. Pylkänen, and J. Niemi-Kiesiläinen (eds.), *Nordic Equality at a Crossroads: Feminist Legal Studies Coping with Difference* (Ashgate, Aldershot, 2004); A. Hellum, 'Den globale likestillingsnormen', in Svensson

3 Nordic Contribution to Drafting of the UN Convention on the Elimination of Discrimination against Women

3.1 *Gender Roles and the Role of Civil Society*

The United Nations (UN) Convention on the Elimination of Discrimination against Women was adopted by the UN General Assembly on 18 December 1979 in order to set forth gender specific approaches to promote non-discrimination and equality rights, providing a definition of discrimination.[12] It has been ratified by 188 states. The CEDAW also pursues a holistic perspective, uniting civil, political, social and economic rights, as well as public and private perspectives to address political, cultural, economic, social and family life. In terms of external promotion of women's rights, the Nordic delegations provided important input in the drafting of the CEDAW, which reflected their own experiences of emancipation of women and evolution of gender roles. For example, Sweden prompted the preambular paragraph 14: "Aware that a change in the traditional role of men as well as the role of women in society and in the family is needed to achieve full equality between men and women".[13] Denmark, Finland, Norway and Sweden sought recognition of "the role of both parents in the family and the upbringing of children".[14] Subscribing to this perspective, Sweden stated that "true equality between men and women could not be introduced by means of measures dealing exclusively with women: some measures aiming to bring about changes in the traditional role of men would be required.[15]

Nordic countries have a strong tradition of turning to the Parliament to solve societal problems. Nevertheless, in relation to Article 2, Denmark noted that legislative measures should not be the only means of achieving the

---

et al., ibid.; I. Ikdahl, 'Et lærestykke: Kvinneretten og internasjonaliseringen', in K. S. Bull and M. Halvorsen (eds.), *Det juridiske fakultet gjennom 200 år. Kontinuitet og fornyelse* (Akademisk Publisering, Oslo, 2013) pp. 151–164; R. Nielsen, 'The Impact of EU Law on Scandinavian Law in Matters of Gender Equality', in Nielsen and Tvarnø, *ibid.*, p. 63.

12 UN General Assembly, Convention on the Elimination of All Forms of Discrimination Against Women, 18 December 1979, United Nations, Treaty Series, vol. 1249, p. 13, available at: <www.refworld.org/docid/3ae6b3970.html>, accessed 9 June 2016.

13 L. A. Rehof, *Guide to the Travaux Preparatoires of the United Nations Convention on the Elimination of All Forms of Discrimination against Women* (Martinus Nijhoff, Leiden, 1993) p. 40.

14 *Ibid.*

15 Sweden underscored the importance of men sharing responsibility for family/children so that women could achieve equality in the labor market and education. Rehof, *supra* note 13, pp. 54 and 126.

objective of the Convention.[16] Hence they endorsed training and educational programmes to promote social awareness and change of attitudes.[17] Furthermore, Sweden emphasised attention to discrimination within civil society and organisations and entities beyond public authorities, underscoring the importance of non-state actors in gender discrimination. Thus, Article 2 calls for "appropriate measures to eliminate discrimination against women by any person, organization or enterprise".[18] Yet, Anne Hellum notes that civil society women's organisations appeared to lack funding and were often marginalised or excluded by the state when trying to influence national legislation and policy.[19] However, the CEDAW Committee did prompt Norway to strengthen the non-governmental organisation (NGO) shadow reporting mechanism, and this has proved to be a valuable contribution to the transnational evolution of women's human rights.

The fact that there appeared to be a Nordic emphasis on looking beyond formal law-making and the state when addressing compliance is particularly interesting because at present the CEDAW Committee conclusions to Nordic states actually commence with formalistic perspectives on the role of the Parliament. As an example, one may consider CEDAW's concluding observations to Denmark's eighth periodic report which "stresses the crucial role of the legislative power in ensuring the full implementation of the Convention ... It invites the parliament of Denmark and the parliaments of the territories of Greenland and the Faroe Islands, in line with their mandates, to take the necessary steps regarding the implementation of the present concluding observations ...".[20] CEDAW issues an identical conclusion to Finland in its concluding

16 On Nordic majoritarian democracy, *see* M. Wind, 'When Parliament comes first. The Danish Concept of Democracy Meets the European Union', 27:2 *Nordic Journal of Human Rights* (2009) pp. 272–288.

17 *Ibid.*, p. 53.

18 *Ibid.*, p. 57.

19 *See* A. Hellum, 'Making Space and Giving Voice: the CEDAW in Norwegian Law', in A. Hellum and H. S. Aasen, *Women's Human Rights: CEDAW in International, Regional and National Law* (Cambridge University Press, Cambridge, 2013) pp. 603–605. She cites a study on women's movements in Norway, B. Halsaa, C. Thun and L. N. Predelli, 'Women's Movements: Constructions of Sisterhood, Dispute and Resonance: The Case of Norway: Feminist Citizenship in Multicultural Europe: The Impact of Contemporary Women's Movements (FEMCIT)', FEMCIT Working Paper No. 4 (Centre for Gender Research, University of Oslo, and Department of Social Science and Centre of Research in Social Policy, Southbororough University, 2008).

20 CEDAW, *Concluding Observations on the Eighth Periodic Report of Denmark*, CEDAW/C/DNK/CO/8 (11 March 2015), para. 8 (hereinafter CEDAW CO Denmark).

observations on the seventh periodic report, as well to Norway in its concluding observations on the eighth periodic report, to Sweden in its concluding observations on the combined eighth and ninth periodic reports, and to Iceland in its concluding observations on the combined seventh and eighth periodic reports.[21] It does not appear that CEDAW has sufficiently heeded Denmark's original concern regarding the importance of holistically evaluating implementation measures beyond formal law-making.

3.2 *Additional Contributions to Women's Rights*

The Nordic countries were very progressive in supporting recognition of rights which had proved essential for Nordic women's own historical emancipation. Indeed, in June 2015, Denmark celebrated the 100th anniversary of its constitution that gave women the right to vote, marked by a speech by the country's first female prime minster, Helle Thorning-Schmidt.[22] It was Denmark which endorsed the articulation of women's right "to vote in all elections and public referenda and to be eligible for election to all publically elected bodies" in Article 7 of the CEDAW.[23] Denmark also promoted recognition of the "significant roles which rural women play in the economic survival of their families, including their work in the non-monetized sectors of the economy …", reflected in Article 14.[24]

The provision of state parental support may well be the cornerstone of the advancement of women in the Nordic labour market, and it is almost taken for granted within the region, while it remains a mere aspiration in many other regions in the world. Hence, Sweden formulated the wording of Article 11 which

---

21 CEDAW, *Concluding Observations on the Seventh Periodic Report of Finland*, CEDAW/C/FIN/CO/7 (10 March 2014), para 7. (hereinafter CEDAW CO Finland); CEDAW, *Concluding Observations on the Eighth Periodic Report of Norway*, CEDAW/C/NOR/CO/8 (23 March 2012), para. 8 (hereinafter CEDAW CO Norway); CEDAW, *Concluding Observations on the Combined Eighth and Ninth Periodic Reports of Sweden*, CEDAW/C/SWE/CO/8-9 (7 March 2016) para. 9 (hereinafter CEDAW CO Sweden); and CEDAW, *Concluding Observations on the Combined Seventh and Eighth Periodic Reports of Iceland*, CEDAW/C/ISL/CO-7-8 (7 March 2016) para. 6 (hereinafter CEDAW CO Iceland). As pertaining to Iceland, the CEDAW Committee stressed "the crucial role of the legislative power in ensuring the full implementation of the Convention". It placed responsibility on the Parliament to take necessary steps for implementation of the Concluding Observations.

22 'Denmark marks 100 years of women's rights', *The Local* (4 June 2015) available at: <www.thelocal.dk/20150604/denmark-marks-100-years-of-womens-right-to-vote>, visited on 17 March 2016.

23 Rehof, *supra* note 13, p. 96.

24 *Ibid.*, p. 157.

calls upon states to take appropriate measures "to encourage the provision of the necessary supporting social services to enable parents to combine family obligations with work responsibilities and participation in public life, in particular through promoting the establishment and development of a network of child-care facilities". Further, Denmark and Sweden advocated Article 12, which sets forth the state's obligation to provide services for pregnancy and post-natal periods.[25]

Among the most important contributions are Sweden, Denmark and Norway's espousal of the recognition of equal civil and legal status, the right to enter into contracts, enforcement of property rights, and equal treatment in all stages of procedures before judicial authorities, all contained within Article 15.[26] Yet, at present, the Nordic countries struggle with a lack of research, legislation and inconsistent case law addressing gender-based disparities between spouses and problems relating to dissolution of marriage and distribution of marital assets, concealment of property, *etc.*[27]

3.3 *Common Objections to Reservations Incompatible with the Object and Purpose of* CEDAW

Of special significance, Sweden, Denmark and Norway objected to reservations to CEDAW made by states which claimed that accession cannot conflict with the laws on personal status derived from the Islamic Sharia (such as Libyan Arab Jamahiriya), stating that this is incompatible with the object and purpose of the Convention.[28] The clash between women's human rights and religious mores continues to be a perplexing challenge which the Nordic countries engage with both externally and internally.[29]

These examples illustrate the significant contribution of the Nordic states towards the normative evolution of women's human rights at the universal level which merit reflection and recognition at present. In spite of this, scholars have noted that the CEDAW has been marginalised, for example "as a source

25 *Ibid.*, p. 146.

26 *Ibid.*, p. 164.

27 *See generally* J. Asland *et al.*, *Nordic Cohabitation Law* (Intersentia, Antwerp, 2015). CEDAW CO Iceland, *supra* note 21, paras. 49–50; CEDAW CO Sweden, *supra* note 21, paras. 38–39; CEDAW CO Sweden, *supra* note 21, paras. 41–42; CEDAW CO Finland, *supra* note 21, paras. 38–39; CEDAW CO Norway, *supra* note 21, paras. 37–38; and CEDAW CO Denmark, *supra* note 20, paras. 41–42.

28 Rehof, *supra* note 13, pp. 276 and 280.

29 *See e.g.* A. Hellum, 'Transnational challenges to international and national law: Norwegian-Pakistani women at the interface', in C. Bailliet (ed.), *Non-State Actors, Soft Law and Protective Regimes* (Cambridge University Press, Cambridge, 2012) p. 151.

of Finnish legal reform and in court praxis".[30] Indeed, there remain internal challenges within all the Nordic states where neither the CEDAW nor 'women's law' have been sufficiently incorporated within legal instruments nor institutions, in spite of the fact that gender equality may be regarded as constituting a shared cultural value within the region.

4 Current Internal Challenges

4.1 *Legal Guarantee of Equality*

Although the Nordic states played a key role in drafting the CEDAW, they have failed to sufficiently reform their domestic legislation to incorporate the equality guarantees that they advocated.[31] Indeed, within Norway, the women's rights movement fought for ten years to have the CEDAW incorporated into the Human Rights Act.[32] At present, regarding Norway, the Committee on the Elimination of Discrimination against Women is concerned "at the lack of guarantee or definition of gender equality in the State party's Constitution or other appropriate legislation. The Committee is also concerned that the use of gender neutral legislation, policies and programmes might lead to inadequate protection of women against direct or indirect discrimination and hinder the achievement of substantive equality between women and men".[33]

The Committee called upon Norway to: "Embody the principle of equality of women and men into the Constitution or other appropriate legislation in accordance with Article 2 of the Convention, adopt a more gender-specific approach for its legislation, policies, and programmes".[34] It is noteworthy that although the Norwegian Constitution was recently reformed to include additional human rights, it remains gender neutral.[35] There is an equality and anti-discrimination bill that will be considered by the Parliament in 2016 that also pursues a gender neutral approach.[36] Further, Norway was criticised for lacking

30 K. Nousiainen and M. Pentikäinen, 'Rise and Fall of the CEDAW in Finland: time to reclaim its impetus', in Hellum and Aasen, *supra* note 19, pp. 557 and 558.

31 In terms of definition in Article 1, they defended recognition of the purpose of the Convention to be the elimination of discrimination based on sex. Rehof, *supra* note 13, p. 46

32 Hellum, *supra* note 19, p. 595.

33 CEDAW CO Norway, *supra* note 21, para. 9.

34 *Ibid.*, para. 10.

35 The Norwegian Constitution § 98: "Alle er like for loven. Intet menneske må utsettes for usaklig eller uforholdsmessig forskjellsbehandling".

36 *White Paper on Equality in Practice (2015–2016)*, available at: <www.regjeringen.no/no/dokumenter/meld.-st.-7-20152016/id2456562/?ch=1&q=>, visited on 17 March 2016. For

implementing legislation to guarantee equal pay for work of equal value, and the persistence of a wage gap.[37]

Similarly, regarding Denmark, the CEDAW Committee offered the critique that since the CEDAW is not incorporated into Danish national law, it has a secondary status.[38] The lack of legislation on discrimination would render marginalised women more vulnerable; hence the Committee "reiterates its call upon the State party to reconsider its decision not to incorporate the Convention into its national legal order, or at least to adopt a comprehensive law on the prohibition of sex discrimination in all areas covered by the Convention".[39]

As pertaining to Iceland, the CEDAW Committee suggested that Iceland fully incorporate the Convention and make it an integral part of its national legislation without delay, as well as recommending the adoption of a comprehensive anti-discrimination legislation.[40] Furthermore, the Committee expressed concern that although Iceland has an Act on Equal Status and Equal Rights of Women and Men, the gender wage gap has persisted at 7–18 per cent over the past years, and the Centre of Gender Equality lacks sufficient human and financial resources to monitor compliance by companies.[41]

Finally, with respect to Sweden, the CEDAW Committee called upon the state to ensure that the provisions of the Convention are duly incorporated into the domestic legal system and directly applicable in the national courts.[42]

It is important to note that the Nordic states have advanced in the area of equality by way of reference to EU legislation and regulations; hence the lack of incorporation of the CEDAW or of constitutional guarantees should not be interpreted to mean that there has been no progress.[43] At present, there appears to be an interest in harmonising the different legal regimes in order to provide a holistic approach to guaranteeing equality.[44]

---

arguments against gender neutral legislation, *see* V. Blaker Strand, 'Forenklingsjuss – En trussel mot individers vern mot kjønnsdiskriminering?', 8 *Lov og Rett* (2015); Hellum, *supra* note 19, pp. 611–616.

37 CEDAW CO Norway, *supra* note 21, paras. 29–30.

38 CEDAW CO Denmark, *supra* note 20, para. 11.

39 *Ibid.*, para. 12.

40 CEDAW CO Iceland, *supra* note 21, para. 10.

41 *Ibid.*, para. 30.

42 CEDAW CO Sweden, *supra* note 21, para. 15.

43 *See* R. Nielsen, 'The Impact of EU Law on Scandinavian Law in Matters of Gender Equality', in Nielsen and Tvarnø, *supra* note 10, p. 63.

44 *See e.g.* K. Nousiainen, *Gender Equality and Anti-discrimination Law, Equality Bodies, Equality Planning and Cooperation in Equality Matters in Finland* (09.11.2011), available at:

The need to pursue further incorporating legislation at the domestic level indicates that the CEDAW was perhaps considered to be of more relevance externally than internally. Indeed, Kevät Nousiainen and Merja Pentikäinen wryly point out that:

> In Finland the CEDAW and human rights in general have been emphasized more in the context of Finnish foreign policies and international cooperation rather than as matters of relevance at home. It is quite telling that in the area of state administration, the CEDAW appears particularly in the work of the Ministry of Foreign Affairs.[45]

4.2 *Knowledge of Rights*

The CEDAW Committee is also concerned about the lack of knowledge among Danish, Icelandic, Swedish and Norwegian women of their rights under the Convention, and hence called upon the states to "raise awareness of their rights under the Convention and of legal remedies available at the national and local levels, including through information campaigns and the media".[46]

In relation to Norway and Iceland, the CEDAW Committee is also concerned at the:

> general lack of awareness of the Convention and its Optional Protocol in the State party, in particular, among Government officials, the judiciary and other law enforcement officials; at the lack of case law, including Supreme Court case law, referring to the Convention.

And in relation to Norway "that it had not been included in the new judicial training programme mentioned by the Minister during the dialogue".[47]

<www.regjeringen.no/globalassets/upload/bld/sla/skjeieutvalget/rapport_likestilling sapparat_finland.pdf>.

45 Nousianen and Pentikäinen, *supra* note 30, p. 586.

46 CEDAW CO Norway, *supra* note 21, para. 10; CEDAW CO Iceland, *supra* note 21, para. 7; CEDAW CO Denmark, *supra* note 20, para. 10; and CEDAW CO Sweden, *supra* note 21, para. 12.

47 The Committee further called upon the state to: "Take the necessary steps to ensure the adequate dissemination of the Convention, the Optional Protocol and the Committee's general recommendations among all stakeholders, including Government ministries, parliamentarians, the judiciary jury and law enforcement officers; Include the Convention, the views adopted on individual communications and inquiries under the Optional Protocol and the Committee's general recommendations into judicial training programs; and Intensify its efforts to raise awareness among women on their rights under the Convention and the communication and inquiry procedures by its Optional Protocol".

The CEDAW Committee expressed similar observations regarding the lack of invocation of the Convention within the Finnish and Swedish courts as well.[48] It called upon Finland and Sweden to promote capacity building programmes for judges, prosecutors and lawyers on the Convention, the Optional Protocol, *etc.* in order to enable them to invoke these instruments before domestic courts and interpret domestic legislation accordingly.[49] Hence, there appears to be a general lack of dissemination about women's rights within the judicial branches within the region, weakening implementation of rights.

4.3 *Intersecting Forms of Discrimination and Lack of Access to Justice*

As Nordic states have become more multi-cultural, due to immigration, the issue of discrimination evolved to address different groups. The CEDAW Committee recommended that "Denmark consider the enactment of a comprehensive law on the prohibition of discrimination covering all internationally recognized grounds and the establishment of institutionalized structures to exchange and coordinate information among its various bodies for tackling discrimination, with a view to ensuring legal clarity and consistency, especially for women who are victims of intersecting forms of discrimination".[50]

CEDAW issued a similar conclusion to Finland, emphasising that "reforms explicitly affording protection to women against multiple or intersecting forms of discrimination in all national gender equality and anti-discrimination laws are [to be] adopted in a harmonized matter".[51] This was responding to the fact that the Act on Equality between Women and Men and the Non-Discrimination Act do not currently provide adequate protection to women against multiple or intersecting forms of discrimination. Furthermore, the CEDAW Committee called upon Finland to address access to justice: "strengthen measures to eliminate discrimination against migrant women, both in society at large and within their communities and develop targeted programmes and strategies to increase the awareness of migrant women of their rights and access to education, professional training, employment, health care and other basic services, as well as to free legal aid and effective remedies if their rights have been violated".[52] Similarly, Sweden was asked to revise the scope

CEDAW CO Norway, *supra* note 21, paras. 11 and 12 and CEDAW CO Iceland, *supra* note 21, para. 7.

48 CEDAW CO Finland, *supra* note 21, para 8; CEDAW CO Sweden, *supra* note 21, para. 12.

49 CEDAW CO Finland, *supra* note 21, para. 9; and CEDAW CO Sweden, *supra* note 21, para. 13.

50 CEDAW CO Denmark, *supra* note 20, para. 12.

51 CEDAW CO Finland, *supra* note 21, para. 11.

52 *Ibid.*, para. 31.

of protection within its Discrimination Act to ensure that it covers intersecting forms of discrimination against women.[53] The CEDAW Committee called for rights awareness campaigns to target Sami women, Roma women, migrant women, asylum-seeking and refugee women, and women with disabilities.[54] Of most importance, it also called upon the state to address access to justice approaches:

> to take all necessary measures to remove barriers for women victims of discrimination and enable them to effectively use the Discrimination Act to claim their rights, including by allocating adequate human, technical, and financial resources … The Committee further recommends that the State party ensure that the Equality Ombudsman is provided with adequate resources to effectively fulfil its broad mandate.[55]

In relation to Norway, the CEDAW Committee was also concerned at the lack of attention in some laws and policies to the specific needs of minority groups of women, including women with ethnic minority background and women with disabilities, often leading to intersectional discrimination.[56] The Committee addressed access to justice approaches to protection, specifically calling on Norway to strengthen the Equality and Anti-Discrimination Ombud by providing it with adequate human and technical resources and consider authorising the Ombud and the Tribunal to hear cased of sexual harassment and to raise awareness about the Equality and Anti-Discrimination Ombud, in particular, among women with a minority background. CEDAW called upon the state to "enhance programmes of capacity-building for women of minority background to encourage their participation in public and political life". It called upon the state to raise awareness of the nature of indirect discrimination and the principle of equality for all women, including women from ethnic minority backgrounds and women with disabilities, among government officials, the judiciary and the general public.

4.4 *Violence against Women*

The Nordic region is confronted with violence against women, characterised by the vulnerability of minority women, deportation of migrants (including those at risk of gender related persecution), prevalence of domestic violence,

53 CEDAW CO Sweden, *supra* note 21, para. 15.

54 *Ibid.*, para. 13.

55 *Ibid.*, para. 17.

56 CEDAW CO Norway, *supra* note 21, paras. 9 and 18; *see* A. Hellum and J. K. Olsen, *Like Rettigheter og ulike liv* (Gyldendal Copenhagen, 2014).

rape, prostitution, and human trafficking, which limit the achievement of gender equality and respect for women's rights. In keeping with Nordic feminists' attention to pluralistic dimensions of discrimination, the CEDAW Committee is straightforward in addressing challenges within each state.

The CEDAW Committee, upon reviewing Norway's report, expressed concern at the prevalence of violence against women, the high levels of acquittals, and the lenient sentences imposed on perpetrators in Norway. It called upon the state to "train lay judges on the subject of violence against women".[57] It also called for free legal aid for victims of trafficking, regardless of their availability or willingness to testify against their traffickers. In the matter of Denmark, the CEDAW Committee criticised the used of detention of victims of trafficking and called upon the state to support women, especially non-nationals, who wish to leave prostitution.[58] It also expressed concern that the use of gender-neutral approaches in the Criminal Code would negatively impact collection of data on domestic violence.[59] Regarding trafficking in Finland, the CEDAW Committee called upon the state to assess the risk of deportation of victims of trafficking and called for a broad range of assistance to be provided.[60] It also called for reform of the legislation on rape, *inter alia* to remove the requirement of force or threat in the case of sexual assault and instead place consent at the centre of the definition and to increase the conviction rates in cases of rape.[61]

With regard to Iceland, the CEDAW Committee also expressed concern about the high number of discontinuances in criminal proceedings for charges of violence against women, in particular rape and sexual violence, by the state prosecutor and the low number of convictions, as well as the lack of a legal analysis of the high number of acquittals in sexual violence cases.[62] The Committee also criticised the lack of a national action plan against sexual and domestic violence that would take into account the specific needs and vulnerabilities of migrant women and women with disabilities.[63] It called upon the state to strengthen prosecution and conviction of perpetrators of sexual violence and address the causes of acquittals, as well as calling for ratification and incorporation of the Istanbul Convention in order to strengthen the legal protection of women from domestic violence.[64]

---

57 CEDAW CO Norway, *supra* note 21, para. 24.

58 CEDAW CO Denmark, *supra* note 20, paras. 19–22.

59 *Ibid.*, paras. 39–40.

60 CEDAW CO Finland, *supra* note 21, para. 21.

61 *Ibid.*, para. 19.

62 CEDAW CO Iceland, *supra* note 21, para. 19.

63 *Ibid.*

64 *Ibid.*, para. 20.

As pertaining to Sweden, the Committee expressed concern for the low reporting rates of cases of violence against women, including rape, and low prosecution and conviction rates, resulting in impunity for perpetrators; thus it called for a study of the root causes and improved efforts to eliminate barriers to reporting, as well as evaluation of response by police and the judiciary to complaints of sexual crimes, and mandatory capacity building for judges, prosecutors and the police, and systematic collection of data on violence against women, protection measures, prosecution and sentencing.[65] Further, it called for amendment of the criminal code to ensure that rape is defined on the basis of lack of consent of the victim.[66] The Committee also indicated concern for the reversal of Sweden's asylum policy which may have particularly negative consequences for women and children asylum-seekers, and hence called for implementation of the non-refoulement principle and the adoption of a gender sensitive approach to ensure that the needs of asylum-seeking and refugee women and girls are addressed as a priority concern.[67]

The lack of sufficient response by the judiciary and other actors to situations involving violence against women is inconsistent with the Nordic profile as a leader in gender equality.[68] The need for a significant structural overhaul and institutional cultural change in order to provide a better foundation for prevention and protection of women is underscored.

4.5 *Conclusion on Internal Promotion of Women's Rights*

If we move from marginalised groups to those aspiring towards leadership, the CEDAW Committee is concerned about the underrepresentation of women in academic institutions and in the private sector, especially at decision making levels, and in particular in technical areas. In relation to Norway, the CEDAW Committee is also concerned about the low number of women professors. Across the Nordic region, 80 per cent of professors are men.[69] Women's

---

65 CEDAW CO Sweden, *supra* note 21, paras. 26 and 27.

66 *Ibid.*, para. 15.

67 *Ibid.*, paras. 10 and 11. *See also* CEDAW, *M.E.N.* v. *Denmark*, Communication No. 35/2011, CEDAW/C/55/D/35/2011 (19 August 2013), dissent by Committee member Ms. Dubravka Simonovic, joined by Ms. Ruth Halperin-Kaddari, Ms. Violeta Neubauer and Ms. Silvia Pimentel, criticising Denmark for failing to recognise gender related persecution and sex-based discrimination in an asylum case involving a woman who had been gang raped in Burundi.

68 *See* U. Andersson, 'Våld mot kvinnor i straffrätten', in Svensson *et. al.*, *supra* note 10, p. 405.

69 Nordic Information on Gender, 'The Nordic Countries Dealing with Gender Inequality in Academia' (24 April 2015), available at: <www.nikk.no/en/news/the-nordic-countries-dealing-with-gender-inequality-in-academia/>, visited on 17 March 2016.

income is still at only 60 per cent of men's income.[70] The labour market remains segregated; most women work in the public sector and most men in the private sector. Men hold the majority of key political, economic and other decision making positions. There is a need to strengthen the internal promotion of women's rights; the gaps regarding faulty implementation of the Convention, lack of knowledge of rights, structural challenges, lack of access to justice and the prevalence of violence against women indicate that the Nordic region cannot regard women's rights as an external issue.

On a positive note, Norway's Ministry of Children, Equality and Inclusion issued a White Paper on Equality in Practice in 2015 which presents the government's policies addressing equality within Norwegian society, broadly spanning the family, kindergarten, schools, workplace, violence, forced marriage, rape, sexual harassment, hate speech, health, business and international cooperation.[71] Similarly, Sweden recently launched a "He for She" initiative which seeks to close the gap between women and men in pay and employment, advance women leaders in sectors and address gender inequities in health.[72] Finally, the Nordic states have a joint programme, Together for Gender Equality – A Stronger Nordic Region (2015–2018), which promotes cooperation for equality within the Nordic countries.[73] This indicates that there appears to be a strong regional push to address equality issues internally, and thus it will be interesting to measure the results of these initiatives in the future.

5 External Actions: The Promotion of Development and Peacebuilding

The Nordic Countries are renowned for promoting women's rights externally. They cooperate with the United Nations (UN) and EU agencies to pursue

70 OECD, 'Closing the Gender Gap: Norway', available at: <www.oecd.org/norway/Closing%20the%20Gender%20Gap%20-%20Norway%20EN.pdf >, visited on 17 March 2016.

71 White Paper on Equality in Practice, Meld. 7 Likestilling i praksis (2015–2016), available at: <www.regjeringen.no/no/dokumenter/meld.-st.-7-20152016/id2456562/>, visited on 17 March 2016.

72 "He for She" is located at: <//www.heforshe.org/>, visited on 17 March 2016. On equality policies within Sweden, *see generally*: <sweden.se/society/gender-equality-in-sweden/>, visited on 17 March 2016.

73 Nordic Information on Gender, *Together for Gender Equality – A Stronger Nordic Region: Nordic co-Operation Programme on Gender Equality 2015–2018 Nordiska ministerrådet, Norden*, available at: <www.nikk.no/en/publications/together-for-gender-equality-a-stronger-nordic-region-nordic-co-operation-programme-on-gender-equality-2015-2018-nordiska-ministerradet-nord/>, visited on 17 March 2016.

equality projects in various countries, such as via UN Women and the EU's PROGRESS programme.[74] These may be taken as examples of 'governance feminism' in which any form of state, state-like or state-affiliated power is capable of being infiltrated by feminists and feminist ideas, often promoted in cooperation with transnational NGOs and experts.[75] There has been some concern that the emergence of 'governance feminism' has depoliticised gender, and it is interesting to note that the Nordic external focus on structural empowerment provides a contrasting example.[76] Given that women within the Nordic region have a long history of participating in agriculture, fishing and even industry, it is understandable that the region opts for promotion of long-term development initiatives addressing education, health care, access to justice, farming, access to energy and political participation as key to the emancipation and enjoyment of women's rights within Africa, Asia, the Middle East and Latin America.[77] One key example is Norway's support for teaching and research cooperation between the Institute of Women's Law at the University of Oslo and the Southern and Eastern Regional Center in Women's Law at the University of Zimbabwe. This research cooperation contributed to the CEDAW Committee's jurisprudence on rural women's social and economic rights, including the right to water for personal, domestic and livelihood uses in General Recommendation 34.[78]

---

74 UN Women is available at: www.unwomen.org/en; the UN Commission on the Status of Women is available at: <www.unwomen.org/en/csw>, both visited on 16 March 2016. The EU Progress programme is available at: <ec.europa.eu/social/main.jsp?catId=327>, visited on 16 March 2016.

75 J. Halley *et al.*, 'From the International to the Local in Feminist Legal Responses to Rape, Prostitution/Sex Work, and Sex Trafficking: Four Studies in Contemporary Governance Feminism', 29:2 *Harvard Journal of Law & Gender* (2006) pp. 335–425, at p. 335; H. Shamir, 'Background Materials before Reading the Draft Chapter – Anti Trafficking in Israel: Nationalism, Borders, Markets', available at: <www.clb.ac.il/images/files/Background%20 Shamir.doc> and <www.law.harvard.edu/students/orgs/jlg/vol292/halley.pdf>.

76 *See generally* American Society of International Law, 'Democracy, Gender and Governance: Questions and Answers', 101 *American Society of International Law Proceedings* (28–31 March 2007) p. 384.

77 *See e.g.* NORAD's *Annual Report on Women's Rights and Equality* (2015), available at: <www.norad.no/en/toolspublications/publications/2015/results-report-2015.-womens-rights-and-gender-equality>, visited on 17 March 2016.

78 *See* A. Hellum, P. Kameri-Mbote and B. van Koppen, *Water Is Life: Women's Human Rights in National and Local Water Governance in Southern and Eastern Africa* (Weaver Press, Harare, 2015); UN Committee on the Elimination of Discrimination Against Women, General Recommendation 34 on the Rights of Rural Women, CEDAW/C/GC/34

One of the most significant areas of international engagement by Nordic women is within peace promotion. The link between the quest for peace and feminism is complex, given disagreements among feminists about the legitimacy of humanitarian intervention (in particular within the context of conflicts involving women as victims of mass rapes and sexual violence).[79] Historically, there were Nordic women's peace marches against nuclear weapons in Europe, in the USSR and USA during the 1980s.[80] Since then, Nordic women have sought to increase their participation in peace negotiation. In Norway, Prime Minister Erna Solberg has underscored the importance of women's participation in peacebuilding. Norway is promoting an Action Plan on Women, Peace and Security (2015–2018) which will seek to promote women's participation in peace processes and help ensure that women's economic and political status and legal rights are given more emphasis in peacebuilding processes.[81]

On 27 November 2015, representatives of the Ministries of Foreign Affairs of Norway, Sweden, Finland and Iceland gathered at the Nobel Peace Centre in Oslo, Norway to launch the Nordic Women Mediators Network.[82] State Secretary Tore Hattrem of the Ministry of Foreign Affairs of Norway explained that this initiative was inspired by a South African network of women mediators. He expressed the belief that the implementation of sustainable peace could only be achieved by including meaningful participation of women in peace negotiations. The persistent lack of women peace negotiators in spite of UN Security Council Resolution 1325 was recognised; between 1992 and 2011 only 9 per cent of peace negotiators and 2 per cent of lead mediators were women.

(4 March 2016), available at: <tbinternet.ohchr.org/_layouts/treatybodyexternal/Download.aspx?symbolno=CEDAW/C/GC/34&Lang=en>, visited on 26 March 2016.

79 *See* J. Huckerby, 'Feminism and International Law in the Post 9/11 Era', 39 *Fordham International Law Journal* (2016) p. 536; G. Heathcote, 'Feminist Perspectives on the Law on the Use of Force', in M. Weller (ed.), *Oxford University Press Handbook on the Prohibition of the Use of Force* (Oxford University Press, Oxford, 2015) pp. 114–128; G. Heathcote, 'Robust Peacekeeping, Gender and the Protection of Civilians', in H. Charlesworth and F. Jeremy (eds.), *Strengthening the Rule of Law through the UN Security Council* (Routledge, Abington, 2015); C. A. MacKinnon, 'Women's September 11th: Rethinking the International Law of Conflict', 47:1 *Harvard International Law Review* (Winter 2006).

80 For an overview of this history, *see* the video by Trine Eklund, available at: <www.youtube.com/watch?v=ZrF9WxGJBhM>, visited on 17 March 2016.

81 Norway's *National Action Plan on Women, Peace and Security 2015–2018* is available at: <www.regjeringen.no/en/dokumenter/women-peace-security/id2395993/>, visited on 16 March 2016.

82 For the programme of the launch, see: <www.prio.org/Events/Event/?x=8379>, visited on 17 March 2016.

Hattrem noted that it was important for the Nordics to lead by example; hence they should ensure that their own delegations and negotiation teams are gender balanced and address gender issues, as well as support the appointment of women as UN special envoys, special representatives, ambassadors and other offices. He concluded by stating: "It is not about counting women, it is about making women count". There was discussion about the common heritage of the Nordic countries in implementing gender equality through public education, health care, child care, social safety nets, *etc.* In addition, 'Nordic' was considered to be a good brand name in international affairs that could help push the aspiration of promoting gender empowerment throughout the world. Hilde Frafjord Johnson, former Special Representative of the Secretary General (SRSG) and Head of the UN Mission in South Sudan (2011–2014), observed that since women are more seldom belligerents they are more often excluded from cease fire negotiations. She indicated that peace negotiations should ideally be divided into different stages, separating the cease fire stage from the state building/peace building stage, which would address political and social issues relating to marginalisation and exclusion that should include women. The objectives of this network are:

- To increase the number of Nordic women that are actively involved in international peace mediation efforts.
- To connect with and promote networks of women mediators in the South, both at country level and in regional organisations.
- To serve as a pilot for similar initiatives in other regions or at the international level, through close coordination with the UN.

Indeed, in May 2016, the UN launched the network internationally at a meeting on "Women in Mediation" in New York.[83] The Norwegian mediators visited Cyprus that month. This initiative indicates that there is a possibility that a Nordic feminist foreign policy may be emerging, and this is further explored in the next section.

6 The Myth of a Nordic Feminist Foreign Policy

It may be argued that among the Nordics, Sweden is leading in terms of promoting a vision of a feminist foreign policy. Both Sweden and Norway issued action plans, respectively addressing feminist foreign policy 2015–2018 and women's

83 PRIO, *Gender Peace and Security Update*, Issue 2, 3 (2016).

rights and equality in foreign policy 2016–2020. These action plans highlight the aims of combating sexual violence, promoting sexual and reproductive rights, political rights, economic rights, education, and sustainable development. The most progressive aspects of these action plans are their approaches to addressing women's access to education (from primary to tertiary), land and property ownership/inheritance rights, gender responsive budgeting, access to productive and inclusive work, women's rights as workers, business opportunities and network, as well as inclusion in development and corporate social responsibility plans. Personifying the feminist foreign policy is Sweden's minister of foreign affairs, Margot Wallström, noting: "Striving toward gender equality is not only a goal in itself but also a precondition for achieving our wider foreign, development, and security policy objectives".[84] However, visionaries are often attacked, and hence Wallström encountered significant blowback after she commented on Saudi Arabia's violation of women's rights.[85] None of the other Nordics stepped forward to defend Wallström; she remained isolated. The response by Saudi Arabia was strong, as it withdrew its ambassador, issued a freeze on visas to Swedish businessmen, and prompted cancellation of Wallström's speech at the Arab League.[86] In *IntLawGrrls*, Professor Milena Sterio grimly related the significance of the silence by the West:

---

84 J. Nordberg, 'Who's Afraid of a Feminist Foreign Policy?', *The New Yorker* (15 April 2015), available at: <www.newyorker.com/news/news-desk/swedens-feminist-foreign-minister>, visited on 17 March 2016.

85 N. Cohen, 'Sweden's feminist foreign minister has dared to tell the truth about Saudi Arabia. What happens now concerns us all', *The Spectator* (28 March 2015), available at: <new.spectator.co.uk/2015/03/swedens-feminist-foreign-minister-has-dared-to-tell-the-truth-about-saudi-arabia-what-happens-now-concerns-us-all/>, visited on 17 March 2016.

86 'Editorial: The Guardian's view on Sweden's foreign policy: admirable, but maybe not entirely high-minded', *The Guardian* (15 March 2015), available at: <www.theguardian.com/commentisfree/2015/mar/15/guardian-view-sweden-foreign-policy-margot-wallstrom>, visited on 17 March 2016. *See also* A. Taylor, 'How Saudi Arabia turned Sweden's human rights criticisms into an attack on Islam', *The Washington Post* (24 March 2015), available at: <www.washingtonpost.com/news/worldviews/wp/2015/03/24/how-saudi-arabia-turned-swedens-human-rights-criticisms-into-an-attack-on-islam/>; M. Beyravesh, 'Gender clash: Why is Saudi Arabia so angry at Sweden?', *Your Middle East* (25 May 2015), available at: <www.yourmiddleeast.com/opinion/gender-clash-why-is-saudi-arabia-so-angry-at-sweden_30834>; I. Carlquist and L. Hedegaard, 'Sweden's Foreign Minister Reviled as an Enemy of the Prophet', *Gatestone Institute* (21 March 2015), available at: <www.gatestoneinstitute.org/5423/sweden-saudi-arabia-wallstrom>, all visited on 17 March 2016. It is of interest that after this event Saudi Arabia granted women voting rights, the right to register as candidates and run for office in municipal elections, although

> The lack of coverage of the Wallström Affair by the western media, and the lack of support for Wallström by western democracies, reveals two geo-political realities. First, it seems that smaller and less influential countries, such as Sweden, may be more easily manipulated into changing their foreign policy stances. Sweden most likely needs to export goods to Saudi Arabia more than Saudi Arabia needs to import the same goods.
>
> Second, it appears that human (and women's rights) always lose to other political and strategic goals. If we were to truly champion human (and women's rights), we would not partner with Saudi Arabia on much of anything, and we would be willing to publicly condemn this country's appalling practices. Sadly, the western democratic regimes have sent the opposite message through their lack of interest for the Wallstrom Affair – that geo-political and business interests trump the protection of human (and women's) rights. Or, "nous ne sommes pas Margot".[87]

The disappointment expressed by this scholar perhaps suggests a need to pursue a new epoch of Nordic promotion of women's rights as well as women within international law generally. Should Nordic states cooperate to enable women to become creators of international law, rather than subjects, we may enter a new phase of women's progress that would be remarkable.

7 Nordic Women as Creators of International Law

A feminist approach to international law seeks to reveal the structural bias which excludes the interests of women while presenting the law as neutral and upholding patriarchal structures in terms of both participation and substantive output.[88] Hilary Charlesworth and Christine Chinkin set forth that:

---

they were forced to sit in separate rooms from men after their election to the municipal councils. 'First Saudi women register to vote', *Al Jazeera* (20 August 2015), available at: <www.aljazeera.com/news/2015/06/saudi-women-register-vote-150621081535058.html>; K. Beckerle,'Those Newly Elected Saudi Women Just Got Pushed Away from the Table', *Women's ENews* (25 February 2016), available at: <womense<news.org/2016/02/those-newly-elected-saudi-women-just-got-pushed-away-from-the-table/>, both visited on 17 March 2016.

87 M. Sterio, 'The Wallstrom Affair: Je Suis Margot', *IntLawGrrls* (27 March 2015), available at: <https://ilg2.org/2015/03/27/the-wallstrom-affair-je-suis-margot/>, visited on 17 March 2016.

88 H. Charlesworth and C. Chinkin, *The Boundaries of International Law: A Feminist Analysis* (Manchester University Press, Manchester, 2000) pp. 60–61.

> Feminist analysis of international law has two major roles. One is deconstruction of the explicit and implicit values of the international legal system, challenging their claim to objectivity and rationality because of the limited base on which they are built. All tools and categories of international legal analysis become problematic when the exclusion of women from their construction is understood ... Investigating the silences of international law is another way of discovering its gendered nature: why are some activities considered capable of international legal regulation while others are not? ... Deconstruction ... reveal[s] 'the partial and partisan instead of the universal or representative position' of patriarchal discourse. The second role of feminist analysis of international law is that of reconstruction. ... It requires rebuilding the basic concepts of international law in a way that they do not support or reinforce the domination of women by men. The benefits of such a reconstruction would not be limited to women.[89]

In order to change international law, women need to become the creators of international law, not just the subject of international law, through participation in treaty making and the issuance of case law as international judges.[90] The pursuit of gender parity within national delegations for treaty drafting and negotiating sessions is essential. Indeed, Gry Larsen, the secretary general of CARE and former state secretary at the Norwegian Ministry of Foreign Affairs, remarked that during her time as state secretary she was often in the minority of women at most of the international meetings she attended, unless the meetings addressed women's rights and equality.[91] Hence she calls for more women

---

89 *Ibid.*

90 Fernando Teson sets forth three feminist critiques of international law: 1) The processes of international lawmaking exclude women, 2) The content of international law privileges men to the detriment of women, 3) International law, as a patriarchal institution, inherently oppresses women, marginalizes their interests, and submerges their experiences and perspectives. Regarding the first issue, Teson addresses the underrepresentation of women within international organisations, diplomatic service and government; he agrees that "imposing on states the duties of non-discrimination and equal opportunity, including affirmative measures where appropriate, is the only way to redress the underrepresentation of women as states agents ... Likewise, in international organizations it may make sense, depending on the circumstances to push to achieve a gender balance in the composition of the organization's personnel". F. Teson, 'Feminism and International Law: A Reply', 33 *Virginia Journal of International Law* (1993) p. 647.

91 G. Larsen, 'Norge burde inspireres av Sveriges feministiske utenrikspolitikk', *Dagbladet* (19 May 2015), available at: <www.dagbladet.no/2015/05/19/kultur/debatt/kronikk/meninger/utenrikspolitikk/39232650/>, visited on 17 March 2016.

within the diplomatic and foreign policy corps, and although there has been some improvement in the delegations, the lead actors are mostly men. She also supports the integration of a feminist perspective within international law, human rights, peace, democracy, education, labour, business and climate change.

Yet, the pursuit of feminist international law in practice may appear to be a bit serpentine.[92] As an example, one may consider the case of the recent climate change agreement, adopted in Paris in 2015.[93] Norway's negotiation team included women; in particular Christina Voigt, who played an important role in the drafting of the agreement.[94] However, the delegation was criticised by NGOs on account of the decision to remove references to human rights, including gender equality, from Article 2,[95] which articulates the aims of the

92 Katherine Bartlett identifies the following feminist legal methods: 1) Identifying and challenging those elements of existing legal doctrine that leave out or disadvantage women and members of other excluded groups (asking the woman question), 2) Reasoning from an ideal in which legal resolutions are pragmatic responses to concrete dilemmas rather than static choices between opposing, often mismatched perspectives (feminist practical reasoning), and 3) Seeking insights and enhanced perspectives through collaborative or interactive engagements with others based on personal experiences and narrative (consciousness-raising). She sets forth that feminist legal methods consider rules to over-represent power structures, and that application of rules have subordination effect; hence feminists value rule flexibility and the ability to identify missing points of view from those who are excluded, peripheral or invisible. K. Bartlett, 'Feminist Legal Methods', 10:4 *Harvard Law Review* (1990).

93 United Nations Framework Convention on Climate Change, Adoption of the Paris Agreement, FCCC/CP/2015/L.)/Rev.1 (12 December 2015).

94 Christina Voigt is a law professor at the University of Oslo who has published extensively in the field of climate change: <www.jus.uio.no/ior/english/people/aca/chrisvo/>, visited on 17 March 2016. She was recently appointed to the Permanent Court of Arbitration's Panel for Environmental Disputes, where she is one of only two women arbitrators: <pca-cpa.org/en/about/structure/panels-of-arbitrators-and-experts-for-environmental-disputes/>, visited on 17 March 2016. Norway's delegation was composed of ca. 70 persons from ministries, political parties, media, *etc.* The group was composed of about 50 per cent women. Among the 12 negotiators who took the floor to speak, four were women.

95 Article 2:

1. This Agreement, in enhancing the implementation of the Convention, including its objective, aims to strengthen the global response to the threat of climate change, in the context of sustainable development and efforts to eradicate poverty, including by:
   (a) Holding the increase in the global average temperature to well below 2 °C above pre-industrial levels and to pursue efforts to limit the temperature increase to 1.5 °C above pre-industrial levels, recognizing that this would significantly reduce the risks and impacts of climate change;

agreement. The reference was placed within the preamble, where it will not be considered to be legally binding or operative text, but instead serve as a context for the agreement:

> Acknowledging that climate change is a common concern of humankind, Parties should, when taking action to address climate change, respect, promote and consider their respective obligations on ... gender equality, empowerment of women, and intergenerational equity.

Voigt explained that it was essential to retain the focus of the agreement on climate change and that human rights would be more adequately addressed in Article 7 of the agreement on adaptation, which calls for gender-responsive approaches to adaptation.[96] Ironically, the Norwegian delegation was characterised as standing with Saudi Arabia in opposing human rights and gender equality.[97]

Hence, the question is whether the Norwegian delegation's strategic negotiation choice was correct in placing the recognition of gender equality within the periphery of the instrument in order to attain agreement among states parties to address the preponderant challenge of climate change. It is possible to both agree and disagree with this choice. If we view this from an ecofeminist perspective, there is a fundamental connection between the treatment of women and the environment that should not be weakened. In addition, it may be argued that the agreement is somewhat of a compromise, given that states retain the right to determine nationally their contribution to the agreement; hence the traditional respect for sovereignty is maintained (adhering

---

(b) Increasing the ability to adapt to the adverse impacts of climate change and foster climate resilience and low greenhouse gas emissions development, in a manner that does not threaten food production;

(c) Making finance flows consistent with a pathway towards low greenhouse gas emissions and climate-resilient development.

2. This Agreement will be implemented to reflect equity and the principle of common but differentiated responsibilities and respective capabilities, in the light of different national circumstances.

96 Interview with Christina Voigt, 1 March 2016.

97 S. Duyck, 'Norway: The Debbie Downer of the Paris Climate Talks', *The World Post* (12 September 2015), available at: <www.huffingtonpost.com/sebastien-duyck/norway-the-debbie-downer-_b_8746932.html>; L. Kastner, 'Human-rights protections at risk in Paris climate talks', *The City Paper* (4 December 2015), available at: <www.citypaper.com/blogs/the-news-hole/bcpnews-humanrights-protections-at-risk-in-paris-climate-talks-20151204-story.html>, both visited on 17 March 2016.

to the 'male' paradigm of law). Nevertheless, the orientation towards international cooperation to diminish the effects of climate change is in keeping with feminist environmental aspirations to address pragmatically the pressing global dilemma.[98] The inclusion of women within delegations negotiating international treaties will not necessarily guarantee an outcome which pursues a feminist approach to international law; nevertheless, their presence is essential from the perspective of democratic representation.

If we move to the second form of international law creation, case law emitted by international tribunals, there is also a need to address the underrepresentation of women as judges or members of monitoring committees.[99] It is estimated that men make up 83 per cent of members of major international courts, while women make up 17 per cent.[100] In September 2015, Norway and Sweden supported the launch of GQUAL, a global campaign which seeks to promote gender parity within international tribunals.[101] GQUAL aims to publicise information on tribunals, promote best practices for parity in nomination and voting, study the underrepresentation of women from the perspective of non-discrimination and work with governments to get states to pledge to nominate and vote for candidates in a manner compliant with gender parity. It appeared that Norway and Sweden would set an example for other countries to ensure that women would enjoy participation in international law tribunals.

However, in 2016, the CEDAW Committee had openings for new members. Ironically, Norway chose to support a male candidate, Gunnar Bergby, secretary-general of the Supreme Court of Norway, for membership to the CEDAW Committee instead of the female candidate, Anne Hellum, the renowned professor of women's law.[102] This came as a shock to the Norwegian and Swedish women's lobby groups, both of which had supported Anne Hellum due to her leadership and scholarship within the Department of Women's Law, Children's

---

98 For an overview of feminist approaches to international environmental law *see* C. C. Joyner and G. E. Little, 'It's Not Nice to Fool Mother Nature! The Mystique of Feminist Approaches to International Environmental Law', 14 *Boston University International Law Journal* (Fall 1996) p. 233. *See also* R. Connell and R. Pearse, *Gender in World Perspective*, third edition (Polity Press, Cambridge, 2015), chapter 7 on gender and environmental change.

99 For the statistics of women judges within the international courts *see*: <,visited">www .gqualcampaign.org/1626-2/>,visited on 17 March 2016.

100 *Ibid.*

101 The GQUAL campaign is available at: <www.gqualcampaign.org/home/>, visited on 17 March 2016.

102 An overview of Anne Hellum's publications is available at: <www.jus.uio.no/ior/english/people/aca/ahellum/>, visited on 17 March 2016.

Law, and Equality and Discrimination Law, teaching and research of women's law in Zimbabwe, and publications on the CEDAW.[103] Mr. Bergby worked with the gender equality ombudsman 30 years ago.[104] Given that the past three candidates nominated to the CEDAW have been men, there appeared to be a contradiction with Article 8 of the CEDAW which sets forth: "take all appropriate measures to ensure to women, on equal terms with men and without any discrimination, the opportunity to represent their Governments at the international level and to participate in the work of international organizations".[105] Norway appears to have completely reversed its commitment to the GQUAL Declaration on gender parity, and hence its leadership in promoting women within international law is diminished. When asked to comment on the reasoning behind the choice of Mr. Bergby, the spokesman of the Norwegian Ministry of Foreign Affairs, Rune Bjøstad, commented on the fact that the CEDAW Committee was dominated by women (22:1), as well as noting that in terms of competence in women's rights, "[t]he Committee has competence in Women's Rights, in part thanks to the experts from the South, which lends particular legitimacy when CEDAW reviews state reports from the South on implementation of their obligations under the Convention".[106]

This underscores the perception that women's rights are considered to be of external application, relevant to states outside of the Nordic region.

As a further point of reflection, to the extent that women are international judges or members of monitoring committees, several serve on international criminal courts or human rights bodies. Indeed, at present there are Nordic women judges within human rights, such as Helena Jäderblom and Pauliine Kauskelo, both judges on the European Court of Human Rights, and Kirsten Sandberg, member of the UN Committee on the Rights of the Child.[107] Women judges are often cited as having contributed by supporting

---

103 The statement of the Swedish Women's lobby is available at: <//sverigeskvinnolobby.se/en/anne-hellum-to-the-cedaw-committee/>, visited on 17 March 2016.

104 Mr. Bergby's CV is available at: <www.domstol.no/en/Enkelt-domstol/-Norges-Hoyesterett/The-Supreme-Court-of-Norway-/Justices/Directors-General/Gunnar-Bergby-Director-General/>, visited on 17 March 2016.

105 C. Martin, 'Article 8 of the Convention to Eliminate All Forms of Discrimination against Women: A Stepping Stone in Ensuring Gender Parity in International Organs and Tribunals' (2015), available at: <www.gqualcampaign.org/claudias-paper/>, visited on 17 March 2016.

106 N. Schmidt, 'Oppnevnte mann til Kvinnekomité', *Advokaten* 21 March 2016, available at: <www.advokatbladet.no/2016/03/oppnevnte-mann-til-kvinnekomite/>, visited 22 March 2016.

107 Pernilla Lindh of Sweden was a member of the European Court of Justice from 2006–2011.

jurisprudence on sexual violence, children's rights or women's rights, such as Navi Pillay.[108] This approach suggests that the interest in having women on the international bench is oriented towards outcome.[109] On the other hand, it has also been noted that "legal orders demand … neutrality in exchange for legitimacy: feminist judges, feminist policy makers, feminist experts must obey the rituals of rule of law, objectivity and legal rationality to stay in power".[110] Hence, there may also be cases of restraint by women judges who may be reluctant to articulate feminist perspectives in their decisions. It may be argued that it is much more salient to orient the discussion of appointment of women judges from the perspective of democratic representation, as with the example of including women within treaty negotiation teams. Yet, it is arguable that it may be imperative to place women on trade and investment tribunals where they have a potential to address structural violence. As stated by Dianne Otto:

> I am concerned that there is no frame for imagining what comes after the enterprise of addressing sexual violence. I am concerned that the institutionalization of feminist ideas, in international law and politics, has divested them of their radical potential. I am also concerned that the urge to think 'after gender', as much as the idea excites me, may destroy the categories that so many of us rely upon as springboards to our critiques of the present and our imaginings of better futures.[111]

These issues merit attention and action because the Nordic region may well be described as having come the closest to being 'post gender'. And yet, due to the uneven Nordic approach to women's rights there is clearly a need to

---

108 B. Bedont and K. Hall-Martinez, 'Ending impunity for gender crimes under the International Criminal Court', *Brown Journal of World Affairs* (1999) p. 65.

109 Nevertheless, with respect to international criminal law (ICL), some feminists have criticised the focus of 'governance feminists' on ICL's prosecution and punishment of perpetrators over reparations and socio-economic assistance approaches which would actually enable women (victims, family members, community) to attain dignity and a means to rebuild their lives. *See* J. Halley, 'Rape at Rome: Feminist Interventions in the Criminalization of Sex-Related Violence in Positive International Criminal Law', 30 *Michigan Journal of International Law* (Fall 2008), providing an engrossing account of the impact of governance feminism on ICL jurisprudence. An additional critique is that ICL is seen as promoting a "hegemony of victimhood" instead of focusing on women's agency. J. Huckerby, 'Feminism and International Law in the Post 9/11 Era', 39 *Fordham International Law Journal* (February 2016) p. 533.

110 Shamir, *supra* note 75.

111 D. Otto, 'Prospects for International Gender Norms', 31 *Pace Law Review* (2011) p. 873.

continue to promote women's human rights both internally and externally. Internal challenges include the continued need for institutional and normative development, as well as improving access to justice for vulnerable women. The Nordic region has always led the world in developing women's rights, and there is great potential to pursue creative approaches to eliminate subordination, marginalisation and exclusion of women.

Conspicuous Absence and Mistaken Presence. A Note on the Ambiguous Role of Scandinavian Legal Realism in Nordic Approaches to International Law

Jakob v. h. Holtermann[1]

> There is an *ambiguity* in the term 'positivism'. It can both be defined as 'what is based on experience' and as 'what is formally established'. The reaction against positivism is justified with respect to the latter, but not with respect to the former meaning. A realistic doctrine of the sources of law is based on experience but recognises that not all sources are positive in the sense that they are 'formally established'.
>
> ALF ROSS[2]

1 Introduction

By way of introduction, I should briefly situate this chapter. Unlike most contributors to this volume, I did not participate in the conference in Oslo with a distinct paper on Nordic approaches to international law. I was part of the

---

1 I am grateful for comments from and discussion with participants at the conference on "A Nordic Approach to International Law?", held 27–29 August 2015 in Oslo, Norway. I remain particularly indebted to the convenor of the conference Astrid Kjeldgaard-Pedersen, and to Dan Priel and Alessandro Serpe for helpful suggestions. Furthermore, I would like to thank participants at the conference "Still Exceptional? Nordic Countries Constitutional Tradition in the 21st Century", held 16–17 May 2016 at the European University Institute in Florence, Italy. Section 4 of this contribution draws closely on the paper "Scandinavian Realism and Nordic Exceptionalism – a Philosophical Mismatch?", which I delivered there. This research is funded by the Danish National Research Foundation Grant No. DNRF105 and conducted under the auspices of the Danish National Research Foundation's Centre of Excellence for International Courts (iCourts).

2 A. Ross, *A Textbook of International Law: General Part* (Longmans, Green and Co., London, 1947), p. 95.

 | DOI 10.1163/9789004343597_014

closing round-table, the aim of which was to round up and suggest further perspectives on the many rich and thoughtful discussions that had taken place during the three days in the beautiful surroundings of Lysebu. The convenor Astrid Kjeldgaard-Pedersen had invited me for this panel not as an international lawyer, but as a legal philosopher – and, in particular, as one who has spent quite some time studying the scholarship of Scandinavian Legal Realism and notably the works of Alf Ross.[3] If beside the notion of a possibly distinct approach to international law, there is anything in law for which our small region has gained international renown, Scandinavian Legal Realism seems to be the best candidate.[4] Kjeldgaard-Pedersen was therefore interested in exploring whether or not, at the closing of the conference, it might be possible to discern traces of congeniality between Scandinavian Realism and Nordic approaches to international law.

At the conference, I therefore made my closing remarks from that perspective, focusing on two main issues, on which I shall also focus in the following. Before doing so, however, I presented some more general methodological reflections in light of the conference discussions and main conclusions on Nordic approaches to international law; reflections on the virtues and vices of the conference's predominant "approach to the approach" so to speak. These remarks did not strictly relate to Scandinavian Legal Realism as such. I shall nevertheless briefly recapitulate the main idea in Section 2 ("Approaches to

3 Besides exegetic work on Ross (*cf.* e.g. J.v.H. Holtermann, 'A Straw Man Revisited – Resettling the Score Between H.L.A. Hart and Scandinavian Legal Realism', 57:1 *Santa Clara Law Review* (forthcoming, 2018)) I have written introductions to and edited new editions both in Danish and English of his own main work (A. Ross, *Om ret og retfærdighed : En indførelse i den analytiske retsfilosofi*, 2nd ed., and a new introduction for this edition by J.v.H. Holtermann ed. (Hans Reitzels Forlag, Copenhagen, 2013); and A. Ross, *On Law and Justice*, trans. Uta Bindreiter, rev. ed., and a new introduction for this edition by J.v.H. Holtermann ed. (Oxford University Press, Oxford, forthcoming 2017) respectively. In the following, I shall occasionally be referencing passages from *On Law and Justice/Om ret og retfærdighed* that Ross for unknown reasons decided to exclude from the 1958 English translation. I have therefore chosen to quote from the new complete translation of the forthcoming 2nd English edition. For consistency, I have further chosen to do so throughout the chapter, i.e. even when quoting passages that Ross did include in the 1958 edition. Since the forthcoming edition has not yet been typeset, this means that I can only refer to Ross's § numbers.

4 It is telling of the continuous influence of Scandinavian Realism that a standard textbook and -compilation like *Lloyd's Introduction to Jurisprudence* contains a separate chapter comprising 42 pages on and by the Scandinavian Realists (*cf.* M.D.A. Freeman, *Lloyd's Introduction to Jurisprudence*, 8th ed. (Sweet & Maxwell, London, 2008), pp. 869–910). The current plans of the Oxford University Press publication of a full new translation of Alf Ross's main work *Om ret og retfærdighed/On Law and Justice* counts to the same effect.

the Approach: Some Methodological Reflections"), because I believe it points to something important also with a view to defining an agenda for future additional research on Nordic approaches to international law. At the same time, this section prepares the ground for the introduction of a distinction between two further aspects of Nordic approaches to international law, which I shall use to structure the remaining parts of the chapter, where I turn to the ambiguous relation between these approaches and Scandinavian realism. Section 3 ("Conspicuous Absence: Carefree Scholarly Engagement in International Legal Politics") discusses the approach taken in the shaping of international law directly at the international level in various international fora such as the United Nations, the Council of Europe, the International Law Commission, international courts, etc. Traditionally, this would be considered a purely *legal political* dimension of international law, where the outcome usually takes the shape of treaties. Then, Section 4 ("Mistaken Presence: the Dubious Linking of Scandinavian Realism with Nordic Exceptionalism in Constitutional Law") examines the approach taken in the domestication of such international law – immediately through the ratification of treaties, but also, and of particular importance in this context, through the integration by national judiciaries of the case law of international courts and tribunals. Traditionally, this would be considered a more *legal doctrinal* dimension of international law, and one relating to domestic constitutional law. Papers and discussions at the conference touched upon both these aspects, and I shall deal with them specifically in relation to Scandinavian Realism in sections 3 and 4 respectively.

2 Approaches to the Approach: Some Methodological Reflections

It is probably fair to say that the overall conclusion – both at the conference and in this edited volume – was, to use a term from natural science, a 'null result'. Although expressed in different ways and with different emphasis and qualifications by different participants, the predominant message was that a distinct Nordic approach to international law could not be identified. This negative conclusion was probably conveyed most clearly – and most bleakly – already on the first day of conference by Gregor Noll in his excellent keynote address "*Nostalghia*: A Nordic International Law". Taking as his point of departure a demonstration of the glaring lack of convergence between the Nordic countries on a number of central issues in international law – the use of force, international recognition and humanitarian law – Noll concluded that a common Nordic approach to international law does not exist. Or, to be precise, he concluded that it does not exist as a matter of doctrinal legal fact.

Instead, Noll asserted, 'Nordic international law' exists today only as a vague, nostalgic memory of the region's greatness in times past: "a mentality that is acutely mindful of past grandeur and therefore sees and laments present decay";[5] a theme which he masterfully played through a parallel reading of the present situation with Tarkovski's film *Nostalghia* (1983).

Without in any way challenging the soundness of Noll's specific reasoning – or of any other conference participant – I suggested, however, that this general picture of a denial of a common Nordic approach might have been somewhat skewed as a function of the participants' nationality and/or disciplinary background. First of all, the participants were all either Nordic nationals or "domesticated" through several years of working and living in the Nordics, and with few exceptions they all had specific training in one or more Nordic legal system. This fact of course bodes well with regard to possession of the relevant legal expertise. However, it also carries with it the risk of succumbing in one's analysis to what Sigmund Freud has aptly dubbed *the narcissism of small differences*, i.e.

> the peculiar fact that peoples whose territories are adjacent, and are otherwise closely related, are always at feud with and ridiculing each other, as, for instance, the Spaniards and the Portuguese, the North and South Germans, the English and the Scotch, and so on.[6]

Feud and *ridicule* definitely do not capture the cordial character of the exchanges at the conference. However, it cannot be excluded that the general picture may have manifested a tendency to exaggerate inter-Nordic differences and downplay similarities. Thus, it was characteristic of virtually all participants that they restricted their set of observations to the international law practices of the Nordic countries to the exclusion of non-Nordic countries. As a means of investigating the possible existence of a distinct Nordic approach to international law this approach thereby seems vulnerable to accusations of committing the error of selecting on the dependent variable – in this case with the possible effect of leading to a false or at least exaggerated negative conclusion. It is after all a well-known law of perspective also captured by Freud's notion of the narcissism of small differences that small differences appear big when perceived up close. The restriction to Nordic practices may, therefore,

---

5 G. Noll, 'Nostalghia: A Nordic International Law', 85:4 *Nordic Journal of International Law* (2016) p. 275.

6 S. Freud, J. Strachey, and A. Dickson, *Civilization, Society and Religion: Group Psychology, Civilization and Its Discontents and Other Works* (Penguin, Harmondsworth, 1991), p. 90.

in the concrete case have produced a bias against perceiving what – in the larger scope of things – could seem more like relative similarities between the Nordic countries. To test for this possibility, in future research on Nordic approaches to international law it might therefore be wise to also include perspectives from non-Nordic researchers and expand the set of observations to non-Nordic jurisdictions.

Furthermore, to the limited degree commonalities in Nordic approaches to international law were in fact asserted at the conference, most participants seemed to agree that these most often did not have the character of tangible similarities in terms of positive law. Rather, several participants described how the Nordic countries stood out internationally in virtue of converging around a distinct *legal mentality* or *legal culture*. Both Johan Karlsson Schaffer and Marlene Wind described in their papers how in the field of human rights the Nordics had a long prehistory of serving as *an aspirational model* in international law and politics; how they were often ascribed and also gladly took upon themselves the role of moral superpowers, global good Samaritans, and agents of a world common good. In the same vein, I drew a parallel at the closing panel between this apparent aspirational role for the Nordics in international law and politics and the role which Francis Fukuyama ascribes to Denmark in his recent study of *The Origins of Political Order*.[7] Referring to a notion introduced by World Bank economists Pritchett and Woolcock,[8] Fukuyama here articulates the problem of creating modern well-functioning political institutions as the problem of "getting to Denmark". Importantly, "Denmark", in this context, is not strictly speaking Denmark but rather an ideal-typical construct devised for Fukuyama's analytical purposes. Thus, he describes "Denmark" as "a mythical place that is known to have good political and economic institutions: it is stable, democratic, peaceful, prosperous, inclusive, and has extremely low levels of political corruption".[9]

Several participants seemed to think that the Nordic countries may generally play (or, in Noll's nostalgic analysis, at least have played) a similar aspirational role in the realm of international law and politics, and thereby to suggest a parallel analysis of the overall project of international law as the project of "getting to the Nordics". This perception of the Nordics as embodying a regulative ideal for international law as such may to a greater or lesser

7 F. Fukuyama, *The Origins of Political Order: From Prehuman Times to the French Revolution* (Farrar, Straus and Giroux, New York, 2011), p. 14, *et seq*.

8 L. Pritchett and M. Woolcock, 'Solutions When *the* Solution is the Problem: Arraying the Disarray in Development', 32:2 *World Development* (2004) p. 192, *et seq*.

9 Fukuyama, *supra* note 7, p. 14.

extent be adopted by Nordic international lawyers and politicians themselves in their efforts to shape international law through various relevant fora be it the UN, the Council of Europe, the law commission, international courts etc. But it may also be adopted by non-Nordics actors in the field in the same way as Fukuyama, Pritchett and Woolcock adopted the project of "getting to Denmark" in political philosophy.

From the point of view of scientific analysis, however, these considerations seem to pose a particular methodological challenge in so far that we are trying to capture what is characteristic of a Nordic approach to international law. It is after all perfectly possible for this approach to exist as an aspirational model/a regulative idea, *without it necessarily manifesting itself in identifiable legal doctrine*. If what we are looking for is a legal mentality or culture – or, more broadly, a political mentality or culture – it is not obvious that the disciplinary lenses of doctrinal lawyers are sufficient. On the contrary, it seems that the study of Nordic approaches to international law could benefit profoundly from supplementing doctrinal lawyers with scholars from other disciplines such as e.g. anthropology, cultural studies, psychology, sociology, and history.[10]

3 Conspicuous Absence: Carefree Scholarly Engagement in International Legal Politics

For the remaining parts of this chapter, I shall be turning to the specific question regarding possible relations between Scandinavian realism and Nordic approaches to international law. First, I shall in this section focus on Scandinavian realism in relation to the role played by Nordic countries in actively shaping international law. In the next section, I turn to Scandinavian realism in relation to the domestication of such international law primarily through the national judiciaries of the Nordic countries.

Concerning the active shaping of international law, the discussions at the conference revealed a somewhat surprising absence of any traces of the key tenets of Scandinavian realism. To see why, we should first remind ourselves of the primary motivations of the realists' programme. The Oxford philosopher

10 Interestingly, this methodological precept seems to be followed at least partly in the newly established network "Nordic Exceptionalism in International Criminal Justice: Myth or Reality" in which the legal doctrinal perspective is supplemented also with criminological and sociological perspectives, *cf.* 'Nordic Exceptionalism in International Criminal Justice: Myth or Reality', < jura.ku.dk/icourts/news/nordic-exceptionalism-in-international-criminal-law/>, visited on 4 April 2017.

J.W. Harris once described the Scandinavian Realists as "wild prophetic figures riding in from the hills with a message for legal philosophers".[11] As a movement or school of thought comprising at least a handful of authors and their prolific writings across at least half a century Scandinavian Realism is of course a great many things. However, if one were to boil down their joined efforts to just one "message to legal philosophers" it would presumably be that above anything else we should secure the foundations of legal science. The Scandinavian Realists were all deeply engaged, almost to the level of obsession, in the project of securing that the doctrinal study of law is possible *as a respectable science*. In particular, they wanted to make sure that this academic endeavour was not in fact merely a pseudo-science – or metaphysics to use their favourite pejorative term.

To the Scandinavian realists, the doctrinal study of law seemed particularly vulnerable to accusations of being just pseudo-science or metaphysics. The doctrinal study of law deals with normative phenomena like rights, duties and competences that at least *prima facie* seem to be more ontologically and epistemologically dubious than the phenomena dealt with in other sciences. To the realists, it therefore simply could not just be taken for granted that our apparently scientific assertions about rights and duties could be given philosophically respectable foundations in the same way as assertions made in the natural sciences. They therefore focused their entire efforts on providing such foundations.

As is well known, the realists believed to have found a fitting framework for dealing with this challenge in the empiristic or positivistic philosophical ideas that figured prominently in the first half of the 20th century.[12] Simplifying somewhat, these ideas implied that an academic discipline could be scientific if and only if its statements could be derived ultimately from sensory experience. Accordingly, the realists attempted to provide a model for the doctrinal study of law that would make this kind of derivation possible thus placing also this discipline, at least in principle, on the same firm epistemological footing as natural and social science.

---

11 Jim Harris as quoted from S. Swaminathan, 'Projectivism and the Metaethical Foundations of the Normativity of Law', 7:2 *Jurisprudence: An International Journal of Legal and Political Thought* (2016) p. 254.

12 In the first phase of Scandinavian realism, these criteria were based on the Uppsala school in philosophy originally associated with the works of Axel Hägerström (1868–1939) and Adolph Phalén (1884–1931). In the second phase, and particularly in the late work of Alf Ross from *Om ret og retfærdighed* (1953) onwards, the specific tenets of the Uppsala school were replaced with those of the fundamentally congenial but internationally more renowned and influential logical positivism movement associated with the Vienna Circle.

In the next section, I shall get back to how this analysis played out in Ross's specific theory of valid law. For now, the key thing to observe is that the price for adopting this approach was that the realists had to sever the ties between legal science and morality. Legal science could, strictly speaking, only deal with the description of objectively valid law. *Qua* science, it had no business discussing the moral value of that law, let alone of proposing changes to it – lest it collapse into metaphysics. In this sense, the realists asserted a categorical divide between the doctrinal study of law (*retsdogmatik*) as a scientific discipline and legal politics (*retspolitik*).

One may agree or disagree with the soundness of these philosophical tenets, and even in the heyday of Scandinavian realism they attracted massive controversy.[13] But most legal scholars seem to agree (even if with regret) that as a matter of intellectual history these realist ideas have in fact been very influential in the Nordic countries.[14] In light of these considerations, it was therefore quite surprising to observe the virtual absence of such epistemological concerns among the international lawyers participating at the conference in Oslo.

To be sure, several participants were not academics but practitioners and they were invited in that capacity, so they can hardly be expected not to engage with legal politics. However, also among the legal academic participants a substantial share did not stick strictly to legal doctrinal issues, but engaged openly with and promoted particular stances on controversial issues of international legal politics. Thus, e.g. in her paper on "A Nordic Approach to a New International Climate Treaty", Christina Voigt recounted and discussed the challenges with regard to promoting a particular environmental agenda that she had encountered as a member of the Norwegian negotiation team in UN climate negotiations.

---

13 For a very influential, but also quite problematic early critique of Alf Ross, *cf.* H.L.A. Hart, 'Scandinavian Realism', 17:2 *The Cambridge Law Journal* (1959) pp. 233–240. More recently, several attempts have been made at putting Scandinavian realism permanently to rest. One prominent example was provided by Jens Evald in his biography of Alf Ross. Here, Evald announced that today Ross only survives "in the mass graves of the libraries": J. Evald, *Alf Ross, et liv* (Jurist- og Økonomforbundets Forlag, Copenhagen, 2010), p. 371. For a reply, *cf.* J.v.H. Holtermann, '"Således består (endnu) al verdens herlighed!" – om Jens Evalds vurdering af Alf Ross' betydning', litterær afdeling, hæfte nr. 16: *Ugeskrift for Retsvæsen* (2011). Here it is argued that while undoubtedly less influential today than in the 1950s and 60s the rumours of Ross's death (and that of Scandinavian Realism more generally) are vastly exaggerated.

14 I shall return to this question in the next section.

In the same vein, in her paper on "Nordic Approaches to Women's Human Rights – Internal v. External Application",[15] Cecilia Bailliet actively engaged with and suggested particular strategies with regard to promoting women's rights in international law. A final example of the open intermingling of the scientific doctrinal study of law with the promotion of particular political agendas in international law was provided – although more indirectly – by Martti Koskenniemi. In his keynote address "Varieties in Formalism: Finnish International Law in the 20th Century",[16] Koskenniemi demonstrated how the most prominent Finnish international lawyers in the 20th century had not only often combined academic work with public service as diplomats and politicians, including government members.[17] He also made the case that their theoretical position as academic doctrinal lawyers (predominantly as legal positivists) had been substantially determined throughout by Finland's precarious geopolitical position vis-à-vis the USSR/Russia.[18]

Characteristic not only of these papers, but also of the discussions throughout the conference, was however, that the participants evinced no particular awareness of what to the realists was the main concern: to distinguish clearly between legal science and legal politics. Papers and discussions moved – indiscriminately it seemed – back and forth across the divide without noteworthy regard to or explicit mention of when participants (or, in the case of Koskenniemi, the scholars whose work he was describing) were promoting a particular legal political agenda, however praiseworthy (the environment, women's rights, Finland's continued existence as an independent nation), and when they were merely aiming to give an objective doctrinal account of currently valid international law.

I hasten to emphasise that this is not to say that we should expect present day scholars of international law to adopt the specific, quite rigid and in many ways archaic empiristic and scientistic epistemology adhered to by the Scandinavian realists. It is not even to say that legal scientists should never be allowed to engage in legal politics. In fact, when pressed on this point at least Alf Ross expressly denounced the notion of the doctrinal legal scholar as a complete

15 Printed in the special issue of *Nordic Journal of International Law* as C. Bailliet, 'A Nordic Approach to Promoting Women's Rights within International Law: Internal v. External Perspectives', 85:4 *Nordic Journal of International Law* (2016) pp. 368–394.

16 Koskenniemi's contribution to the special issue of *Nordic Journal of International Law* (M. Koskenniemi, 'Diplomats, Professors, and Then Some: Notes for a History of International Law in 20th Century Finland', 85:4 *Nordic Journal of International Law* (2016) pp. 322–333) is based on this keynote.

17 *Ibid.*, p. 322.

18 *Ibid.*, p. 327.

political ascetic. He only maintained that the legal scientist should be acutely aware of – and that it should be transparent to others – when she is doing science and when she is doing politics.[19]

One may generally find the realists' notion of a sharp and categorical divide between legal science and legal politics unsound, overstated, or even philosophically naïve. It is, however, a *non-sequitur* to infer from this that any reflection on the difference between the two is moot or that one can move back and forth across the divide as one pleases. In contemporary and more topical terminology one might phrase the realist considerations simply in terms of a demand for epistemological modesty and reflexivity on behalf of the scientist. At least judging from the papers and conversations at the conference, it is however, (with few exceptions)[20] striking how limited a role such considerations seem to play in general academic discussions about Nordic approaches to international law – especially considering the fact that these conversations take place against a backdrop of notions of the Nordics as moral superpowers and global good Samaritans.

4 Mistaken Presence: The Dubious Linking of Scandinavian Realism with Nordic Exceptionalism in Constitutional Law

While the philosophical concerns of Scandinavian realism thus seem to have played only a limited role in relation to Nordic international lawyers' promotion

19 Thus, Ross in the following passage objects to what he takes to be the exaggerated methodological demands that he thinks other Scandinavian realists and the legal positivist Hans Kelsen have derived from the notion of the purity of legal science: "I would like to admit that it is not without uneasiness that I have taken this stance in opposition to Kelsen and his Swedish adherents. The idea of the purity of science is the cornerstone of the professional ethos of the man of science. I embrace it warmly myself, and I am always happy when anyone defends it by attacking that fraudulence of science which follows when this idea is not honoured. Nevertheless, I cannot close my eyes to the fact that the methodological demands which these scholars wished to derive from this idea are mistaken. One might say that they are caused by mixing up, on the one hand, what applies to science qua idea, and, on the other, what applies to science qua profession. *No violence is done to the idea by the profession pursuing both science and policy making, provided that the ideal borderline between them is clearly observed*". Ross, *On Law and Justice*, *supra* note 3, § 84, emphasis added.

20 Arguably. Noll stands out in this regard – although he seems to couch his nostalgic reading of Nordic approaches to international law not so much in considerations about the character of legal science but rather in an explicit scepticism about the actual moral superiority of 'the Nordic'.

of different political agendas in the international arena, the school has repeatedly been ascribed a much more substantive role in relation to the domestication of international law through the national judiciaries. Several conference participants made the observation that in this area the Nordic countries almost completely reverse their traditional pioneering role and become instead reluctant or even outright obstructive vis-à-vis international law.[21] This peculiar feature is often explained in terms of a more general phenomenon in comparative constitutional law sometimes referred to as *Nordic exceptionalism,*[22] i.e. the peculiar constitutional tradition allegedly prominent in the region, which is characterized by the exercise of very limited or no judicial control with the legislative branch of government. Using Ronald Dworkin's terminology,[23] this approach where the courts show virtually unconditional deference to parliament exemplifies a so-called *majoritarian* conception of democratic government. It contrasts with *constitutionalist* conceptions that allow for substantive judicial review of the legislative output from parliament. It is, more precisely, Nordic exceptionalism understood as majoritarianism that is often coupled with Scandinavian realism in general and with Alf Ross's version thereof in particular.

4.1 *Outlining the Alleged Link between Scandinavian Legal Realism and Nordic Exceptionalism*

At the conference, this coupling was primarily promulgated by Marlene Wind in her paper "Do Scandinavian Judges Care about International Law? The Impact of International Law on Scandinavian Supreme Courts: A Citation

21 According to Schaffer, Sweden and Denmark were only number 17 and 26 respectively on a list of top human rights treaty ratifying countries, and the other Nordic countries were even further down the list. Wind, in her original and comprehensive study of citation practices in Scandinavian supreme courts, convincingly demonstrates the reluctance with which especially Danish and Swedish courts cites the case law of the ECJ and the ECtHR, *cf.* M. Wind, 'Do Scandinavians Care about International Law? A Study of Scandinavian Judges' Citation Practice to International Law and Courts', 85:4 *Nordic Journal of International Law* (2016) pp. 281–302. *Cf.* also Bailliet, *supra* note 15. The Danish Supreme Court arguably stepped into the category of obstruction or defiance when it recently decided to openly disregard a preliminary ruling by the ECJ, *cf.* *DI som mandatar for Ajos A/S mod Boet efter A*, 6. December 2016, Danish Supreme Court, online at <http://www.hoejesteret.dk/hoejesteret/nyheder/Afgorelser/Documents/15-2014.pdf>, visited on 4 April 2017.

22 For instance, Nordic exceptionalism was the subject of the conference "Still Exceptional? Nordic Countries Constitutional Tradition in the 21st Century", held 16–17 May 2016 at the European University Institute in Florence, Italy.

23 *Cf.* R. Dworkin, *Freedom's Law: The Moral Reading of the American Constitution* (Oxford University Press, Oxford, 1996), notably "Introduction: The Moral Reading of the Majoritarian Premise", pp. 1–38.

Analysis", and the point is repeated and further unfolded in her contributions both to this volume and to the special issue preceding it.[24] In this volume, Wind is also joined by Jens Elo Rytter who briefly refers to Scandinavian realism in order to explain the particular Nordic majoritarian tradition.[25] However, while made with variations and differences in emphasis the contention is indeed widespread that Scandinavian realism can somehow be used to explain the phenomenon of Nordic Exceptionalism generally and hence, in this context, the specific reluctant or even defiant stance of Nordic courts vis-à-vis international courts.[26] In the following, I will therefore not focus specifically on Wind or Rytter but discuss the coupling of Scandinavian realism with Nordic majoritarianism in general.

As indicated by the heading of this section, I have my doubts about the soundness of these attempts to invoke Scandinavian realism in order to explain

24 *Cf.* also M. Wind, 'When Parliament Comes First – The Danish Concept of Democracy Meets the European Union', 27:2 *Nordisk Tidsskrift for Menneskerettigheder* (2009); Wind, *supra* note 21.

25 *Cf.* J.E. Rytter, 'A Nordic Approach to the Interpretation of the European Convention on Human Rights?", this volume. In previous co-authored work Wind and Rytter have also defended the hypothesis that Scandinavian realism is at least partly responsible specifically for the reluctance of the Danish judiciary to engage actively with international case law, *cf.* J.E. Rytter and M. Wind, 'In need of juristocracy? The silence of Denmark in the development of European legal norms', 9:2 *International Journal of Constitutional Law* (2011) pp. 476–477.

26 *Cf.* e.g. A. Follesdal, 'Rawls in the Nordic Countries', 1:2 *European Journal of Political Theory* (2002) p. 182; A. Follesdal and M. Wind, 'Introduction – Nordic Reluctance towards Judicial Review under Siege', 27:2 *Nordisk Tidsskrift for Menneskerettigheder* (2009) pp. 139–140; S. Blandhol, 'Formalisme, pragmatisme, realisme: Teori, metode og grunnlovsforståelse hos Castberg, Knoph og Ross', in Eivind Smith (ed.), *Grundlagens makt: Konstitutionen som politiskt redskap och som rättslig norm* (SNS Förlag, Stockholm, 2002), 59–62; D. Tamm, 'The Danes and Their Legal Heritage', in Børge Dahl, Torben Melchior, and Ditlev Tamm (eds.), *Danish Law in a European Perspective* (Thomson Publishers, Copenhagen, 2002), 56–58; K. Ketscher, *Socialret: Almindelige principper, Retssikkerhed og administration, Grundværdier* (Forlaget Thompson A/S, Copenhagen, 2002), 151–152. An interesting subgroup in this literature is constituted by J.P. Christensen, 'Ross og statsforfatningsretten', in Jakob v.H. Holtermann and Jesper Ryberg (eds.), *Alf Ross: Kritiske gensyn* (Jurist- og Økonomforbundet, Copenhagen, 2006); S. Schaumburg-Müller, 'Parliamentary Precedence in Denmark – A Jurisprudential Assessment', 27:2 *Nordisk Tidsskrift for Menneskerettigheder* (2009). Both Christensen and Schaumburg-Müller draw the connection between Alf Ross's works in constitutional and democratic theory and the Nordic majoritarian tradition but they simultaneously emphasize, in my view correctly, the discrepancy between these thoughts and Ross's general realist program in legal philosophy. I shall return to this question immediately below and again towards the end of this chapter.

the majoritarian tradition of the Nordic countries. In fact, I believe that the running together of Scandinavian realism with Nordic exceptionalism – and thereby with the Nordic reluctance to implement international law in the judiciary – is a philosophical mismatch. The widespread association between the two phenomena is based on a failure to appreciate the distinctiveness of Scandinavian realism, and, in particular, on a conflation of it with legal positivism and rigid formalism. To see why this is so, it is necessary to take a somewhat more detailed look at the central philosophical tenets of Scandinavian realism. Only in this way will it be possible to see clearly why Scandinavian realism properly understood simply does not imply any particular constitutional theory understood as a theory about the correct judicial interpretation of valid law obligating the judiciary.

Before doing so, however, two things should be emphasised. First, there is an ambiguity underlying many of the works that assert this connection, and the direct relevance of the below depends on how this ambiguity is resolved. On the one hand, one might read the attempts to couple Scandinavian realism with Nordic exceptionalism as an exegetic claim to the effect that there is in fact a fundamental congeniality between and even an implicational relationship from the program actually espoused by Ross and others as Scandinavian realism and to the majoritarian constitutional tradition. In this case, the claim is that members of the Nordic judiciaries generally subscribe to these realist tenets and correctly grasp the majoritarian implications thereof and act accordingly in their professional capacity. On the other hand, however, one might so to speak disregard the exegetic question altogether and read the claim *only* as one of intellectual history. In this case, the contention is only that a certain, possibly mistaken idea about Scandinavian realism in general (say, "Scandinavian realism") and about Alf Ross's version in particular ("Alf Ross") has in fact been widely adopted by the members of the judiciaries in the Nordic countries, and that their adoption of these ideas has tended to influence their judicial behaviour in the characteristic majoritarian direction.

In general, I think the former interpretation is closer to the intentions of the majority of the authors who couple Scandinavian realism and Nordic exceptionalism. I should emphasize however, that the main part of the following discussion is directly relevant only on that particular reading of the relation, and that it has no direct bearing if there is no claim about exegetic correctness. That is, if there is merely an assertion of a causal relation between the existence in the minds of Nordic judges of a certain complex of positivistic ideas mistakenly called "Scandinavian realism" and the majoritarian judicial behaviour of these judges vis-à-vis international courts. I shall only touch briefly on the plausibility of this weaker, non-exegetic hypothesis toward the end of this chapter.

Second, I should emphasize that even, or particularly, when approached strictly from the point of view of exegesis, the questions dealt with in this section are complex and wide reaching, and that they deserve a more extensive treatment than what is possible within the scope of this contribution. In particular, the relation between Ross's version of Scandinavian realism on the one hand, and his own doctrinal work in constitutional law[27] and in political philosophical works on democracy[28] on the other is intricate and raises interesting questions that deserve closer scrutiny, and I hope to be able to return to these issues in future research.

In continuation of this point, it seems fitting to make a preliminary concession to those, who, like Wind and Rytter, maintain that the development and consolidation of a strong majoritarian tradition in the Nordic countries is somehow connected with Scandinavian realism. Without agreeing, we can at least acknowledge that it is not entirely incomprehensible why, even apart from the geographical overlap, this belief has arisen among so many legal scholars. If anything, the Scandinavian realists are famous for their blanket rejection of any substantive notion of justice. Time and again justice is denounced as meaningless metaphysics and denied a place in legal theory.[29] And this view would seem to have implications for the notion of judicial review. Broadly speaking, this very notion seems to presuppose *some* substantive notion of justice. Ultimately, justice seems to constitute the only criterion against which it makes sense for courts to review the legality of a piece of legislation.[30] If, on the other hand, as Ross and the other Scandinavians maintained, no such

---

27 *Cf.* A. Ross, *Dansk Statsforfatningsret, bind I & II*, 3. ed. (Nyt Nordisk Forlag Arnold Busck, Copenhagen, 1980 [1959–1960]).

28 *Cf.* e.g. *Hvorfor demokrati?* [Why Democracy?] (Ejnar Munksgaard, Kbh, 1946).

29 Justice was not the only victim of this realist criticism. Thus, Ross famously denounced the notion of a right as meaningless in his article "Tû-Tû" ('Tû-Tû', 70:5 *Harvard Law Review* (1957); in Danish: 'Tû-Tû', in O.A. Borum and Knud Illum (eds.), *Festskrift til Professor, Dr. Juris Henry Ussing* (Nyt Nordisk Forlag Arnold Busck, Copenhagen, 1951)).

30 A famous formulation of this notion is found in Radbruch's formula: "The positive law, secured by legislation and power, takes precedence even when its content is unjust and fails to benefit the people, unless the conflict between statute and justice reaches such an intolerable degree that the statute, as 'flawed law', must yield to justice. [...] Where there is not even an attempt at justice, where equality, the core of justice, is deliberately betrayed in the issuance of positive law, then the statute is not merely 'flawed law', it lacks completely the very nature of law. For law, including positive law, cannot be otherwise defined than as a system and an institution whose very meaning is to serve justice".

substantive notion of justice is forthcoming, it seems natural to settle instead for a more formal, processual notion; a notion which reduces justice in relation to law to the purely formal property of having been duly enacted by parliament. This perspective in turn, as Wind also remarks, seems to reduce the courts' role to the famous "*la bouche de la loi*". In other words, a picture emerges that very much resembles the majoritarian constitutional tradition known as Nordic exceptionalism.[31]

4.2 *What Alf Ross the Scandinavian Legal Realist Really Said – and Why it Sits Badly with Nordic Exceptionalism*

Yet, I maintain that this whole line of reasoning is fallacious. As I shall try to demonstrate, Scandinavian realism and in particular Ross's version thereof, is genuinely agnostic about the propriety of this or that constitutional theory, be it majoritarian or constitutionalist, *if by this notion we mean a doctrinal theory that asserts how the judiciary* ought *to behave vis-à-vis the legislator*. To see why this is so, it is necessary to recapitulate the central tenets of Ross's theory in slightly greater detail.[32]

As already mentioned, Scandinavian realism and in particular Ross's version is first and foremost a program in the philosophy of legal science. Its main concern is with the epistemological question: *can* we have knowledge about valid law? This is the philosophical project and any discussion of Scandinavian realism specifically in relation to constitutional law as a subdiscipline of generic doctrinal legal science has to take this starting point seriously. As also mentioned already, Ross sought a solution to this challenge within a general empiricist or positivistic epistemological framework. It has often been described how this made him vehemently reject the rationalistic, justice-centred approach of natural law (or *material idealism* as he sometimes preferred to call it).[33] However, and here is the fallacy, contrary to what those

---

G. Radbruch, 'Statutory Lawlessness and Supra-Statutory Law', 26:1 *Oxford Journal of Legal Studies* (2006 (1946)) p. 7

31 It transpires from this brief recapitulation that this line of criticism of Scandinavian realism is fundamentally congenial with the *ad nazium* argument so often launched against legal positivism. Thus, e.g. Radbruch, "Positivism, with its principle that 'a law is a law', has in fact rendered the German legal profession defenceless against statutes that are arbitrary and criminal". *Ibid.*

32 The following five paragraphs follow quite closely my previous accounts of Ross's theory provided e.g. in Holtermann, 'A Straw Man Revisited – Resettling the Score Between H.L.A. Hart and Scandinavian Legal Realism', *supra* note 3.

33 In Ross's interpretation, natural law tries to provide foundations for law in universally valid notions of justice to which we all have access in virtue of our (God-given)

who connect Ross with majoritarianism seem to think, Ross manifestly did not infer from this that the only alternative way, then, to secure the scientific ambitions is to embrace rigid legal positivistic formalism, and to make black letter law the bedrock of the doctrinal study of law.

What is often overlooked is that Ross is in fact equally dismissive of (even if less hostile towards) legal positivism – or *formal idealism* as he also called it precisely to group it together with natural law's *material idealism* and contrast both of these with his own legal *realism*. Regardless of his veneration for Hans Kelsen, Ross simply did not think that legal positivism fared much better philosophically speaking than natural law. On the legal positivistic approach, doctrinal legal science is claimed to be possible – propositions about valid law can be scientific – because they can be derived, ultimately, through an inter-normative chain of reasoning from either a Kelsenian *Grundnorm*[34] or a Hartian *rule of recognition*.[35] Unlike the natural lawyers' approach, this positivistic foundational norm provides the foundations for the entire system regardless of its affinity or lack thereof with substantive notions of justice. The *Grundnorm/rule of recognition* is simply valid whenever it is effective, i.e. whenever it has managed to secure broad compliance among the population. Ross however rejects this approach too. He rejects it on the basis that it builds on a naturalistic fallacy, an inference from *is* to *ought*, right at the foundations – the inference from the fact of effective compliance with the historically first constitution/the rule of recognition to the normative validity of that constitution.[36]

The lesson, which Ross draws from these alleged failures, is that the doctrinal study of law can only survive as a science if it becomes a truly empirical

reason – an approach which he dismisses in one of the most memorable passages in *On Law and Justice*: "Like a harlot, natural law is at the disposal of everyone. There is no ideology that cannot be defended by invoking the law of nature. And indeed, how could it be otherwise when the ultimate basis for every natural law is to be found in a private (intra-subjective), direct insight, a self-evident contemplation, an intuition. Cannot my intuition be just as good as yours?" Ross, *On Law and Justice*, *supra* note 3, §63.

34 *Cf.* e.g. H. Kelsen, *Pure Theory of law* (University of California Press, Berkeley, 1967).

35 *Cf.* H.L.A. Hart, J. Raz, and P.A. Bulloch, *The Concept of Law*, 3rd ed., introduction by Leslie Green (Oxford University Press, Oxford, 2012).

36 Strictly, both Kelsen and Hart denies that they *infer* the validity of the Grundnorm/rule of recognition from its effectiveness. Kelsen famously insists that effectiveness is a *conditio sine qua non*, not a *conditio per quam* for the validity of the Grundnorm, *cf.* e.g. H. Kelsen, *General Theory of Law and State* (Lawbook Exchange, Union, N.J., 2009), 119. However, this cuts no ice with Ross in so far that this move essentially renders the validity of the Grundnorm an arbitrary postulate instead, which, epistemologically speaking, is equally unsatisfactory.

discipline on a par with the natural and social sciences. For Ross, this means that the doctrinal study of law has to change its subject. It cannot be *normative*; it has to be *descriptive*. We should however be very careful when stating this point because this is where people (starting with Hart)[37] usually tend to miss the subtle nuances in Ross's position. The important point is that Ross does not take this to mean that any notion of the normative – of legal rules – thereby goes by the board in the doctrinal study of law. What he is saying is that if the doctrinal study of law is to be a science, it can no longer be a normative discipline asserting the validity in the sense of correctness of certain legal rights and obligations; i.e. asserting what legal rights and obligations citizens in general and judges in particular have; how they ought to behave legally speaking. By implication, and of special importance in the present context, Ross is therefore also saying that the doctrinal study of *constitutional law*, if possible as a science, can no longer directly assert the validity of certain legal rights and obligations of the judiciary; it cannot, as held e.g. in Nordic exceptionalist majoritarianism, be about how the members of the national judiciary *ought* to behave vis-à-vis the legislature, or vis-à-vis certain international courts.

Instead, and this is the crucial move in relation to the normative, Ross changes the perspective slightly but decisively and says that the doctrinal study of law has to become a study of *a particular group of people*, i.e. *of judges*, and *their* normative beliefs about legal rights and duties. Instead of being dogmatic and stating the objective existence of rights and obligations, the doctrinal study of law, if it wants to be a science, has to become a social-psychological study of *the beliefs certain groups of people actually hold towards* legal norms about rights and obligations.

In Ross's apt terminology the propositions of legal science therefore cannot be norm-*expressive* as he takes them to be in both natural law and legal positivism; they have to be norm-*descriptive*. Legal science cannot itself *express* certain legal norms *as being valid*; it can only *describe* the fact that certain legal norms *are held to be valid by judges*. In Danish, Ross expresses this distinction terminologically by using two different adjectives for the validity of legal rules. Thus, he uses *gyldig* to refer to the natural law/legal positivist norm-*expressive* notion of correct and legally obligating rules; and *gældende* to refer to the social-psychological norm-*descriptive* fact that judges in a given jurisdiction take certain rules to be thus correct and obligating.

37 Hart particularly misunderstood the point recounted in the following in the aforementioned influential review essay (*cf.* Hart, 'Scandinavian Realism', *supra* note 13). For critical discussion, *cf.* Holtermann, 'A Straw Man Revisited – Resettling the Score Between H.L.A. Hart and Scandinavian Legal Realism', *supra* note 3.

Ross takes this change in focus – from norm-expressively valid (*gyldig*) law to norm-descriptively valid (*gældende*) law – to imply that the doctrinal study of law becomes a study of what he calls *the judge ideology*.[38] As Mikael Rask Madsen and I have demonstrated elsewhere, this notion corresponds closely to what Max Weber earlier, in a very congenial analysis, calls the set of "maxims in the minds of certain men".[39] What is particularly important for present purposes is that Ross was very clear that, as an empirical matter of fact, he by no means took this judge ideology to consist *only* of the set of formally enacted statutory laws. In general, he did not take the "maxims in the minds of certain men" to be only the maxims found in black letter law. On the contrary, Ross took any such theory to be plainly wrong. Any empirically adequate norm-descriptive theory would simply have to countenance the well-known fact that judges consider as valid also legal rules that stem from other sources. In seeming contradiction of the formalistic straw man he is often made out to be, Ross therefore included besides statutory law also precedence, custom and notably what he called the cultural tradition or "the nature of the matter" ("*forholdets natur*") by which he referred to soft notions about justice and morality.[40] As an empirical matter of fact, Ross plainly took all these sources to actively influence the actual "maxims in the minds of certain men", the judge ideology, and thus to co-determine judicial behaviour.[41]

While firmly denying any foundation of these soft notions in a universal human reason Ross therefore maintained that in terms of countenancing sources of law, he was in fact much more in line with natural law than with

38 Ross, *On Law and Justice*, *supra* note 3, § 8.

39 Weber introduces this term in his extremely interesting but often overlooked work M. Weber, *Critique of Stammler* (Free Press, New York, 1977), p. 130. This is the only work in which Weber engages at length with the specific epistemological problems relating to the scientific study of legal norms. For demonstration of the parallels between Weber's and Ross's analyses of legal validity, *cf.* e.g. J.v.H. Holtermann and M.R. Madsen, 'European New Legal Realism and International Law: How to Make International Law Intelligible', 28:2 *Leiden Journal of International Law* (2015) pp. 211–230.

40 *Cf.* Ross, *On Law and Justice*, *supra* note 3, notably Chapter III, "The Sources of Law".

41 Ironically, the implication of this is that if in Wind's picture of the domestication of international law in the Nordic countries there is anything resembling Scandinavian realism it is in fact not the Danish and Swedish judges' majoritarian and formalistic beliefs about (axiologically) valid law. It is Wind's own study of these judges! Her own study comprises precisely a comprehensive attempt, profoundly Scandinavian realist in spirit, to capture the legal ideology that actually occupies the minds of Scandinavian judges. Or, using Weber's term, based on their citation practices Wind suggests a theory about the "maxims in the minds of certain men". Only, Wind reaches the conclusion that this ideology is more formalistic than what Ross actually thought.

legal positivism. Thus, in commenting on the natural law reaction against legal positivism in the wake of World War II Ross writes:

> [T]here is undoubtedly something right in this reaction. There are sources of law other than those positively formulated. In so far one must agree with the naturalist theories. But this does not mean that there are also 'natural' (supersensual, *a priori*) sources of law, but merely expresses the socio-psychological reality that judicial decisions, as described above, are also determined by spontaneous free factors of many kinds.[42]

Considering the unambiguous character of these words, it is more than a little ironic to observe how often Ross's heritage has been interpreted in terms of legal positivism and rigid formalism.

4.3 *History of Legal Ideas and the Wondrous Adventures of "Alf Ross" and "Scandinavian Legal Realism"*

The question is of course where these considerations leave the conference's concern about the relation between Scandinavian realism and Nordic exceptionalism as manifested in the region's reluctant domestication of international law through national judiciaries. I believe that the above brief recapitulation of the fundamentals of Ross's theory demonstrates that the widespread assertion of a link between the two is wrong. Contrary to what is commonly held, there is simply no fundamental congeniality between Scandinavian realism and Nordic exceptionalism, nor is there an implicational relationship going from the former to the latter.

However, I make this assertion solely as a matter of Ross-exegesis. As already touched upon, this does nothing to exclude that "Alf Ross" and, more generally, "Scandinavian realism" (*i.e.*, *certain mistaken ideas* about Alf Ross and about Scandinavian Realism), can have played a factual role in consolidating in the region the particular kind of majoritarianism known as Nordic exceptionalism. Misunderstood ideas can also have empirical consequences. While those who make the inference from Scandinavian realism via formalistic legal positivism to majoritarianism in constitutional law may be wrong, they may not be alone in committing this error. And *this* fact may very well have had empirical consequences. Thus, it is not only possible but also indeed somewhat likely that they exemplify a pattern of reasoning that may have been adopted also by (at least some) members of the Nordic judiciaries, and that

42 Ross, *A Textbook of International Law: General Part*, *supra* note, p. 95.

this mistaken pattern may have guided these members in their actions as judges.[43]

I have already outlined how a superficial reading of Scandinavian realism's scepticism about justice can be said to invite these mistakes. But there are other factors that may have reinforced this tendency. Ross himself called attention to one such factor already in the continuation of the above passage where he emphasized an ambiguity inherent in the term positivism:

> There is an *ambiguity* in the term 'positivism'. It can both be defined as 'what is based on experience' and as 'what is formally established'. The reaction against positivism is justified with respect to the latter, but not with respect to the former meaning. A realistic doctrine of the sources of law is based on experience but recognises that not all sources are positive in the sense that they are 'formally established'.[44]

Keeping this distinction in mind is certainly a virtue that too often is not exercised in legal scholarship. However, it probably only captures part of the story how Ross's realist theory has come to be connected with legal positivism. In the introduction to the second Danish edition of *On Law and Justice*,[45] I pointed to two additional factors. First, I alluded to a peculiar feature of at least the Danish reception of Scandinavian realism, and in particular of Alf Ross's work. On the one hand, it is well known that Ross's name has for many years played and continues to play a very active role in various debates in the legal academy. On the other hand, however, it seems that only a minute fraction of the members of the legal academy actually go through the trouble of reading the philosophical

---

43 However, one might question the independent causal work actually done by this "Alf Ross" in creating and sustaining Nordic exceptionalism. As emphasized by e.g. Skinner paths of influence are a complex matter, *cf.* Q. Skinner, 'Meaning and Understanding in the History of Ideas', 8:1 *History and Theory* (1969) p. 24 *et seq.* Considering the lack of actual exegetic support for "Alf Ross" it is tempting to see *both* this construct *and* Nordic Exceptionalism as the joint result rather of something more fundamental in Nordic political/legal culture. (I am grateful to Dan Priel for suggesting this option.) Below, I shall get back to the possible role of a more fundamental Nordic or at least Danish culture of this kind.

44 Ross, *A Textbook of International Law: General Part, supra* note 1, p. 95.

45 J.v.H. Holtermann, 'Introduktion', in A. Ross and J.v.H. Holtermann (ed.), *Om ret og retfærdighed : En indførelse i den analytiske retsfilosofi* (Hans Reitzels Forlag, Copenhagen, 2013), pp. 17–19.

writings of Ross.[46] My contention in the introduction was that this contrast signifies how, by a curious turn of events in intellectual history, the actual Alf Ross has been replaced by a largely fictitious "Alf Ross". Apparently, the function of this "Alf Ross" is to serve more as a reference point in an ongoing positioning battle among members of the legal profession in Denmark – between old and new; the capital and the provinces; legal positivism and natural law; formal and material justice; black letter law and soft humanistic principles. For these purposes, the actual writings of Alf Ross seems simply to have become superfluous because everybody more or less agrees what the positioning game is all about; what one is either con or pro. Nobody seems to have sufficiently strong incentives to actually sit down and study closely what Ross has in fact written. In this context, I therefore suggested that the republication of *Om ret og retfærdighed* after all these years could be seen as the equivalent of finally confronting the elephant in the room of law and justice – and finding out that it was in fact a giraffe.

The second feature I mentioned in the introduction had to do with the internal consistency of Ross's own work. Thus, it seems that in spite of apparently unambiguous passages like the one above (about the difference between two kinds of positivism and Ross's realism only fitting one of them), Ross was not always equally careful in distinguishing his own realist position from legal positivism. In particular, it seems that he may not always have practiced *as a doctrinal scholar*, or indeed as a political philosopher, what he preached *as a legal philosopher*. Thus, the case can at least be made that Ross's own actual doctrinal work in Danish constitutional law does indeed seem to come close to the kind of majoritarian analysis of the division of power between.

Jens Peter Christensen has produced a very strong and very critical argument to this effect[47] – an argument on which Wind relies when holding Ross at least co-responsible for the reluctance of national Scandinavian judiciaries to incorporate international law. Much depends, however, for Christensen's specific argument on the fine point whether Ross's work in constitutional law does in fact come out, on a close reading, as a norm-expressive or a norm-descriptive study; i.e. whether it comes out as a theory about what Danish (Swedish etc.) judges *should* do legally speaking (i.e. they *should* show deference to the legislature) or a theory about what they *habitually tend to feel they*

46 This is evidenced at least anecdotally by the fact that the first Danish edition of Ross's main work *On Law and Justice* (*Om ret og retfærdighed*, 1953) had in 2013 been allowed to remain out of print for several decades.

47 *Cf.* Christensen, *supra* note 26.

should do. I believe that more research is still needed before anything certain can be concluded in this regard.

In the meantime, however, there are two reasons why Wind and others may not wish to rely too heavily on Christensen's unrelenting critique for the specific purposes of connecting Ross's realism with Nordic majoritarianism. First, Christensen is one of the leading voices of the Danish Supreme Court of which he has been a member since 2006. In other words, those who are making the connection between Ross and majoritarianism are trying to explain the behaviour of this particular court by reference to its alleged adherence to a constitutional theory, which at least one of its key members denounces as fundamentally wrongheaded. Secondly, the very reasons Christensen cite for rejecting Ross's constitutional theory are almost verbatim the same as those he uses for criticizing the ECJ and the ECtHR, and which strongly echo the reasoning found in the recent Ajos-judgment where the Danish Supreme Court openly reject the ECJ's interpretation of EU-law. Thus, Christensen rejects Ross on the grounds that:

> [...] he led constitutional law astray because of his obsession with abstract concept formations and logical reasoning. As a constitutional lawyer, Ross was excessively fascinated by philosophy and logic. By his own example, he did not help law students throughout the years to understand that law is more about ones practical identification with the concrete legal issues of life as it is actually lived than it is about abstractions, logic and fierce parlance.[48]

Ironically, this compares very closely with Christensen's critique of the reasoning of the ECJ and the ECtHR:

> Good law does not consist of conceptual gymnastics and academic math exercises but of sound common sense anchored in an understanding of real life. [...] Do we start from concepts and academic reasoning and infer the solution to the problems of real life from there? Or do we start from the problems of real life and adjust the concepts and arguments in a way that makes the result practical and sensible? [...] The inclination toward worshipping of concepts and legal quibbling is particularly outspoken with the European Court of Human Rights and the European Court of Justice. This is contrasted with the traditional Danish legal culture where

48 *Ibid.*, pp. 100–101, my translation.

the good judge never lets the concepts take control but takes reality as his starting point and tries to solve the real problems in the cases at hand".[49]

In other words, in terms of legal reasoning Christensen is in fact pitching Ross *together with* the ECJ and the ECtHR, and *against* the Danish Supreme Court.[50]

5 Conclusion

I introduced this contribution in Section 2 by making a few, more general methodological reflections about how future research on Nordic approaches to international law might usefully supplement the many valuable studies found in this volume. In this connection, I pointed to the importance of expanding both the object of study and the prisms through which we observe it. On the one hand, it might be useful to expand the object of study (i) beyond the footprint of international law in Nordic law so as to avoid selecting on the dependent variable, and (ii) beyond legal doctrine so as to include vaguer objects such as Nordic legal culture and the widespread international legal ideal of "getting to the Nordics". On the other hand, it might be useful in future research to expand

49 J.P. Christensen, 'Jura og sund fornuft', *Jyllands-Posten*, 27 September 2015, 34, my translation. One might add to this that if there is any truth to Christensen's description of traditional Danish legal culture (and it is further corroborated by Børge Dahl in the quote in the next footnote) then it is simply not very likely that Alf Ross would have had many followers. (I am grateful to Dan Priel for bringing my attention to this point.)

50 Former president of the Danish Supreme Court Børge Dahl provides another example of the same line of reasoning in: 'Juridisk argumentation og retsanvendelse', in Børge Dahl, Thomas Riis, and Jan Trzaskowsk (eds.), *Liber Amicorum Peter Møgelvang-Hansen*, ed. 1 (Ex Tuto Publishing, Copenhagen, 2016). Considering this central role ascribed to – and not least the diverse uses of – high praise of sound common sense (and, inversely, the disdain for anything that can be described as "abstract" and "academic" reasoning), it might be worth a closer look in future research on Nordic constitutional law and especially on the argumentative strategies of the Danish Supreme Court. Immanuel Kant for one solemnly warned against (implicitly referring to Hume) references to common sense as argumentative strategy: "I must forbid [...] decision by means of the divining rod of so-called *sound common sense*, which does not bend for everyone, but is guided by personal qualities". I. Kant, *Kant: Prolegomena to Any Future Metaphysics: With Selections from the Critique of Pure Reason* (Cambridge University Press, Cambridge, 1997). doi:10.1017/CBO9781139164061, pp. 122–23 Along the same lines, it is tempting in the present context to consider the relevance of a slightly paraphrased version of Alf Ross's famous dictum: "Like a harlot [*common sense*] is at the disposal of everyone". cf. Ross, *On Law and Justice*, *supra* note 3, § 63.

the prism both by supplementing the group of researchers with non-Nordic lawyers and by supplementing the primarily doctrinal approaches with various interdisciplinary approaches.

In sections 3 and 4, I turned towards specific issues regarding possible relations between Scandinavian realism and Nordic approaches to international law. In Section 3, I made the observation that the traditional overarching concern of the Scandinavian realists, i.e. of securing that the study of law is scientific, appeared to be conspicuously absent in the majority of the contributions. In spite of the fact that many of the discussions took place against a backdrop of notions of the Nordics as moral superpowers and global good Samaritans, it was striking how limited a role such epistemological concerns seemed to play.

Finally, the upshot of the rather long discussion in Section 4 was that we should treat with considerable caution the contention so often presented as a commonplace that Scandinavian realism and in particular Alf Ross are connected with and cause Nordic exceptionalism. If interpreted as an exegetic claim about the actual congeniality and implicational relationship between the former two and the latter a close textual study reveals it to be simply wrong. *Qua* legal realist, Ross was anything but the rigid legal positivist and black letter lawyer he is so often made out to be. However, if treated more carefully solely as a claim about the history of ideas and the actual influence of these mistaken interpretations, of "Scandinavian realism" and of "Alf Ross", the connection is somewhat more plausible. However, the general picture also becomes more muddy. There is certainly reason to believe that "Scandinavian realism" and "Alf Ross" may at least in earlier times have been sympathetically held by many Nordic jurists. However, there is also reason to believe that the essentially legal positivistic beliefs that seem to (co-)determine the majoritarian judicial behaviour of the Nordic supreme courts vis-à-vis international courts are at least sometimes held *by the very judges themselves* to be antithetical to Ross's realism.

Index

www.ingramcontent.com/pod-product-compliance
Lightning Source LLC
LaVergne TN
LVHW020635300926
849161LV00004B/715
* 9 7 8 9 0 0 4 3 4 3 5 8 0 *